CURRICULUM REFORM IN ONTARIO

'Common Sense' Policy Processes and Democratic Possibilities

This first full account of curriculum policy formulation in 1990s Ontario helps readers understand the real-life experiences of policymakers both within the province and internationally. Having worked as a policy analyst for the Government of Ontario, a public school teacher, and a university professor, author Laura Elizabeth Pinto is uniquely positioned to tackle the key issues of policy formulation: the politics and tensions among different policy actors; the relationships between democracy in education and in policy formation; and the hidden role of privatization.

Based on interviews with key policy actors, including ministry bureaucrats, curriculum policy writers, stakeholder consultation participants, and political staffers, *Curriculum Reform in Ontario* provides a critique of conventional policy formulation processes. Pinto also suggests possibilities for more participatory approaches to policy formulation that can better support the critical role played by schools in creating democratic societies.

LAURA ELIZABETH PINTO is an assistant professor in the Educational Leadership Program at Niagara University.

Curriculum Reform in Ontario

'Common Sense' Policy Processes and Democratic Possibilities

LAURA ELIZABETH PINTO

UNIVERSITY OF TORONTO PRESS
Toronto Buffalo London

EDUC

LB
1629.5
.C3
P56
2012

© University of Toronto Press 2012
Toronto Buffalo London
www.utppublishing.com
Printed in Canada

ISBN 978-1-4426-6154-7 (cloth)
ISBN 978-1-4426-1285-3 (paper)

Printed on acid-free, 100% post-consumer recycled paper
with vegetable-based inks.

Library and Archives Canada Cataloguing in Publication

Pinto, Laura Elizabeth
Curriculum reform in Ontario : common sense policy processes
and democratic possibilities / Laura Elizabeth Pinto.

Includes bibliographical references and index.
ISBN 978-1-4426-6154-7 (bound). – ISBN 978-1-4426-1285-3 (pbk.)

1. Education, Secondary – Curricula – Ontario – Planning – Case studies.
2. Curriculum planning – Ontario – Case studies.   3. Education and
state – Ontario – Case studies.   I. Title.

LB1629.5.C3P56 2012   373.1909713   C2012-900026-4

This book has been published with the help of a grant from the Canadian
Federation for the Humanities and Social Sciences, through the Aid to
Scholarly Publications Program, using funds provided by the Social
Sciences and Humanities Research Council of Canada.

University of Toronto Press acknowledges the financial assistance to its
publishing program of the Canada Council for the Arts and the Ontario
Arts Council.

 Canada Council   Conseil des Arts
for the Arts   du Canada
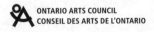 ONTARIO ARTS COUNCIL
CONSEIL DES ARTS DE L'ONTARIO

University of Toronto Press acknowledges the financial support of the
Government of Canada through the Canada Book Fund for its publishing
activities.

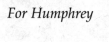*For Humphrey*

Contents

Preface

Large-scale, centralized education reform has occurred in a variety of jurisdictions in recent years. Such reforms usually include new approaches to funding and major changes to policies governing school board organization, curriculum, student assessment, and teacher working conditions. Education reforms are shaped by the processes undertaken to develop them and by the variety of individuals and groups involved. While a great deal of contemporary research concerns the outcomes and impacts of educational policies, few studies examine the process of education policy development and its relationship to democracy in education.

This book is concerned with curriculum policy production in a democracy: the ways in which agendas are constructed, as well as the ways in which compromises over policies are brought under the leadership and overall outlook of dominant groups. Walter Werner (1991, 107) poses an important question: *who should have the right to determine curriculum goals and content?* The significance of curriculum policy documents is that they define what is to be taught and often how it is to be taught. Curriculum policy documents also may indicate why the curriculum decisions were made. As a result, curriculum policy reflects a certain set of values, defining priorities and legitimating what is worth learning. Whose voices and values are reflected within curriculum policy is dependent upon the policy production process in any given jurisdiction.

Specifically, this book reconstructs and critiques curriculum policy production during an important period in Ontario's political history. Second, it investigates and analyses the degree to which this moment in policy production reflected the ideals of democracy. Finally, it offers possibilities for the democratization of education policy production based on the experiences of other jurisdictions and the growing body of literature on participatory policymaking.

My investigation is based on a reconstruction and analysis of Ontario's Secondary School Reform (SSR) curriculum policy formulation based on interviews with policy actors and data collected through archival and historical documents. My research focuses exclusively on the curriculum policy component of a larger-scale reform of education in the province, with analysis focused on the extent to which principles and practices associated with a framework of critical democracy were demonstrated within the policy formulation and in its outcomes. The case study I present in this book is the first to provide a full account of the curriculum policy formulation in Ontario[1] and provides a contribution to the literature through its application of a post-positivist framework to understand the process, viewed through the lens of critical democracy.

The broad significance of this book encompasses both theoretical and practical aspects of critical-democratic policymaking. First, from a theoretical perspective, my work builds on that of Schneider and Ingram (1997) – who also look at democratic practice in the policy process – and advances the literature by describing components of a critical-democratic policy process that incorporates elements from philosophy, education, and the policy sciences.

Second, this book contributes to a growing body of literature on education policy processes and privatization in education. Intense concern about the outcomes of large-scale reform trends (see, for example, Levin 1999; Hogan 2000; Earl et al. 2002; Rezai-Rashti 2003) can be effectively addressed on the basis of better understanding of how the policy process works and what features of it give rise to its impacts.

Third, because the research is presented as a case study, this book provides a basis for further comparative analysis of policy processes. In particular, this is the first study of Ontario's policy process in SSR. Thus, the research provides a detailed snapshot of curriculum development that can, in the future, be compared with other policy initiatives in these and other jurisdictions.

Finally, from a practical perspective, the case study offers both an opportunity for critique and concrete examples of possibilities that might be considered by other jurisdictions. For those who have an interest in adapting models of policy processes that successfully include citizens (see, for example, Wagle 2000), my research enhances understanding the sorts of components that promote successful, critical-democratic citizen participation. I provide not only a critique of a conventional policy formulation characterized by elitism, efficiency, and politicization to 'get things done' in the policy arena, but also and more importantly suggest possibilities for more democratic approaches to policy formulation. The possibility of alternate approaches is especially important to education since schools play a critical role in creating democratic societies. Unless schools engage students in thinking about possibilities for change towards a more just and more democratic society, it is unlikely that such change will occur. Without a more rigorous accountability structure that privileges critical-democratic (and therefore social justice and equity) ideals as envisioned by Carr (2007) and Skrla et al. (2001a, 2001b), democratic schools will not exist. Finally, I address the question of whether there is another way, in light of the analysis of Ontario's policy process. To examine alternatives, I describe the curriculum policy formulation undertaken in Porto Alegre, Brazil, during roughly the same timeframe as in Ontario. Using Porto Alegre as an analytic foil, I provide a discussion that highlights the possibilities and limitations of alternative forms of policymaking.

Position of the Researcher

I come to this research both as an insider and an outsider to curriculum policy formulation. In 1998, I was, quite unexpectedly, invited to participate in Ontario's secondary school curriculum reform as a writer contracted by the Ministry of Education. The circumstances were unique: one particular curriculum policy document – a pair of International Business courses for grades eleven and twelve – had to be rewritten from the ground up. I, along with two others, was called in at the last moment and given approximately one week to create a new curriculum policy document for this pair of courses. I did not experience any sort of 'application' procedure for my participation – instead, I received a call from a ministry bureaucrat asking if I was available and willing to participate in this capacity. As a relatively new teacher with no policy experience, I was both surprised and honoured to be given this opportunity. Given the short timeline, my co-authors and I jumped into the task and created a curriculum policy document within the timeframes, working on a ministry laptop in a makeshift office. This resulted in little time for reflection, for research, or for looking at the broader process. In the weeks and months after the submission of our policy document, I received occasional electronic correspondence from the ministry bureaucrat to whom I had reported, providing me with bits of feedback from 'consultations' to which I was asked to respond or incorporate into policy documents or respond in writing. No information about the consultations was offered.

Being an active participant in the policy process gave me insider status, with access to information and participant insight into the process. Once the process was complete and the curriculum policy documents were finalized, I had an opportunity to reflect on my experience. As I contemplated the process, the task of writing a policy document, and the completed policy text, more and more questions arose. My understanding was limited to the narrow 'slice' of work that I undertook – working exclusively with two other policy writers, not privy to how feedback was gathered or what happened during consultation meetings in the weeks and months that followed. This experience led me to wonder what occurred leading up to the development of the policy documents. How were decisions made about courses offered, and which policy documents were approved or not approved? How were other writers (like myself) selected or appointed? Who was responsible for reviewing and approving policy texts? What was the nature of the feedback/ consultation? Who else was involved, and in what capacity?

My research began with my investigation into the 'black box' of this policy process, seeking answers to some of these questions. I soon realized that reconstructing the process was a difficult task, since little information was publicly available. To further complicate matters, it became increasingly apparent that others, like me, knew about only their piece of the process, not the whole of it. In my attempts to better understand, I was an 'outsider' with respect to access to information and insight into the involvement of other individuals and groups.

As more information came to light through my initial investigation, I observed some troubling aspects – particularly the practice of outsourcing the writing of policy texts, and what appeared to be a problematic selection for policy actors in all aspects of the process. In a democracy, I wondered, is this the way that policy ought to be developed? I eagerly discussed my findings with friends and colleagues. In conversations, others often remarked, 'This was an efficient method to create policy. What other way could there possibly be to create this sort of policy?'

This led me to engage in deeper investigation into policy processes. I wondered if the method undertaken in the province of Ontario was generally accepted in other jurisdictions, and what alternatives might exist elsewhere. I learned that Porto Alegre, Brazil, undertook curriculum reforms, within a larger-scale education reform effort, during roughly the same timeframe. I was intrigued by its democratic nature, which, when compared to Ontario's secondary school reform process, provided a stark contrast. From this rough comparison, I became interested in further investigation about similarities and differences in process, as well as the outcomes.

Methodology and Rationale

To provide a holistic account of policy formulation in Ontario, the case study is the most relevant method for this research. A case study is 'an in-depth, multifaceted investigation, using qualitative research methods, of a single social phenomenon. The study is conducted in great detail and often relies on the use of several data sources' (Orum et al. 1991, 2). The case study research design yields several fundamental advantages, in that they provide information from a number of sources over a period of time, resulting in a holistic study of complex actions associated with policy formulation, including webs of social processes and political interaction. As such, researchers constructing case studies 'consider not only the voices of actors of focal concern, but also the perspectives and actions of other relevant groups and the interactions among them' (Snow and Anderson 1991, 149). Furthermore, case studies examine processes within a specific context, draw on multiple sources of information, and relate a story, usually in a chronological order. Moreover, they are ideal for revealing 'information patterns' that might not appear in official documentation (Sjoberg, Williams, Vaughan, and Sjoberg 1991). As such, the case study is ideal for reconstruction and analysis of the policy formulation process. Case studies allow for analysis of how or why particular phenomena occur through rich, textured descriptions of social or infrastructural processes (Scanlon 1997), such as the focus for this research.

The case study is ideal for the study of policy formulation, particularly given its ability to report and analyse the process of policy formulation (deLeon 1997; Wagle 2000). For this research, the case study takes the form of a 'social history' (Orum et al. 1991, 5) of the curriculum policy process in Ontario. This case study is bounded by the timeframe of policy formulation – it begins at the time of announcement of curriculum policy formulation (and SSR) within the 'Common Sense

Revolution' (1994) and ends with the enactment of these new curriculum policies. As such, the timeframe is 1994 through 2000. In order to construct the case study, I collected data in several forms:

• Primary and archival documents and reports reconstruct the policy process and determine the content and nature of policy outputs, including reports obtained under the Freedom of Information Act.
• Interviews with key policy actors involved in the process contribute primary data, and that allows me to reconstruct the policy process as well as to understand and report policy actors' perceptions about salient aspects of outcomes.
• Selected secondary literature provides detail about the enactment and the nature of policy outputs, as well as further support for themes that arise out of interviews.

I selected participants purposefully through 'snowball' or 'chain sampling' (Patton 1990). This approach 'identifies cases of interest from people who know people who know people who know what cases are information-rich, that is, good examples for study, good interview subjects' (182). Purposive sampling allowed me, as a researcher, to select a sample that would 'yield the most comprehensive understanding of [the] subject of study' (Babbie 1992, 292). I began by reviewing my professional network of colleagues. From my own involvement in this policy formulation, I knew a number of individuals who had participated in Ontario's policy process and were regarded as competent professionals among colleagues. Their experience and reputations suggested that they would be able to contribute significant insight. I contacted a total of nine (bureaucrats, writers, and individuals who were known to have been involved in consultations) with invitations to be interviewed, and asked them to recommend others. Most recommended at least one additional potential candidate. Subsequent referrals resulted in sixteen interviews conducted in Ontario. I received multiple referrals for three interviewees who were perceived by others I contacted to be fair-minded, intelligent, and exceptionally involved in the process. While I made attempts to identify as many types of representation as possible, participants include only those comfortable participating in the research.

I interviewed sixteen individuals in Ontario between April and June 2006. Of these, six participated in the curriculum reforms as members of contracted writing teams, five in a bureaucratic or central-government role, and five by attending consultation sessions. I use pseudonyms to preserve participant anonymity, and I identify them by the roles they played, avoiding information about participants' subject area, and, where possible, organizational or departmental affiliations. Writing team members interviewed represent the following subjects: history, science, civics, business studies, English, and the arts.

I analysed the data in several phases, following Yin's (1994) two-phased strategy for general use in case study analysis. The first phase involved reviewing the three subsets of data gathered (public and archival primary documents, secondary data, and interview transcripts), then analysing deductively and then inductively. Approaching the data deductively, I flagged passages using a thematic coding scheme tied to my conceptual framework. By using inductive analysis, I was able to identify patterns, themes, and categories that 'emerge out of the data rather than being imposed on them prior to data collection and analysis' (Patton 1990, 390), using constant-comparative analysis (Heck 2004). This first phase of analysis resulted in the identification of ideas, perceptions, and relationships. With the first phase complete, I set out to construct the case study. Using all three subsets of coded data from interviews, I began compiling and organizing information within the timeframe, relating it the conceptual framework of critical democracy, and triangulating to verify its strength and accuracy (Heck).

To address the question of whether there is another way, in light of the construction and analysis of the Ontario case study, I sought an analytic foil to offer a contrast and extend the critique offered in the case study analysis. To achieve this, I relied on published sources and supporting historical documents in order to describe curriculum policy production undertaken in Porto Alegre during roughly the same timeframe as the Ontario case study. Using Porto Alegre as an analytic foil, and not a comparative case study, I am able to offer a discussion that highlights the possibilities and limitations of alternative forms of policymaking.

As a case study, the limitations characteristic of qualitative methodologies apply to this research. First, Ontario data are limited to available documentation and willing research participants. By embarking on a multi-perspective study with three data subsets (interviews, secondary documents, and primary archival documents), the subsets overlap and to fill in one another's gaps.

Second, the accuracy of interview data is limited to the knowledge, recollection, perceptions, and honesty of each participant. Some respondents may give an answer they feel will be appreciated by the researcher or one that will result in their responses appearing more progressive or democratic. Again, because this research relies on multiple data subsets and the perspectives of interview participants from all sides of the policy formulation 'table,' triangulation offsets individual interview limitations. As well, I limit my discussion of outcomes to those issues raised by participants. Thus, outcomes (and their implications) may not necessarily reflect my position or the accounts in secondary research.

Third, my own biases and value judgments – as a policy 'insider' to the policy writing process in Ontario, as an outsider to other aspects of policy formulation in Ontario, and as a researcher and citizen – weigh heavily on my research. In describing societal, cultural, institutional, and political contexts, I am also subject to them. However, through the collection and analysis of a multitude of sources, I attempt to reconstruct, as accurately as possible, the policy formulation process undertaken in Ontario. Furthermore, as I emphasized earlier in this chapter, wherever possible, I allow the policy actors' voices to speak for themselves through direct quotations, rather run the risk of (mis)interpreting their words.

Organization of Book

The organization of this book follows a conceptual framework that builds on the work of Anne Schneider and Helen Ingram (1997), using their scheme of contexts (societal, institutional, and policy formulation) to organize and describe Ontario's policy process. By examining policy formulation in relation to these three contexts, I am able to illustrate 'how policy affects citizens and other aspects of democracy within the society' (Schneider 1998). I advance this framework by exploring each context with respect to critical-democratic criteria, thus incorporating elements from philosophy, education, and the policy sciences. In doing so, I am able to analyse the data I gather for the degree to which it reflects the ideal of critical democracy. This organizing framework is classified as post-positivist, since it is concerned with the 'multidimensional complexity of social reality' within a broader interpretive framework (Fischer 1998, 129) and relies on qualitative data. Because the conceptual framework is situated within the critical-democratic ideal, it is critical-theoretical in nature. As such, this framework shares the following characteristics associated with critical-theoretical policy analysis (Schneider and Ingram 1997; Schneider 1998):

- A multidimensional structure such that the framework addresses context, with attention to inclusiveness, participation, deliberation, power, and social justice
- Examination of policy text content that addresses the extent to which texts 'reflect the values, beliefs, and social constructions that produced the policy' (Schneider 1998, 10)
- The capacity to capture (1) social constructions of citizens, (2) social constructions of knowledge used to develop policies, and (3) format and content of policy deliberations

This conceptual framework organizes the case study and its analysis within the three contexts as well as outcomes.

Chapter 1 begins with an elaboration of the ideal of critical democracy. Within the critical-democratic ideal, democracy becomes a way of life, and issues of inclusion, empowerment, and social justice become central concerns. I compare critical democracy to several other conceptions of democracy, and explore various models for citizen participation in the policy process. A central feature of critical-democratic policy formulation of conceptual framework is agonistic exchange, as defined by Chantal Mouffe (1997, 2000a, 2000b, 2005). In the chapters the follow, I reconstruct Ontario's curriculum policy production, analysing various aspects of the process against the democratic ideal laid out in this chapter. Criteria to analyse the degree to which Ontario achieves the critical-democratic ideal are woven into chapters 2 through 7 and reflect the critical-democratic ideal laid out in this first chapter.

Chapter 2 explores the societal context surrounding Ontario's reforms, with particular attention to underlying neoliberal and neoconservative ideologies. I provide details about the Common Sense Revolution, the political platform devised prior to the 1995 election, and how it lays out a series of sweeping and significant political changes. I also provide an overview of the actual policy and legislative changes made, and analyse their implications, with particular attention to race and the construction of the other. Finally, I discuss the framing of these issues in the public sphere, with attention to resistance among citizens.

Following the overview of Common Sense Revolution policies and changes as a whole, I turn to Ontario's education restructuring, in chapter

3. The Common Sense Revolution affected education as a whole – not just the curriculum policy process studied in depth. A brief history of education reform in Ontario describes the shifts in thinking about education in the province leading up to the period of reform studied. This sets the context for the curriculum policy process I examine in detail.

Chapter 4 explores how the Ministry of Education's institutional culture during the period of reform relied on privatization to carry out policy functions traditionally left to bureaucrats and education professionals. I describe how changes to public sector values shape the way in which work was done, and describe the mechanics of the private-sector outsourcing model used.

Chapters 5 and 6 describe the policy formulation context. Chapter 5 focuses on the process of policy text production, with attention to the tensions between writers on the one hand, and bureaucrats and political staff on the other. Chapter 6 describes the nature and content of stakeholder consultations, and offers perspectives of all categories of policy actors interviewed. Together, these two chapters flesh out the intricacies of Ontario's curriculum policy formulation process and point to a democratic shortfall, despite other gains.

Chapter 7 describes policy outcomes from the perspective of those interviewed. The outcomes I discuss – structure of policy texts, an absence of continuity, value-neutrality, concerns about streaming, a career-focus, and an absence of social justice – are triangulated by an exploration of other accounts, especially secondary research. When measured against the ideal laid out in chapter 1, they, like the policy formulation process, suggest a shortfall of critical democracy.

Chapter 8 provides an alternative for curriculum policy formulation, based on the process and outcomes of Porto Alegre's education reform during roughly the same time. Using data from secondary sources, I describe the approach undertaken by Porto Alegre in order to construct an analytic foil, which allows me to underscore how Ontario's process is not the only way to approach policy production, and that indeed, there are possibilities for different approaches that feature meaningful participation. A comparative discussion reveals that, despite a few similarities in the societal context, there are stark contrasts in the approach undertaken in each jurisdiction.

Finally, chapter 9 concludes the book, offering a summary of broad themes and discussing the sorts of structures and initiatives that might provide an alternative, more democratic approach to policy formulation and jurisdictions like it.

CURRICULUM REFORM IN ONTARIO

'Common Sense' Policy Processes
and Democratic Possibilities

1 The Ideal of Critical-Democratic Policy Production

Democracy requires dialogue, participation, political and social responsibility, as well as a degree of social and political solidarity ... before it becomes a political form, democracy is a form of life.

— Paulo Freire 1978, 28–9

The obligations of allegiance to democracy may thus entail obligations to struggle for a just society ... [T]his means sharing a common obligation to resist the unjust social order and to struggle to transform society into a more just democracy.

— Ronald Glass 2000, 292–3

'Democracy' continues to be a wildly popular slogan among politicians and pundits in the media, equally so in research and academic circles, raising questions over the politics and the mechanics of public policy and their democratic significance. In particular, recent (and controversial) grassroots movements (such as the Tea Party and Coffee Party) who claim to act as democratic agents have garnered public attention, and their popularity appears to be increasing. But what conceptions of democracy are operating in this public dialogue? What are the criteria for truly democratic policy production? In this chapter, I lay out the conditions of the critical-democratic ideal, which lead to a fuller articulation of what a critical-democratic policy process might entail in the chapters that follow.

The possibility of democratic approaches to policy production is especially important to education, since schools play an essential role in creating democratic societies. There are several rationales for a more inclusive policy process. Meaningful citizen participation in policy formulation is essential to achieving a critical-democratic ideal. Moreover, creating policy in a way that is perceived as fair has been empirically shown to lead to citizens' acceptance of outcomes as legitimate (see, for example, the meta-analysis by Tyler 2000) – thus a more democratic process can also serve governments. In recent years there have been scattered efforts to engage in more participatory policymaking and decision-making (see, for example, Button and Mattson 1999; Schneider and Ingram 1997; Weeks 2000; Baiocchi 2001; Fields and Feinberg 2001). These suggest real government interest in revisiting citizen engagement and involvement. By investigating, critiquing, and proposing criteria for inclusive, democratic policy processes, jurisdictions can move closer to achieving better forms of policymaking.

Curriculum policy is highly political, regularly garnering attention from politicians and the media. What students ought to learn, and what teachers ought to teach, is argued to have an impact on the social fabric of society and on a nation's or region's ability to compete globally. But remarkably, and despite popular attention to curriculum content, few have investigated how central governments make curriculum policy decisions. My concern in this book is with the degree to which Ontario's process and outcomes reflect democracy – and more specifically, critical democracy.

Emerging Interest in Policy Production

While academic interest in the policy process encompasses areas that range from social to fiscal to environmental policy, this book is concerned specifically with curriculum policy production. Studying the features and dynamics of processes used in policy formulation contributes to the analysis and a better understanding of the policy itself as well as its outcomes. Renewed interest in policy production emerges, in part, from developments in theoretical approaches that describe power and control in governance. This interest highlights 'the need to go beyond the study of content of social policies to embrace the study of processes through which policies are made and enacted' (Newman 2002, 347). Janet Newman goes on to say, 'A concern with the dynamics of [the] policy process itself, set in the context of contemporary theories of governance, power and the state, is essential for those seeking to analyse and understand what is going on in social policy' (353).

Since the mid-1990s, a body of literature has emerged that describes the extent to which policy processes reflect democratic principles and practices. Myriad conceptions of democracy appear within it. Some define democracy as primarily procedural, with citizen participation occurring via formal politics (for example, elections and referendums), while other conceptions provide a substantive democratic ideal, in which citizens actively participate in democracy as a way of life, which includes direct involvement in policy formulation (see the work of Mouffe 2000a, 2000b, 2005; Barber 2003; Gutmann and Thomson 2004, as examples of more substantive democratic ideas, which I discuss later on). The common element, regardless of the conception of democracy appealed to, is the central idea that democracy requires citizen participation in public decision-making, and that idea can be applied to public decision-making about educational curriculums.

A number of studies have described theories and models of citizen participation (see, for example, deLeon 1997; Schneider and Ingram 1997; Dahl 1998; Wagle 2000; Gutmann and Thompson 2004; Dryzek 2009, and others). Such models have the potential to achieve inclusion and equity in policy processes. As Udaya Wagle explains, 'It is the outcomes of policymaking that matter to citizens and it is the citizen participation that ensures democratic policymaking. In this regard, citizen participation is not the end, rather it is a means to democratic policymaking which contributes to the overall wellbeing of citizens' (2000, 214). When citizens participate in policy processes, the advantages go beyond policy outcomes – though the presumption is that participation leads to better outcomes. Ideal democratic models, in this view, encourage learning, dialogue, empowerment, equity, and a shared spirit of inquiry (Fischer 1993; Fischer and Forester 1993; Wagle 2000). They also require a fundamental change to the roles of both citizens and governments. Power must be redistributed to citizens to allow for meaningful and legitimate decision-making to occur, and that may require governments to surrender some degree of authority. As well, bureaucrats' roles must shift, at least to some degree, from experts in policy to facilitators of citizen deliberation and decision-making.

I explore various conceptions of democracy in more detail later in this chapter. However, as I stated earlier, my analysis relies on one very specific conception – that of *critical democracy* – as the ideal. Critical democracy goes beyond participation, encompassing the ideal of a fundamental redistribution of power to achieve inclusion and empowerment for all citizens. As well, it calls for the inclusion of those who are often marginalized from political activity, emphasizing equity, diversity, and social justice. As such, critical-democratic policy formulation strives for meaningful citizen engagement in policy decisions. However, there are very few examples of processes that reflect robust critical-democratic processes and outcomes. Moreover, no comprehensive conceptual framework to describe how a critical-democratic policy process might operate has been articulated.

Because critical democracy remains an emergent theoretical paradigm in education and in the policy sciences, examples that illustrate a critical-democratic policy process have yet to be developed. Moreover, critical-democratic criteria for evaluating policy processes have been neither proposed nor empirically investigated. It is impossible to identify a single, concrete design structure that would exemplify critical-democratic policymaking – rather, any number of design possibilities at various stages in the process could be modified in different ways to reflect a critical democracy. In this chapter, I sketch out the components of such a process with the aim of arriving at critical-democratic policy making. I use these to ground the case study analysis that follows, and elaborate upon critical-democratic criteria in subsequent chapters.

The Ideal of Critical Democracy

While a variety of conceptions of democracy appear in the literature, I situate my analysis of Ontario's policy production within the ideal of critical democracy as articulated by Antonia Darder, Joe Kincheloe, Shane O'Neill, John Portelli and Patrick Solomon, Ricardo Blaug, Landon Beyer, and others. This conception of democracy arises primarily out of John Dewey's philosophy, with roots in his definition of democracy as 'more than a form of government; it is primarily a mode of associated living, of conjoint and communicated experience. The extension in space of the number of individuals who participate in an interest so that each has to refer his own action to that of others, and to consider the action of others to give point and direction to his own, is equivalent to the breaking down of those barriers of class, race and national territory which kept men from perceiving the full import of their activity' ([1916] 1966, 84–5).

Within the critical-democratic ideal, democracy is a personal, social, and political experience rather than a form of government (Blaug 2002). Popular contemporary conceptions, several of which I describe in the sections that follow, view democracy as a form of rule that has only to do with government-sanctioned citizen activities such as voting or town halls, most of which are narrowly political. By contrast, critical democracy as personal experience concerns itself with a set of values, dispositions, and behaviours that go far beyond citizen involvement in official, narrow, political functions. Consistent with the contributions of John Dewey described above, the work of Paulo Freire has strongly influenced the critical-democratic ideal. He writes, 'Democracy requires dialogue, participation, political and social responsibility, as well as a degree of social and political solidarity . . . before it becomes a political form, democracy is a form of life, characterized above all by a strong component of transitive consciousness. Such transitivity can neither appear nor develop except as men are launched into debate, participating in the examination of common problems' (1978, 28–9). As this passage emphasizes, critical democracy becomes a way of life that includes concern for meaningful engagement among citizens in all aspects of lived experience in which individuals become agents of social change. This emphasis on personal agency also provides unique legitimacy to the outcomes arising out of critical-democratic processes (Blaug 2002), equally emphasizing substantive issues and processes.

Social Justice as Central to Critical Democracy

Critical democracy differs from other, more widely discussed conceptions of democracy through its requirement of a certain type of participation. Specifically, critical democracy strives to establish a way of life that 'should show us how to transform our form of life in an emancipatory manner' (O'Neill 2000, 503–4). To that end, 'critical-democratic theorists seek to explore how contentious issues of moral and cultural pluralism might be dealt with in a way that minimizes the potential for oppression, alienation and violence. This means that incommensurability must not be taken as a given, or as something to be celebrated. Nor should it be brushed aside as something that will inevitably be overcome' (505). As Shane O'Neill reminds us in this passage, critical democracy necessarily leads to requirements of inclusion and empowerment, with particular attention to those who are often marginalized from political activity. Beyond traditional democracy's narrow concern with equality, critical democracy embraces equity as a goal with genuine and inclusive participation that 'seriously and honestly acknowledges the importance of equity, diversity and social justice' (Portelli and Solomon 2001, 15).

Indeed, social justice is a central component of critical democracy. Social justice is a contested term with multiple meanings (Beilharz

1989; Rizvi 1998; Caputo 2002). Broadly speaking, the literature reflects three dimensions of thinking about social justice: procedural justice or representation (concerned with the freedom to pursue goals, civil liberties); (re)distributive justice (concerned with the allocation of benefits and burdens); and relational justice and recognition (concerned with equity in all aspects of social and economic life as well as cultural recognition) (Gerwirtz 1998; Caputo 2002; Merrett 2004). A full conception of social justice must expand beyond distribution of goods in a society to include all aspects of institutional rules and relations associated with relational justice (Gewirtz 1998; Gewirtz and Cribb 2002). In other words, social justice must permit all members of society to interact with peers equitably along all three of these dimensions in order to achieve parity of participation (representation, redistribution, recognition) (Fraser 2008, 2010) in economic, cultural, and political aspects of life. This goal of full participatory parity is consistent with critical democracy. In this ideal, social justice is a praxis that acknowledges internalized forms of oppression[1] and privilege, and enacts practical strategies to change social institutions to overcome inequity and exclusion (Kohli 2005; Fraser 2010).

In this way, the critical-democratic conception of social justice outlined here is consistent with Nancy Fraser's in that I treat redistribution and recognition as dimensions of justice that cut across all social movements and positions, including gender, race, and class. This broad and far-reaching notion of social justice can take a variety of forms, depending upon the area of life or policy under consideration and the unique characteristics of any given community or jurisdiction, where the individuals and groups who experience oppression differ. For example, Martha Nussbaum (1999) recognizes that societal barriers restrict self-determination for the oppressed, resulting in a lack of internal or external power to exercise self-determination as a result of material constraints and social constructions. She explains this position using women's oppression as an example. Women have a legal right to education, though they may not have the financial or material resources to exercise those rights. For instance, a repressive marriage or traditional hierarchies in the community might prevent a woman from 'true choices.' As well, social constructions about a woman's role might also prevent her from pursuing such opportunities.

Within the critical-democratic ideal, social justice strives to achieve equity over equality. Equality implies that all individuals have the same opportunities or distribution of goods, whereas equity implies that opportunities are distributed in a way that may be unequal, but compensates for differences that disadvantage one group or person over another. Participatory parity requires both cultural equality (recognition) and material equality (redistribution) (Fraser 2007), and all social conditions must allow all groups to participate as peers in all the major forms of social interaction (Travers 2008). As an example, the absence of legal discrimination as a barrier to women's participation is necessary but not sufficient for social justice with respect to gender. Rather, all aspects of life – social, familial, economic, and so on – must allow participatory parity.

Despite compelling moral, religious, political, and legal arguments[2] supporting its importance, social justice is subject to some criticism. First, social justice has come under scrutiny since there are so many conceptions of it, and it is extremely difficult to pin down. A fundamental disagreement about what fairness and equity are, and how to overcome them, appears across the literature. Second, because public dialogue does not necessarily lead to the reconstitution of existing power relations in a way that might address inequity, social justice has been called a form of 'romanticized localism' (Rizvi 1998; Vincent 2003, 4). Inequities and oppression persist and are difficult, if not impossible, to eliminate. However, proponents of social justice (and critical democrats) would argue that without social justice as a goal, no progress can be made towards their elimination.

The Uniqueness of Critical Democracy in Light of Alternate Conceptions

To better understand critical democracy, it is useful to contrast it with other more traditional conceptions of democracy. Benjamin Barber describes 'liberal democracy' as holding a 'perceived monopoly' on forms of politics (2003, 3). Liberal democracy, present in much of the Western world, is very much a model of representative democracy, in which civic participation tends be the responsibility of elected officials, and citizen participation rarely goes beyond voting and the odd 'town hall' consultation. Both Benjamin Barber and Chantal Mouffe agree that liberal democracy is recognized as the only legitimate form of government – thus limiting critique and making alternatives for consideration scant. Indeed, Mouffe (2000a, 1) claims that 'very few dare to openly challenge the liberal democratic model,' despite evidence of disaffection.

Barber's work characterizes liberal democracy as 'thin' in that it privileges individual interests while undermining democratic practices upon which those individuals and their interests depend. Moreover, this conception limits democracy to a political procedure within official institutions, rather than an experience lived by all citizens. In practice, this 'precarious foundation' of a procedurally oriented liberal democracy (Barber 2003, 4) excludes citizenship, participation, and the public good. Barber proposes a conception of 'strong democracy' that places 'agency and responsibility' at the centre of political activity and requires 'politics as a way of living' (2003, 117).

Jason Glynos (2003) describes additional critiques of liberal forms of democracy that centre on undesirable consequences such as apathy, lack of transparency, absence of trust, and inequality. Though perhaps not as widely accepted as other conceptions of democracy, critical democracy holds promise to address some shortcomings and challenges. To understand these critiques and visions of alternatives and to provide a basis for comparison with critical democracy, in the following subsections I describe three versions of liberal democracy: market democracy, deliberative democracy, and agonistic democracy.

Market Democracy

The literature documents a conception of market democracy (see, for example, Sunstein 1997; Chua 2000; Pettit 2008) arising out of 'a period of mounting enthusiasm for free markets' (Sunstein 1997, 3) in which markets and democracy appear 'luxuriously compatible' (Chua 2000, 378). Market democracy first appears in the work of economist Joseph Schumpeter during the mid-twentieth century, relying on the central idea that the spreading of markets and associated privatization constitutes spreading democracy (Beyer 1998; Barber 2004). Within the conception of market democracy, individuals in the electoral polity divide into consumers and producers, and interact within a 'marketplace' to arrive at policies (Manzer 2003; Pettit 2008). Thus, economic 'choice' and 'consumption' of public goods and services (including education) are taken to be components of 'citizenship.' These consumer-citizens register their preferences in polls (Chua 2000; Pettit 2008). In this way, 'the policies ought to track the trend in preferences expressed by voters' (Pettit 2008, 50).

Critics identify a number of problems associated with market democracy, largely focused on two areas: problems with the market analogy, and an apparent inability to address equity and justice. With respect to the market analogy, the move to equate consumers and citizens neglects the difference in dispositions and skills associated with these two roles.

As Zygmunt Bauman explains, 'Consumer skills emphatically do not include the art of translating private troubles into public issues, and public interests into individual rights and duties – the art that constitutes the citizen and holds together the polity as the congregation of citizens' (Leighton 2002, 15). In this way, market democracy has a 'tendency to paralyze and delegitimate political thinking as a gateway to political action,' in which individuals are mistakenly thought to be 'utility maximizing' rational decision-makers (Birchfield 1999, 30). This fails to take other factors that influence citizens' preferences and beliefs into account. For example, 'market criteria are insufficient' to address social problems, given that 'solely procedural criteria for fairness and competition are insufficient for achieving social justice' (Rizvi 1998, 54). Similarly, Peter Beilharz argues that social justice is a *non sequitur* outside the logic of markets': 'The dominant usages of "social justice" are not interested in arguments about needs, but rather in facilitating the pursuit of desert of fairness principles within the matrix of existing market relations' (1989, 95).

Amy Chua describes how market democracy is mediated by material, political, and ideological devices that 'de-escalate the conflict between market-generated wealth disparities and majoritarian politics' (2000, 290). For instance, 'A system aspiring to social justice aspires to liberty, and a system of free markets seems to promise liberty, because it allows people to trade goods and services as they wish. In fact, a system of free markets seems to promise not only liberty, but equality of an important sort as well, since everyone in a free market is given an equal right to transact and participate in market arrangements. This form of equality should not be trivialized or disparaged. For example, race and sex discrimination has often consisted of exclusions of certain classes of people for the market domain' (Sunstein 1997, 3). Along those lines, this 'depersonalized logic of market forces' (Beetham 1997, 76) leads to power imbalances (Beetham 1997; Birchfield 1999), which further exacerbate problems of inclusion and social justice in policy formulation processes and outcomes. The result is a collection of policy directions that benefit capital rather than citizens (Purcell 2009). Critical democracy, by contrast, seeks to deal specifically with inclusion, equity, and social justice, without concern for promoting the interests capital.

Deliberative Democracy

Another set of conceptions of liberal democracy are classified as 'deliberative democracy' models. These emerge in response to critiques of liberal democracy such as those by Amy Gutmann, Dennis Thomson, and Benjamin Barber, and the recognition that liberal democracy fails to recognize the centrality of deliberation (Dryzek 2009). The term *deliberative democracy* describes a number of approaches to citizen participation whose goal is to engage citizens in all phases of policy formulation through deliberation. Tatsuo Inoue (2003) observes that it has become a 'prevailing catchword,' especially popular in the political science literature where it is accepted as a 'normative theory that suggests ways in which we can enhance democracy and criticize institutions that do not live up to the normative standard' (Chambers 2003, 308). Its theoretical popularity has resulted in an empirical turn, and recent research has transformed it from a 'theoretical statement to a working theory' (Bächtiger et al. 2010).

While advocates disagree about its features and its configurations vary, two main versions of deliberative democracy exist: one put forward by John Rawls, the other by Jürgen Habermas. The Habermasian version, based on critical theory, is concerned with empowerment and inclusion in the policy process through 'communicative action' – citizens engaging in discourse in good faith. Habermas envisions an 'ideal speech situation' in which citizens engage in unforced argument, without manipulation, and without time constraints (Habermas 1984). In his view, deliberation (either official or unofficial) legitimizes legal and political institutions. Some classify Habermasian versions of deliberative democracy as proceduralist, since they emphasize process over content (Gutmann and Thompson 2004).

The Rawlsian perspective emerges out of John Rawls's *Theory of Justice* (1971). Rooted in the tradition of liberalism (unlike the Habermasian roots in critical theory), it upholds liberal values. Rawls's version of deliberative democracy is founded in the concept of 'public reason' as a means for dialogue. The concept of public reason is discussed at length by Rawls and scholars who follow in his tradition. For the purpose of this summary, a brief overview highlights the nature of this concept: 'Public reason concerns the kinds of reasons appropriate for government decisions and political argument and justification addressed to the public ... public reason must rely on principles, values, and methods of reason and assessing evidence shared by reasonable doctrines under conditions of a free and democratic society' (Freeman 2003, 39–40). Thus, public reason relies on rational argument in a formal venue and on officially sanctioned issues, resulting in a constitutionalist orientation (Gutmann and Thompson 2004). Rational consensus becomes the aim of public reason among citizens. The central features of this version of deliberative democracy are:

- Ongoing citizen participation
- Institutional structure that requires deliberation to arrive at decisions
- Commitment to plurality of values and aims among citizens
- Acceptance of deliberative procedure as the source of legitimacy
- Recognition and respect for each other's deliberative capacity (Cohen 1989)

The Habermasian and Rawlsian versions of deliberative democracy share several elements. First, both advocate greater and structured citizen participation in political decision-making, with the intention of enhanced democracy. As such, they blend procedural and substantive democracy, albeit to different degrees. Second, both aim to preserve a conception of liberalism as a key component of their respective democratic conceptions, Rawls more so than Habermas. Critics call attention to the apparent contradictions between liberalism and democracy (Mouffe 2000a, 2000b), suggesting that individual interests privileged in liberalism cannot coexist with a vision for a common good associated with democracy. To some degree, Habermas addresses this through his defence of 'co-originality' – essentially, individual will cannot exist without rights, and rights cannot exist without some popular sovereignty (Chambers 2003).

Third, the Habermasian and Rawlsian versions of deliberative democracy also share a belief in the need for a prescribed format for democratic process and decision-making that emphasizes rationality (public reason for Rawls, communicative rationality for Habermas). This notion of rationality – whether the goal is agreement or consensus – is arrived at through the 'exchange of arguments among reasonable persons guided by the principle of impartiality' (Mouffe 2000a, 4). Unforced consensus is impossible in a political context, since there is an ever-present implicit threat of a political decision being imposed if consensus is not reached (McGann 2005).

Agonistic Democracy

In response to these critiques of participatory models, Chantal Mouffe proposes an alternative conception of democracy aimed at genuinely inclusive citizen involvement. Mouffe's agonistic democracy acknowledges the inevitability of conflict in political life, as well as the impossibility of coming to final, rational, and neutral decision procedures, resulting from power structures and the plurality of values. The primary problem with a liberal democracy model, she writes, 'is its incapacity to come to terms with the nature of the political.[3] In one of its versions, it reduces politics[4] to the calculus of interests. Individuals are presented as rational actors moved by the search for the maximization of their self interest' (Mouffe 1997, 25). She asserts that 'one of the main tasks of democracy consists in envisaging how it is possible to diffuse the tendencies to exclusion that are present in every construction of collective identities' (26). To address this, agonistic democracy 'emphasizes permanent conflict rather than consensus, the primacy of power over morality, hegemony rather than consensus, and the passions rather than reason. At the same time it seeks to diffuse or tame antagonism, converting it into agonism which involves respect for the freedom and equality of persons and toleration for their views even if we oppose them' (Crowder 2006, 10).

As this passage suggests, Chantal Mouffe's conception of democracy rejects the inevitability of consensus and acknowledges the centrality of conflict. This conception of democracy also redraws the lines of politics and the political. Politics are the practices, discourses, and institutions that attempt to establish order and organize human life in conditions that are always in conflict because of the political. The political, on the other hand, is the site of struggle in which groups with opposing interests vie for hegemony. Political conflict is a force to be channelled into political and democratic commitment to tame the agon, rather than a problem to be overcome. In this way, she critiques deliberative democracy's desire to eliminate conflict since, in her view, it is simply a part of the democratic process, and attempts to eliminate it lead to destructive, antagonistic conflict.[5]

At its core, agonistic democracy is founded upon Wittgenstein's critiques of rationalism – that for agreement of opinions, first there must be agreement in forms of life. What constitutes a good life, Mouffe contends, is not an absolute. Thus, agreement is not always possible, and this limits the possibility of rational consensus, which is a central component of deliberative democracy. 'The fact that power is constitutive of social relations' (Mouffe 2000b, 98) is a second key foundation of agonistic democracy. As a consequence, the focus becomes 'how to constitute forms of power more compatible with democratic values,' rather than try to eliminate power (100).

Agonism is Chantal Mouffe's solution to these limits. Agonistic democracy calls on citizens to view the 'other' as an adversary – 'somebody whose ideas we combat but whose right to defend those ideas we do no put into question ... a legitimate enemy one with whom we have some common ground' (Mouffe 2000b, 102) – rather than an illegitimate enemy or opponent. Adversaries, in this view, share principles of equity and liberty but disagree on the meaning and implementation of those principles. The key to the adversarial relationship is that both recognize that rational persuasion will not change the other's political identity. The goal of agonistic confrontation, then, becomes compromise rather than consensus – where a compromise is recognized as 'temporary respite from ongoing confrontation' (102).

While, arguably, other versions of deliberation might be adapted to reflect critical democracy, Mouffe's conception of agonistic exchanges best characterizes the type of deliberation suited to critical democracy. A critical-democratic policy formulation process requires a mechanism for citizen engagement to ensure that democratic structures and procedures are substantive and engage and empower citizens. This agonistic approach to understanding the 'other' as well as to recognizing the permanence of conflict within politics and the political realizes the critical-democratic ideal; moreover, mutual concern and respect among opponents supports critical democracy's aims of equity, diversity, and social justice.

Certainly, Mouffe's conception is not without critiques. First, some have argued that Chantal Mouffe lacks detail about structure and procedures to facilitate agonistic democracy (Crowder 2006; Erman 2009). Mouffe herself states, 'It is in our power to create the practices, discourses and institutions that would allow those conflicts to take an agonistic form' (2005, 130). While this lack of specificity may be true in her theoretical work, a broader body of literature is emerging in which others have proposed structures and procedures (see, for example, Dahlgren 2005). More importantly, empirical investigation is emerging that points to specific approaches to institute the sorts of democratic practices that Mouffe describes (for example, Pløger 2004; Goi 2005; Bäcklund & Mäntysalo 2010, and others, which are described in greater detail in chapter 9).

Second, agonistic democracy has been criticized for a reliance on irrational decision-making (Dryzek 2005; Crowder 2006). This is based on Mouffe's claim that there cannot be rational decision-making on some issues, and that passion and emotion are necessarily part of agonistic exchanges among citizens. The failure of rationalist models in political science and critiques of them suggest, however, that Mouffe may be correct. A version of this criticism, which suggests that passion is reduced to unproductive, uncivil, or disrespectful chaos (Dryzek 2005), is an unfounded caricature of Mouffe's rejection of dispassionate and reasoned deliberation. Indeed, there is a general recognition within the literature on reasoning and argumentation that emotion can be civil and has a legitimate, important, and positive role to play in argument (Walton 1992; Gilbert 1997, 1999, 2001; Carozza 2007). From a feminist perspective, this inclusion of passion and emotion is a strength, which supports more inclusive approaches to citizen participation. For instance, Claudia Ruitenberg (2009) argues that agonism addresses the dangers of masculinist rationality central to deliberative democracy, and Deborah Thien (2007) asserts that Mouffe is correct her in acknowledgment that a full dismissal of emotions fails to accept the place of emotions as vital to political engagement.

A third critique of agonistic democracy is that its failure to support consensus is unproductive and incorrect (Dryzek 2009; Erman 2009). This line of criticism argues that 'at least consensus implies that decisions get made' (Dryzek 2009, 221). However, these critics fail to acknowledge that Mouffe's conception of compromise indeed calls for a decision, albeit a temporary one. Moreover, the critics fail to acknowledge that some issues (for instance, the pro-life/pro-choice debate, illustrated in Simona Goi's 2005 research) are matters of value and belief and cannot be resolved through consensus. Moreover, Mouffe (2005) forcefully argues that acts of consensus are necessarily built upon exclusion and simply reinforce hegemonic power. By removing the condition of consensus, power relations are acknowledged and have the potential to be addressed.

A fourth critique is that agonism's encouragement of passionate exchanges among citizens would lead to greater societal conflict, rather than temporary compromise, particularly in divided societies in which extremism and zealotry are present (Olson 2009). In particular, Eva Erman points to a lack clarity about how or why it would be possible for citizens to achieve agonal respect for one another or even an interest in politics. Contrary to these criticisms, Mouffe (2005) insists that agonism makes for a more harmonious and safer society over time by taming and diffusing antagonism, such that the 'enemy' would be transformed into the adversary. One might envision this functioning as in organized sport (Tally 2007). Consider the football game: rival sides compete in an unambiguously agonistic struggle for dominance, with a clear winner and loser. Rival teams play by certain rules, unwilling to destroy the sport itself in order to achieve a particular goal. The goal is not consensus, but victory for a particular match. The winner is triumphant, and the loser must regroup and try again later. Like in agonistic democracy, a clearly defined 'we' fights competes against the 'they,' but the aim is to win, not to destroy 'them' or the sport itself. In this way, a shared understanding of the rules of engagement might achieve a level of agonal respect. Expansion of democracy by including more citizens and deepening their participation, Mouffe (2005) argues, will lead to greater common understandings and result in more harmonious coexistence. While the question of citizens' interest in politics would require empirical investigation to fully respond, disengagement from political institutions does not necessarily mean a lack of interest in politics – rather, it may be simply an indication of discontent with existing political processes (Cameron 2002; Dahlgren 2007).

'Redescribing'[6] Citizens' Involvement in Policy

Several criteria must be met in order to achieve critical democracy in policymaking. First and foremost, the nature and characteristics of a critical-democratic policy formulation require substantial involvement of citizens, compared to other models of citizen involvement. The literature on policy formulation models and research methods associated with democracy focuses on citizen involvement, relying largely on 'participatory policy analysis' (PPA) under the deliberative democracy rubric, though agonistic democracy can be considered a form of participatory policy analysis. Citizen participation tends to be the principle concern of the policy research under the PPA and deliberative democracy rubrics. Peter deLeon (1997) suggests that PPA models generally share several features: (1) a rejection of positivism, (2) a view of phenomenology as a 'better way' to interpret knowledge, and (3) acceptance of an interpretive paradigm of inquiry. Unlike more traditional (and narrow) models of consultative meetings or referendums, PPA models require citizens' commitment to working through problems in order to come to policy advice. PPA also emphasizes an educative objective of participation – citizens learn about a particular issue, about other individuals' and groups' perspectives, and cultivate their citizenship skills. Robert Dahl (1998), who advocates PPA, outlines five criteria for genuinely democratic policymaking across the literature:

- Inclusion in which all citizens have full rights
- Political equality so that when decisions are made, each citizen has an equal and effective opportunity to participate
- Enlightened understanding so that, within reason, citizens have equal and effective opportunities to learn about relevant policy alternatives and their consequences
- Control of the agenda so that citizens have the opportunity to decide which matters are placed on the public agenda and how
- Effective participation so that before a policy is adopted, citizens have equal and effective opportunities to make their views known to other citizens

While research and theory describing PPA (see, for example, Forester 1993; deLeon 1997; Schneider and Ingram 1997; Dahl 1998; Weeks 2000) emphasize the need for citizen involvement, they do not necessarily call for – nor result in – democratic processes aimed at social change, empowerment, enlightenment, and emancipation, which would be necessary to achieve the critical-democratic ideal. Rather, theories of deliberative democracy in the literature tend to follow the Habermasian ideal. As a consequence, most PPA models call for citizen participation that includes certain characteristics as a primary focus: inclusion with equal citizen access, political equality among citizens, an educative component, and devolution of political agenda control to citizens.

Despite the improvements PPA offers over representative democracy, the deliberative version of PPA is not without limitations. Critiques of models that draw on 'ideal speech situations' (see, for example, those raised and addressed in Kohn 2000; Mouffe 2000a, 2000b; Glynos 2003; Gutmann and Thomson 2004) address a failure to acknowledge how power relations circumvent any attempts to 'level the playing field' (Glynos 2003, 189): 'Dialogue itself cannot achieve its own necessary preconditions, e.g., the equality and reciprocity which are prior to any mutual exchange. For this, we need another definition of politics, rooted in contestation, struggle and resistance' (Kohn 2000, 417).

A democratic policy process must, in Shane O'Neill's words, reconcile 'the demands of inclusion and reasoned agreement' (2000, 519). To achieve this, the critical-democratic ideals of citizen participation, deliberation, and empowerment must be realized. Thus, participation must go beyond inclusion and reasoned argument to address social justice and equity. To achieve this critical-democratic ideal, conventional PPA approaches are insufficient. Moreover, as Ricardo Blaug suggests, critical democracy requires that excluded voices and marginalized perspectives can be empowered only by challenging existing institutions. 'On the one hand, effectiveness is seen solely as a product of properly institutionalized activity. On the other, effectiveness is seen to derive from anti-institutional activity' (2002, 107).

While a number of jurisdictions have applied PPA models for various policy issues (see, for example, Schneider and Ingram 1997; Button and Mattson 1999; Weeks 2000; Baiocchi 2001; Fields and Feinberg 2001; Fung and Wright 2001), work in developing practical tools for deliberative democracy is in its early stages (Weeks 2000; Dryzek 2009), with 'a surprising lack of empirical case studies' to describe structures and procedures conducive to citizen deliberation (Bohman 1998, 419; Ryfe 2005). Moreover, it 'cannot be understood as a unified process' because it is open-ended (Button and Mattson 1999, 619). Despite the instances of success reported in the literature, the question of practical feasibility in time, cost, and citizen motivation remains.

First, deliberations obviously require time to plan, organize, and carry out. The actual increase or decrease in the time PPA requires depends on its structure. For example, the participatory education policy process used by Porto Alegre, Brazil (see chapter 8), was time-efficient. Other analyses of PPA models in the literature (for example, Schneider and Ingram 1997; Button and Mattson 1999; Baiocchi 2001; Fields and Feinberg 2001) fail to cite efficiency as a problem. Second, cost is a potential issue. Incremental costs associated with PPA depend on the model applied, and cost has not been identified as a barrier. Finally, citizens must be motivated to participate, and that involves time, energy, and inclination. Some may argue that low voter turnout rates suggest political apathy (see Cameron 2002; Glynos 2003). Though low voter turnout often is considered a signifier of political apathy, others challenge this notion. For example, Peter Dahlgren postulates, 'The ostensible political apathy and disaffiliation from the established political system may not necessarily signal a disinterest in politics per se. That is, if we look beyond formal electoral politics, we can see various signs that suggest that many people have not abandoned engagement with the political, but have rather refocused their political attention outside the parliamentary system. For example, many groups are directly targeting large global corporations for their activities in regard to the environment, working conditions, or other issues rather than going via the formal political system' (2007, 34). However, such levels of interest may not actually lead to participation. While political interest is a necessary condition, it is not sufficient to ensure action. Individuals' personal commitments and responsibilities may limit participation in deliberative forums. Those working more than one job or long hours, or those with unpaid care responsibilities in the home, would likely have less time and energy for participation. For example, research on participatory processes in Porto Alegre, Brazil, reveals that some groups, especially women, are less able or inclined to participate because they have responsibilities in the home (Baiocchi 2001, 2005; Wilkinson 2007). Alternative forums for deliberation (for example, through information and communication technologies) might overcome some of these problems.

Another challenge surrounds the tension between citizen empowerment and ensuring that decisions are made in the end. Where citizens disagree and no consensual solution can be reached (which, in Chantal Mouffe's view, is the reality), how can a temporary resolution be reached? If a government or other institution mandates a process and a means for resolution, does that detract from democracy? Different approaches to PPA approach resolutions in different ways. Some, such as Amy Gutmann and Dennis Thomson (2004), aim for consensus through rational argument. Mouffe (2000b), on the other hand, calls for compromise as temporary resolution until the next time the issue comes up for consideration.

Despite the challenges, research suggests that participatory policy formulation models are not only feasible, but effective. For example, Weeks (2000) reports on four large-scale participatory initiatives, each addressing controversial and politically charged, in municipalities ranging in population between 100,000 and 400,000. He concludes large-scale deliberative processes are feasible and enable governments to take effective action on otherwise intractable issues. Fung and Wright (2001) report on the successes of five different participatory experiments. And Button and Mattson (1999) summarize the results of six deliberative efforts, ranging in size, and conclude that participatory processes can be effective within representative democracies. Finally, over a decade of research into Porto Alegre's participatory budgeting (*orçamento participativo*, or OP, which I describe in detail in chapter 8) suggests not only effectiveness, but sustainability of participatory processes over time (see, for example, Santos 1998; Baiocchi 2001; and others). Thus, achieving a critical-democratic policy process represents a very real possibility.

Concluding Comments

The definition of critical democracy I present here positions this democratic ideal as a mode of associated living (rather than an institutional form) that is both committed to and requires dialogue, inclusive citizen participation, and social justice in both process and outcomes. A central feature of critical-democratic policy formulation in my elaboration of the conceptual framework is agonistic exchange, as defined by Chantal Mouffe. The literature suggests that participation tends to produce better policy decisions, based on the premise that the inclusion of more voices and genuine discussion result in more legitimate and fair decisions (see, for example, Forester 1993; Tyler 2000; Rosenberg 2005; Dryek 2009).

The remainder of the book investigates how Ontario's curriculum policy production during the 1990s measures up to this ideal, resulting in both a critique and an exploration of possibilities to further democratize it. Subsequent chapters follow a conceptual framework building Anne Schneider and Helen Ingram's (1997) scheme of contexts (societal, institutional, and policy formulation) to organize and describe the case study as I describe in the preface. By examining policy formulation in relation to these three contexts, I am able to illustrate 'how policy affects citizens and other aspects of democracy within the society' (Schneider 1998). I advance this framework by exploring each context with respect to critical-democratic criteria, thus incorporating elements from philosophy, education, and the policy sciences. Within each chapter, I outline criteria by which curriculum policy production can be analysed with respect to critical-democracy, focusing on outlining criteria rather than mandating particular designs or structures.[7] These criteria are specific to the aspect of policy production described in that chapter and relate back to the theoretical underpinnings described here.

2 The Politics of 'Common Sense' Policy Production

The 'Common Sense Revolution' is a remarkable document. 'Government isn't working anymore. The system is broken,' it begins, and then goes on to outline a program of reform based on a tax cut, a balanced budget and enormous cuts to government spending, with people on welfare taking the biggest hit.

– John Ibbitson 1996

Policy production cannot be separated from the societal context, which influences procedural aspects and shapes values adopted by policy actors. All the ingredients of public life (physical, social, psychological, political, and historical) simmer, swirl, and combine in the societal context, resulting in a sort of 'primeval soup.'[1] A variety of policy actors interact in the societal context – individual citizens, elected officials, the media, members of social groups, interest groups, and political parties. Through these actors, tensions over values related to policy issues and solutions emerge. This chapter illustrates how neoliberalism and neoconservatism operated in the province, how they were crucial to reframing public policy, and how they compromised democracy in the province.

In describing Ontario's societal context in this chapter, I present the 'historical moment of policy formulation' that 'shapes the framing of policyproblems and solutions' (Stein 2004, 14). A volatile political environment characterized by neoconservative and neoliberal ideologies shaped the province's policy production across all public policy domains, including education. This reveals how elected officials' unprecedented political will and predetermined priorities resulted in discriminatory policies that failed to promote social justice and caused public resistance.

Despite citizens' dissenting voices, the government proceeded with sweeping policy reforms, which set the stage for extraordinary changes to education and compromised the possibility of critical democracy to flourish in policy production and outcomes.

A Highly Politicized Neoconservative and Neoliberal Environment Surrounding Education Reform

To understand Ontario's societal context at the time of reforms, it is necessary to understand the political environment that influenced policy production, content, and outcomes. The highly politicized nature of provincial reforms emerges out of a particularly volatile period in Ontario's recent political history and is influenced by the shifts in education policy during previous political reigns. Ontario is Canada's largest province in terms of population with over 12 million people, second largest in area, and responsible for the production of over 40 per cent of Canada's GDP. Politically, Ontario is a parliamentary democracy, operating under a three-party system comprising the Liberal Party, the Progressive Conservative Party, and New Democratic Party (NDP). The Progressive Conservative Party (commonly referred to as the Tory Party, or Tories) dominated Ontario's political system between 1943 and 1985 in majority and minority leadership governments, earning the nickname 'Big Blue Machine.' During this period, the party was led by a succession of 'red Tory'[2] premiers: George Drew, Leslie Frost, John Robarts, and Bill Davis. Their respective governments created some of the province's most progressive social legislation (including the Ontario Code of Human Rights), created most of Ontario's social programs and Crown corporations, and are considered responsible for strong economic growth. The Tories were reduced to a minority government between 1975 and 1977, then returned with a majority government in 1981. Interestingly, while the provincial legislature has been dominated by Tory governments, Ontario supported the Liberal Party at the federal level over most of the century (Cameron 2002).

As was the case in Ontario during the period of reform studied, neoconservative and neoliberal ideologies have driven recent education reforms in a variety of jurisdictions, most notably in the United States, Canada, and the United Kingdom. Ideologies play different roles, depending on the context of the jurisdiction, often leading to systems of values that emerge 'unsystematically from beliefs entertained by individuals and groups' (Kogan 1985, 18) and become policies when power is gained and those values are made legitimate by individuals and groups in power (Kogan 1985; Manzer 2003). Thus, a predominant neoliberal and neoconservative ideology shapes which values are privileged in the political sphere and play an important role in the resulting policy environment and outcomes.

The terms *neoconservative* and *neoliberal* are often used interchangeably. However, while related, there are key differences between them. Neoliberalism grew out of liberalism and shares some similarities: 'Whereas classical liberalism represents a negative conception of state power in that the individual was to be taken as an object to be freed from the interventions of the state, neo-liberalism has come to represent a positive conception of the state's role in creating the appropriate market by providing the conditions, laws and institutions necessary for its operation. In classical liberalism, the individual is characterized as having an autonomous human nature and can practice freedom. In neo-liberalism the state seeks to create an individual who is an enterprising and competitive entrepreneur' (Olssen 1996, 340, qtd in Apple 2005, 14). Thus, neoliberal language and policies tend to focus on 'the market' and privatization of public goods, and emphasize competition and choice. Resulting neoliberal education foci include school privatization, career-focused education, and accountability through testing and other measurable indicators, often with punitive consequences for under-performance (e.g., funding tied to high-stakes test scores) (see, for example, Apple 2001b; Purcell 2009).

Neoconservatism, on the other hand, prioritizes the market and individual liberty as secondary to restoring traditions constructed around themes such as nationalism, allegiance, authority, and natural order (Apple 2001b; Loxley and Thomas 2001). To do so, neoconservatives use rhetorical devices that invoke traditional conservatism and classical liberalism (terms including *autonomy, individualism,* and *small government*) for ends very different from those of traditional conservatives – persuasion, consolidation of power, and subordination of citizens (Loxley and Thomas 2001; Shudak and Helfenbein 2005). Neoconservatives tend to 'celebrate a mythic past' (Reddick 2004, 73) with reference to strong nuclear families, effective schools that had a traditional, uncontestable curriculum, and within which crime, drugs, and violence were not issues. In education, neoconservative policies advocate for centralized control of curriculum content, standardized curriculum and testing as mechanisms for accountability and 'excellence,' and emphasis on 'back to basics' schooling (Apple 2004).

Despite their famous compatibility, the neoconservative and neoliberal frames contradict one another on several fronts. One might use the slogan coined by Michael Apple (2001a, 66), 'new markets, old traditions,' to describe their seeming incompatibility. The discourse of competition, markets, and choice on the one (neoliberal) hand, and accountability, standards, and common culture on the other (neoconservative) hand appear contradictory. Free markets are said to be natural and neutral and to reward effort and merit; attempts to restore a glorified set of cultural norms and lost traditions seem contrary to laissez-faire market direction, since they aim to subordinate and control citizens through authority.

However, while they embody different tendencies, they do reinforce one another in interesting ways. When the neoconservative and neoliberal frames come together, symbolic language emerges within public educational discourse, evident in many contemporary reforms: competition, choice, excellence, standards, accountability, and 'common sense' (Levin 1998c; Apple 2004). Two principles guide resulting reforms: (1) priority of markets, and (2) the substitution of consumers for citizens, where democracy is defined less by common public choice than by private market decisions. For instance, stemming from these principles, 'investment' in education through reform is purported to be the solution to economic problems by creating a better workforce. However, the idea that education can solve economic problems is a myth lacking empirical evidence (Welch 1998; Taylor and Henry 2002). Moreover, prioritization of these aims shifts scarce resources away from 'emphasis on equity issues' in reform efforts (Welch 1998) that conflicts with the critical-democratic ideal.

Between 1985 and 2000, Ontario politics experienced a period of volatility. In 1985, the Tory party made a shift to the right on the political spectrum with the election of Frank Miller as leader after the retirement of Premier Bill Davis. After forty-two years of Tory rule in the province, the 1987 election resulted in a Liberal party majority government. In 1990, the Liberals called another election, which resulted in an unexpected NDP majority government, with Bob Rae as premier. Faced with a budget deficit during a time of recession, the NDP introduced cutbacks to social spending as well as the Social Contract, an initiative that forced public-sector workers to take unpaid Rae Days and froze wages. The Social Contract led to discontent in the labour movement, with many traditional NDP supporters vowing to bring this government down. Rae also introduced unpopular revenue-raising taxes and operations. Thousands of party members resigned from the NDP, and it became evident that the party was headed for a defeat in the 1995 election.

At that time, the Tories led by soon-to-be premier Mike Harris campaigned on a controversial but straightforward platform called the Common Sense Revolution, promising to solve Ontario's economic problems with lower taxes, smaller government, and pro-business policies intended to create jobs. As a political platform, the Common Sense Revolution was presented in plain language, offered concrete (and arguably over-simplified) 'solutions' to the provinces woes, and remarkably never mentioned the Progressive Conservative party in its text. This was a specific response to research and polling undertaken by Harris and his advisors, which suggested that Ontarians were fearful about their futures and angry at government for not providing leadership (Blizzard 1995; Ibbitson 1996). It was launched on 3 May 1994 through a province-wide marketing campaign, including a press conference, an 800-number television campaign, a provincial bus tour, and the distribution of 2.5 million hard copies of the twenty-one page document (Woolstencroft 1997). The 'Common Sense Revolution' (1994) begins,

> The Chief Economist at Midland Walwyn, one of Canada's most respected securities firms, concludes . . .
> *This plan will work. The Mike Harris plan to cut provincial income tax rates by 30% and non-priority services spending by 20% will give Ontario a balanced budget within four years, and create more than 725,000 new jobs.* – Mark Mullins, Ph.D. (Economics)
> The people of Ontario have a message for their politicians – government isn't working anymore. The system is broken.

The Common Sense Revolution strongly reflects neoliberal and neoconservative ideologies. The term *common sense* itself is associated with neoconservative and neoliberal rhetoric (Gandin 2002; Apple 2004; Fleury 2005). Some have drawn parallels to Thatcherism and Reaganism (see, for example, Keil 2002). More importantly, the framework laid out in the 'Common Sense Revolution' offers solutions that include lowered taxes, smaller government, and policies favouring business. The analysis that follow describes how this played out in a variety of issues. The Harris government's use of 'distinct ideological underpinnings' (Locke 2006, 7) caused a great deal of tension (White 1997a; Locke 2006) in the province. As I make clear in the next sections of this chapter, government framing of social problems cloaked in neoliberal and neo-conservative frames were well executed and especially powerful. This ideological framing was prominent in media coverage and among policy actors.

In its first year in the public sphere, the Common Sense Revolution was dismissed by mainstream media, elites, and much of the business community as 'unjustified, petty, divisive, mean-spirited, and cruel' (Blizzard 1995, 73–4; White 1998, 261). Some Common Sense Revolution claims misrepresented or oversimplified Ontario's actual situation. For instance, the 'Common Sense Revolution' (1994) states that 'Ontario is among the highest-taxed jurisdictions in North America,' yet White (1997a) reports that Ontarians' taxes were lower than most Canadians' and that the OECD reports that the average production worker in the United States pays higher taxes than her Canadian counterpart. The Common Sense Revolution claims that Ontario's spending was out of control failed to acknowledge that, as a percentage of GDP, Ontario was well below the provincial average (ibid.).

However, despite these criticisms, the Common Sense Revolution platform resonated with voters. The 1995 election resulted in a large Tory majority, though no longer under the traditional, red Tory agenda. Rather, the party espoused a neoconservative ideology with emphasis on accountability, smaller government, and policies that favour business (intended, in the spirit of trickle-down or supply-side economics, to strengthen the economy). According to Elections Ontario, 62 per cent of eligible voters participated in the 1995 election, and the Tory party became the first party to jump from third place to first in the legislature since 1923.

The Harris government rejected traditional approaches to policy agenda-setting. Instead, a group of insiders nicknamed 'the whiz kids' and 'right young things' by the media drafted the 'Common Sense Revolution' and advised the premier on policy during the first few years of his leadership (Blizzard 1995). None of the whiz kids had a political background – in fact, they had careers in the private sector, and all were in their twenties and thirties. Despite their collective limited backgrounds in politics and public policy, they held power within the ranks of elected leadership. 'They are the power elite of the administration, and the guardians of its ideological purity. On their good days, they imbue the government with fresh-faced optimism. On their bad days, they sound like an infomercial' (Ibbitson 1996). While the whiz kids appeared to be successful in their work publicly, not all members of the party were pleased. Indeed, some Tory members of provincial Parliament (MPPs) publicly expressed concern that the whiz kids had more power than elected officials in setting direction and policy (Ibbitson 1996).

To fulfil the Common Sense Revolution mandate, Harris was quick to enact changes. Income taxes were cut, municipalities and school boards amalgamated, hospitals closed, labour laws repealed, education spending slashed, and welfare payments cut. The Tories enacted aggressive 'downloading' that transferred the cost of various programs and responsibilities to municipalities. A research participant who served as a political staffer during the time of reforms explained, '"The Common Sense Revolution," which really was the guidebook for all political staffers at that time had, I think, very thin but clear references that were designed to communicate directly to all public reform ... And that a new, clearer curriculum was something the government was committed to doing.'

Table 2.1 summarizes promises made in the 'Common Sense Revolution,' details (including some targets) articulated in the original document, and highlights of the swift actions taken by the Harris government upon taking control of the Legislative Assembly of Ontario. Bill 26, the Savings and Restructuring Act 1996, nicknamed the Omnibus Bill, was reported to be the first example of this government's curtailing of the democratic process. Its moniker refers to its scope – it amended forty-seven laws, to allow the government to proceed with its downsizing plans without interference. The proposed legislation was drafted in secrecy, since the finance minister was to introduce it along with a sensitive economic statement in November 1995. The premier's staff and ministers saw the wording for the first time the night before it was introduced in the House. Riddled with errors, it was 'highly flawed' when introduced, and ministers were expected to defend their respective sections, even though they had not been involved in the writing (Crittenden 2001). Initially, a strategy of downplaying the bill resulted in a lack of attention, since most journalists mistook it for a 'process bill,' without any hard policy directions (Ibbitson 1997). Soon its magnitude became apparent. While the Tories were intent on passing it before Christmas, the opposition was intent on stopping it. After 'humiliating' moments in the Legislature, the bill passed after 160 amendments (Crittenden 2001) in January 1996. As Randall White observes, 'It's hard not to be impressed by the speed

Table 2.1 Summary of Common Sense reforms

Common Sense Revolution promise	Details articulated in Common Sense Revolution	Highlights of actions taken
Lower taxes	• Cut provincial income tax rates by 30% in three years (by 15.0%, 7.5%, and 7.5% annually) • Disallow municipal tax increases • Introduce 'fair share' health care levy	• Taxes were cut, but initially by 3.4% in year one, 12.5% in year two, and the balance in year three.
Reduce government spending by 20% in three years	'Protected priority services' • Health care • Law enforcement • Education 'Savings found so far' • Reduce number of politicians • Reduce bureaucracy • Reform welfare (workfare/learnfare, children in need, seniors and disabled, fraud) • Reform education • Eliminate jobsOntario • Cut grants and subsidies (art is mentioned) • Reduce capital budget, including $300 million from Ministry of Transportation • End public housing • Reform legal aid	• Government spending increased by 21% during the Harris tenure. • 20% of social assistance costs were downloaded to municipalities and benefits were reduced benefits by 22%, while the cost of education was uploaded to the province from municipalities. • jobsOntario was eliminated. • Bill 81, the Fewer Politicians Act 1996, reduced the number of seats in the provincial legislature from 130 to 103. Bill 25, the Fewer Municipal Politicians Act 1999, reduced the number of municipally elected representatives. In addition, the government imposed a uniform, regional government through the creation of 'mega-cities,' thereby reducing the number of municipalities from 815 to 447. Specific program and budget cuts: • 390 co-op and non-profit housing projects cancelled, and rent control eliminated • Ministry of Health budget reduced by $1.5 billion and hospital budgets by 18% in 1995 • Arts funding reduced by 28% ($220 million) (continued)

Table 2.1 Continued

Common Sense Revolution promise	Details articulated in Common Sense Revolution	Highlights of actions taken
		• K–12 and post-secondary funding reduced and JK made optional • 30 hospitals closed in 1997 in response to recommendations by Health Services Restructuring Commission; recommendation made that health-care spending increase overall • Bill 26, the Savings and Restructuring Act 1996, repealed laws governing clean-up of abandoned mines and forest protection Examples of privatization: • In 1999 the Ontario provincial auditor raised health and safety concerns resulting from privatized highway maintenance • In 2001, U.S.-based Management and Training Corporation won a bid of $79 per inmate per day (56% of average cost in Ontario), to run controversial penitentiary in Penetanguishene
Cut government barriers to job creation, investment, and economic growth	• Abolish the job-killing payroll health tax for small business • Eliminate all red tape and reduce regulatory burden • Freeze Ontario Hydro rates for five years • Cut employer Workers Compensation premiums by 5% • Repeal the NDP's job-killing labour legislation – Bill 40	• A Red Tape Commission was formed but made little headway, as was a Restructuring Secretariat whose role was to identify and advocate cultural and operational change within government.

- End inter-provincial trade barriers through bilateral negotiations
- Encourage private sector to provide childcare for working parents

- Bill 7, Labour Relations Employment Statutes Law Amendment Act 1995, passed, which dismantled the NDP's Bill 40, allowed 'replacement workers,' and allowed employers to mount anti-union campaigns. Bill 31, the Economic Development and Workplace Democracy Act 1998, completed the stripping of workers' rights, so there was no penalty for harassment during a union organizing drive. Finally, Bill 49, the Employment Standards Improvement Act 1996, among other things, made it more difficult for unionized workers to make claims against employers and collect wages owed. Bill 8, the Job Quotas Repeal Act, eliminated legislation for employment equity.
- Arbitration for public sector workers was constrained through Bill 26, the Savings and Restructuring Act 1995.
- The Ministry of Labour was reduced by half, including layoff of one-third of employment standards inspectors.
- The government repealed Bill 79, the Employment Equity Act, 1993, and eliminated the Anti-Racism Secretariat and its counterparts in various ministries.
- Childcare subsidies were eliminated.

(continued)

Table 2.1 Continued

Common Sense Revolution promise	Details articulated in Common Sense Revolution	Highlights of actions taken
Reduce size of government, saving $500 million	• Reduce government • Sell assets, including LCBO	• Overall government structure remained, with minor adjustments to ministry configurations, but ministry 'vertical silo' organization remained. Internally, ministries were directed to identify and concentrate on 'core business' and reduce or eliminate peripheral activities, especially if private or volunteer sectors could perform them as 'alternate service delivery.' The OPS decreased from 81,000 to 61,000 FTE. According to the provincial auditor, the rate of privatization increased – outside consultant spending rose from $271 million in 1998, to $662 million in 2002. Some bureaucrats left their permanent positions and returned immediately as consultants at triple their salaries; in some cases duplicate contracts were issued and paid for the same work, suggesting misuse of funds. • A 1999 task force recommended what assets the province should and should not privatize. LCBO and TVO convinced some ministers that 'conservative' principles meant government agencies should compete in the marketplace while adopting business practices. However, the sale of Highway 407 to a Spanish-Quebec consortium in 1999 for $3.1 billion was the largest privatization in Canadian history. Critics suggest that the proceeds of the sale were far less than had the government paid off the highway over several of decades while collecting tolls, and were later revalued at $9 billion.

- In 1999, Management Board announced the government would sell $200 million worth of property (totalling 4 million square metres) the government no longer needed, part of its $5 billion in assets. Sales of these assets were questioned when Ontario Realty Corporation was found to be selling land to an unusually large number of Tory campaign contributors, sometimes below market value, and costing taxpayers as much as $11 million.
- In 1998, when the Electricity Competition Act was introduced for second reading, the minister of energy, science, and technology told the Ontario Legislature, 'We're not talking about privatization.' Harris's 2001 announcement that the government planned to sell Hydro One was stopped in April 2002 by the Ontario Superior Court of Justice (Payne v. Ontario) ruling that the Ontario government did not have legal authority to relinquish public control of Hydro One.

Balance the budget within four years	'The tax and spending reductions and the creation of more than 725,000 jobs will all combine to ease the financial burden on government and bring the deficit down to zero.'
	- When the books became public after the 2003 election, Ontario was left with a $6 billion deficit. Sales of assets, which were promised to go towards deficit reduction, were instead used for operating budgets.

and dispatch with which Mike Harris and his party seized control of the provincial ship of state' (1998, 247).

While the Harris government was very quick to act on their promises, and indeed accomplished a great deal in an extremely short time, their progress resulted in some interesting contradictions. The platform and policy directions are clearly a hybrid of neoconservative and neoliberal philosophies.

Though the large number and scale of changes are far too numerous for analysis here, several salient examples shed light on their nature and scope. First, we see a neoconservative emphasis on control as the answer to social problems defined by the Common Sense Revolution (e.g., welfare, education). In this way, the highly prescriptive policy that, as I will illustrate in the next section, failed to address racism and diversity. While conforming to the neoconservative position, the prescriptive nature of social policy directions is at odds with a neoliberal laissez-faire philosophy.

Second, the 'Common Sense Revolution' defines a neoliberal economic philosophy that calls for smaller government – specifically, less spending and less government intervention in 'barriers to job creation, investment and economic growth.' While the Harris government preached neoliberalism and small, laissez-faire government, they became one of the most interventionist governments in Ontario history (Ibbitson 1997; Keil 2002). Similarly, campaign promises to reduce government spending and balance the budget were not met, in fact increasing spending by 21 per cent, and increasing the deficit to $6 billion – ironic, given political rhetoric about the 'tax-and-spend' left.

Third, the Common Sense Revolution espouses a neoliberal emphasis on cuts to taxes to stimulate the economy, and provide incentive for political support. While the Harris government did follow through on a 30 per cent tax cut, it applied only to the top marginal tax rate, thus benefitting only the wealthiest Ontarians (White 1997a) and was largely offset by user fees and increased costs to provide services privately, including a health care levy (Dare 1997). In this way, the effects of tax cuts, and the benefits, may not have been as far-reaching as the Common Sense Revolution promised.

Race, Discrimination, and Construction of the 'Other' in Common Sense Reforms

As Jean Trickey asserts, 'It is not easy to talk about racism in the best of times' (1997, 113). However, given critical democracy's concern with social justice, attention to racism must address the degree to which Ontario's reform process approaches this ideal. The perceived need to tighten control, to centralize decision-making, and to re-establish a 'common culture' (and a common curriculum for the province) cannot be fully understood unless needs such as these are situated within the role of race and the fear of the 'other.'

The Common Sense Revolution, in keeping with the neoliberal frame, implies that white, managerial, and middle-class people are the norm (Trickey 1997). However, this position fails to recognize that race is always present in every social configuration (Ladson-Billings 1998) and is especially salient in the context of public policy.

Not surprisingly, the origin of the Common Sense Revolution itself was a small group of white, middle-class Harris insiders, all men with the exception of one woman, Leslie Noble (Blizzard 1995, White 1998). Indeed, the 1995 Tory caucus of eighty-two members included only eight women. Randall White describes the 'mood and style' of this government as a 'boys' club' (1998, 257). This phenomenon of white, middle-class men dominating politics has been documented elsewhere (Gillborn 2005; López 2005), and, while it may not have been a conscious plan, the politics of whiteness and white privilege have been enormously effective in the formation of coalitions that unite people across cultural differences, across class and gender relations, and against their best interests (Apple 2001; Dyer 1997). In *White*, Richard Dyer explains, 'There is no more powerful position than that of being "just" human. The claim to power is the claim to speak for the commonality of humanity. Raced people can't do that – they can only speak for their race. But, non-raced people can, for they do not represent the interests of a race. The point of seeing the racing of whites is to dislodge them/us from the position of power, with all of the inequities, oppression, privileges, and sufferings in its train, dislodging them/us by undercutting the authority with which they/we speak and act in and on the world' (Dyer 1997, 2, qtd in Apple 2001, 209).

This failure to acknowledge the politics of race, the invisibility of race as experienced by many whites, is what Apple (1999, 2001a) refers to as an absent present. Indeed, the critical-democratic ideal requires serious attention to social justice in order to reconstitute power relations with the ultimate goal of addressing inequity and oppression. The Common Sense Revolution treatment of difference stems from its neoconservative and neoliberal roots. While neoconservatism seeks to preserve white advantage through denial of race difference (where race is something to be overcome), the neoliberal stance attempts to limit white advantage through the denial of race difference (where attempts are made to narrow differences that divide) (Winant 2004). Both tend to ignore the issue of systemic racism, and in doing so, the resulting 'refusal to engage in "race thinking" amounts to a defense of the racial status quo, in which systemic racial inequity, and yes, discrimination as well, are omnipresent' (8). For this discussion, I share the position of Michael Omi and Howard Winant that race is neither an ideological construct nor an objective position. While sometimes (and incorrectly) considered a discrete category, race is not separate from other aspects of identity or 'modalities of power': 'Race, class, and gender all represent potential antagonisms whose significance is no longer given, if it ever was ... [R]ace, class, and gender (as well as sexual orientation) constitute "regions" of hegemony, areas in which certain political projects can take shape' (Omi and Winant 1994, 68).

These issues of race and racism are enormous and cut across a broad swath of social issues. While it is impossible to address all of the overt and subtle issues adequately within this section, I will describe some of the general problems presented by race and support them with selected policy examples. Through the Common Sense Revolution, the Harris government promoted a resurgence of racism through absent presence in three ways: (1) ideology that relied on particular images and coded language, (2) a structure that cut programs and services for immigrants and minorities and eliminated employment equity, and (3) a process that tacitly incites racist sentiments while failing to provide services and recourse for victims of inequity and oppression (Trickey 1997). I elaborate upon each of these in the subsections that follow.

Racism in Common Sense Revolution
Ideology and Language

Previous federal and provincial governments acknowledged inequities based on race, gender, and other identity forms through their legislation and program initiatives. Indeed, Ontario had been considered a leader in addressing issues of social justice, equity, and anti-racism prior to 1995 (National Anti-Racism Council of Canada 2002; Rezai-Rashti 2003; Carr 2006). The Common Sense Revolution was laden with conscious and deliberate efforts in the framing and policy process to keep such issues under wraps.

Racism in the Common Sense Revolution was perpetuated through denial of racism and race inequity, as well as representations of other groups as the 'problem.' The Harris government employed a 'politics of polarization' by which it distracted people from the real issues at hand by directing citizens' anger against the poor, sidetracking the real agenda, which was increasing benefits for the already privileged (Dua and Robertson 1999). For instance, 'frontal attacks on the poor' (Keil 2002, 589) through constructions of the 'other' as a drain on the system, a self-serving 'special interest group,' or illegitimate immigrants were created. In these images, the disadvantaged 'deserved' their state because they had not worked hard enough, or failed to assimilate into mainstream, middle-class white culture. Thus, failure boiled down to a perceived lack of character (Apple 2001a). Such rhetoric 'paints a picture that excludes some and incites fear and opposition towards the "other"' (Trickey 1997, 114).

For example, media coverage about the so-called quota bill (Bill 79, the Employment Equity Act 1993, discussed in more detail in the next section) reported that 'discrimination against white males in hiring, needs to be rescinded' (Thornton 2008, 7). By using language and characterizations of 'others' threatening white male privilege, the Harris campaign evoked strong emotions on job quota legislation and other issues that proved crucial to their success (Thornton 2008). A similar technique was used in television advertisements. The narrator of one advertisement said, 'Mike Harris will require welfare recipients to work for benefits. Lyn McLeod opposes work for welfare' (8). This second example positions the dangerous 'other' as a welfare recipient, implying he or she is able to work but chooses not to. This is akin to Catherine Lugg's (1998) observation that 'political kitsch' is an effective strategy to demonize the other, using stereotype. At the same time, and despite these dangerous characterizations of 'other,' the Conservatives elected to banish the words *racism, anti-racism,* and *equity* from all policies, programs, initiatives, public pronouncements, and institutional dealings (Corson 2002; Carr 2006). Thus, 'by controlling the political agenda, the Harris government was able to not mention the word racism publicly for eight years, thus ensuring that there would not be a single anti-racism initiative' (Carr 2006). In doing so, Harris reinforced colour-blindness through the 'gaze of whiteness as the unacknowledged norm' (Apple 1999, 15) and attempted to absolve the government of having to face difference and equity. Behind this refusal to acknowledge difference is a fear of the other, in that it implies that acknowledging diversity or race might divert the ideology from restoring an idealized and romanticized past when people purportedly shared a common culture (Apple 2001a).

Common Sense Revolution Structure and Program
Cuts That Undermine Social Justice

Racist structures maintain white property in the form of public goods through both policy texts and funding (Ladson-Billings 2009). By shifting funding away from social programs that would benefit marginalized groups, governments reinforce white privilege while exacerbating race inequity. The Common Sense Revolution included numerous structure and program cuts that not only blatantly eliminated anti-racism initiatives and services to advocate for victims of discrimination but also contributed to perpetuating the marginalization of groups (especially women, minorities, the poor, and Aboriginals). Under the previous government, an Anti-Racism Secretariat was created, as well as its counterparts within other ministries (Bedard and Lawton 2000; Carr 2006). Paul Carr describes the challenges faced by the Ministry of Education's branch: 'One of the shortcomings of the Ministry of Education's Anti-racism and Ethno-cultural Equity Education Branch was that almost all of the staff, the majority of whom were racial minorities, came from the school board sector, and they did not have experience in government, which represented a radically different institutional culture. The Branch was not seen to be an integral part of the Ministry but, rather, an outside entity, almost a "special interest group," and this fact disadvantaged it greatly' (2006).

The branch released a resource guide for anti-racism and equity education, and issued Policy and Program Memorandum 119 in 1993, requiring all school boards to develop anti-racism and equity policies by March 1995 and to plan for implementation within five years. These initiatives were dismantled within weeks of the election. Ontario's Royal Commission on Learning (described in the next chapter) even went so far as to suggest that there was systemic racism in education, and that such data should be collected, though the Tory government removed the ability to do so. The Anti-Racism Secretariat, the Race Relations and Policing Unit at the Ministry of Solicitor General, Racism and Ethno-Cultural Equity Education Branch, and other similar structures were eliminated almost immediately. Their elimination sent a strong message about the political priorities and the degree to which the Harris Tories were willing to acknowledge race and discrimination as issues facing Ontarians.

The Common Sense Revolution platform included a commitment to eliminate Ontario's Employment Equity Commission, a newly

established agency with a mandate to advance the workforce representation of women, visible minorities, Aboriginal Canadians, and
the disabled. Within a week of taking office, the new premier fired
the head of the Employment Equity Commission (Hucker 1997). As
well, the Common Sense Revolution promised to repeal Bill 79, the
Employment Equity Act 1993, attacking it as the 'quota bill.' While Bill
79 was weak,[3] it attempted to address systemic discrimination that disadvantaged women, racial minorities, Aboriginal people, and people
with disabilities (Dua and Robertson 1999). In its elimination through
Bill 8, the Job Quotas Repeal Act, the government eliminated what
little support there was to battle these forms of discrimination. These
programs and legislation were dismantled quickly, keeping the campaign promise. Through the government's actions in dismantling pay
equity, 'some 100,000 women stood to lose $81 million in pay equity
payments. The government insisted that low wages are determined
by the market, and direct comparison between women's and men's
jobs was not possible' (Dua and Robertson 1999, 138).

Additionally, subsequent legal action found that two aspects of the
Common Sense Revolution were in violation of the Canadian Charter
of Rights and Freedoms with respect to discrimination. First, in the 2002
case Falkner v. Ontario (Director of Income Maintenance, Ministry of
Community and Social Services), the Ontario Appeals Court ruled that
the 'spouse in the house' rule under the Family Benefits Act, depriving
sole-support mothers of welfare when they begin to live with a man,
violates section 15 of the Charter. The court found that Act discrim-
inated against women on the grounds of sex and marital status and
was also discriminatory on the basis of receipt of social assistance, in
view of the economic disadvantage and stigma experienced by welfare
recipients (Jackman 2006). Second, in the 2001 case Dunmore v. Ontario
(Attorney General), the Supreme Court of Canada found the exclusion
of agricultural workers from the province's labour relations regime was
a violation of section 2 (d) of the Charter. Evidence showed that agricultural workers suffered repeated attacks in efforts to unionize, com-
pounding their historic vulnerability to social isolation and economic
exploitation. The Court found it is the duty of the state to ensure the
right to freedom of association.

I offer a final example that identifies the effect of budget cuts in education. The number of teachers for special needs students was decreased
to meet funding formula targets (Corson 2002), further disadvantag-
ing this vulnerable group. Interestingly, special education has received

similar downsizing during neoliberal education reforms in other jurisdictions, including the United Kingdom (Apple 2001a). Research by the
National Anti-Racism Council of Canada found that reduced school
board budgets had tremendous negative effects on other services available to diverse student populations. They report,

> The boards of education of the other larger urban centres in the province,
> are currently fighting with the government of Ontario to stave off any
> further budget losses which would result in further compromises of the
> boards' equity and human rights commitments. These boards of education
> have collectively refused to work any further behind the scenes to squeeze
> more money from the province, and have either passed deficit budgets or
> refused to pass a balanced budget containing the program cuts which they
> consider to be unacceptable. Some of the most dramatic cuts to date have
> been made to ESL, heritage language, literacy, adult education programs,
> and related supports, which primarily affect racialized and Aboriginal
> learners. Library resources for racialized and Aboriginal communities are
> also dwindling. There are very few targeted resources for smaller groups,
> such as Francophones of colour. The histories, contributions and perspec-
> tives of Aboriginals and people of colour are thus becoming more and
> more difficult to teach and increasingly devalued. (National Anti-Racism
> Council of Canada 2002)

These structural and program cuts, beyond their symbolic significance,
chipped away at any progress that might have been made towards
participatory parity for those affected by these government actions.
The repeal of employment equity legislation was a blow to representation and recognition and aimed to reduce redistribution for minority
groups. In addition, program cuts, particularly in education, represented a move away from redistributive equity in schools for diverse
student populations, and they failed to recognize those members of
the school who had benefited from the previous policy.

Anti-Democratic Processes in the Common Sense Revolution

The Harris government's withdrawal from anti-racist initiatives resulted
in its functioning as a racist government with little regard for social justice. Indeed, 'the dismantling of progressive policies and programs is
an abdication of the leadership necessary in a complex, multicultural

society. Just as the government's images have moved us toward fear and resistance, anti-racist images could have led us in the opposite direction' (Trickey 1997, 119). The Ontario Human Rights Commission (OHRC) is mandated to enforce the Ontario Human Rights Code in the province. During the Harris government's tenure, the OHRC reduced its size from sixteen offices in 1990, to eleven in 1997, making it less accessible to the public. According to the Ontario Government's report to Committee on the Elimination of Racial Discrimination (CERD), the percentage of race-based complaints received by the OHRC from 1994 to 1997 ranged from 23 to 26 per cent every year. However, what the government report omitted was that, over the same period, the percentage of race-based complaints that were dismissed by OHRC increased from 31 per cent in 1994/5 to 49 per cent in 1997/8 (National Anti-Racism Council of Canada 2002). To dismiss claims, OHRC used section 34 of the Ontario Human Rights Code to dismiss many claims (National Anti-Racism Council of Canada 2002). Under this section, OHRC has the discretion not to deal with a complaint if 'the complaint could or should be more appropriately dealt with under another Act' – an action consistent with the government's 'core business' mandate.

Those working in the defunct Anti-Racism and Ethno-Cultural Equity Education Branch at the Ministry of Education describe instances of bureaucratic resistance training about anti-racist initiatives, and a general unwillingness to recognize systemic racism, reported by Carr (2006) and Harney (2002). Paul Carr, who worked at the Ministry of Education during this time, offers several examples of anti-racism discussions being shut down.

> In a late-afternoon discussion about the context for, and analysis of, a few proposals we were developing in relation to school councils, parental involvement and at-risk students, I made the point that without focusing on the whole community, including marginalized, racial minority groups, and without gathering data to document and develop measures and outcomes for the whole system in an inclusive way, we could be causing and amplifying systemic barriers destined to enshrine the re-productive, non-progressive nature of schools.
>
> The response by a senior official, in a slightly exasperated tone, was clear. While pointing to the door, the official stated: 'You know where the door is; if you don't like it you don't have to stay.' I inferred that public servants were not there to provide strategic advice, to consider the research,

to caution government of the implications, and, especially, not to discuss social justice when it does not intersect with plans originally designed for the business world . . .

There were a number of complaints from people saying they resented 'being treated like a racist' at anti-racism training sessions. One incident sums up the imagery of the White educators collectively making the symbolic cross-sign with arms intersecting to ward off the demons: a colleague in the Anti-racism area attended a committee meeting of a variety of Ministry staff working on a document intended for middle-school children related to values, influences and peers, and was told the moment he entered the room that 'this is not an anti-racist committee,' to which he responded, without missing a beat, 'oh, it must be a racist committee.' (2006)

The dynamic of white privilege was brought to the fore, since bureaucrats perceived the Anti-Racism and Ethno-Cultural Equity Education Branch staff as attempting to disrupt the conventional, accepted educational terrain. Through their policy changes, the government removed ministries' ability to collect or maintain data on racial origin, thus making it impossible to even identify areas of inequity (Carr 2006), let alone work towards recognition as a means of contributing to participatory parity.

In addition to this particular recommendation, the government failed to follow up on other initiatives to address race. In 1995, the *Report of the Commission on Systemic Racism in Ontario's Criminal Justice System* made recommendations to address racism within the system. The Harris government failed to follow up on or implement the commission's recommendations, which are so critical during a time of government-imposed cutbacks to social programs, increasing poverty levels, and reduced opportunity for marginalized groups. In their 2002 federal report, which examined a multitude of indicators for each province, the National Anti-Racism Council of Canada concluded that during the time of the Harris government, 'on every front, Ontario has failed to provide and sustain effective education initiatives, public awareness, policies, and activities that would promote acceptance, inclusion and diversity' (National Antiracism Council of Canada, 2002). This collection of changes in ideology, language, programs, and processes amounted to a total disregard for social justice by the political leadership. More importantly, these changes represented a step backwards, since gains made in equity-focused programs were dismantled as a first priority of the newly elected government.

Resistance and Public Dialogue in Response to the Common Sense Revolution

The Harris government's actions caused waves of protest among citizen constituencies (Gidney 1999; Robertson 1998). This government 'had campaigned on a platform promoting "direct democracy"' (Clarkson 2002, 116) yet ignored a non-binding referendum indicating 76 per cent of citizens opposed and disregarded the limited public hearings, underscoring their discontent with the Harris approach to policy production. In October 1996, labour leaders organized Days of Action, initially planned to be a five-day protest against the Harris government. Ultimately, between 1995 and 1998, Ontario labour organized eleven one-day citywide strikes in protest of the Harris government. Nothing like this had ever happened on this scale in the province (Goldfield and Palmer 2007). Despite the 'constant fire of resistance, civil disobedience, and alternative developments ... attacks on the legitimacy of public protest challenged but did not break the movement' (Keil 2002, 597). First, because the government viewed the Days of Action as illegal, and because workers shut down their workplaces, unions were initially worried about repercussions. Workers' contracts contained no-strike clauses, so organizers deliberately avoided the term *strike*, settling on *day of action*. Second, to protect workers, organizers developed a strategy called 'cross-picketing,' whereby individuals picketed at a location other than their own workplace (Goldfield and Palmer 2007). Private and public sector workers walked off the job, and thousands of people attended rallies to voice their discontent.

In 1998, a series of protests aimed at stopping Bill 160, the Education Quality Improvement Act (its contents discussed in detail in the next chapter) arose – ranging from marches at Queen's Park to a teacher work stoppage (Basu 2004; Kozolanka 2007; Reshef 2007). The legislation was perceived as particularly controversial – both in its content and in its approach to enactment. Its chief architect was rumoured to be prominent Toronto lawyer and Harris insider Guy Giorno, though Giorno went to great length to downplay his role in Bill 160, despite a media perception that he was largely responsible. When asked what expertise he had in education, Giorno admitted he had none (Schmidt 2001, 68). Law professor and former advisor to the Peterson-era government Patrick Monahan pronounced the powers granted in Bill 160 unconstitutional: 'I think there are real, significant constitutional issues that are raised. I think you could attack these on completely open-ended grants of discretion to the cabinet. It is a problem of this government, generally, in drafting legislation. It is a very troubling approach' (White 1998, 281).

Various political actors attempted to reframe the 'problem' of Bill 160. In particular, the Ontario Teachers' Federation (OTF) attempted, though unsuccessfully, to shift the frame from 'self-interest' towards 'justice' with the message that 'teachers are fighting to protect publicly-funded education for our students' (Kozolanka 2007, 187). Indeed, the Harris government rejected 'quality-based' criteria to evaluate the effectiveness of social policy, and privileged 'competition-motivated' reductions in government in the form of quantitative measures (Clarkson 2002). Similarly the non-profit organization People for Education attempted to address the issue of Bill 160 by emphasizing that the proposed changes within it were going 'too far, too fast' (Kozolanka 2007, 188). Despite the protest, Kirsten Kozolanka's analysis of press coverage suggests media coverage 'did not reflect the burgeoning public opposition' (191). Government success in minimizing dissent and acquiring buy-in has been attributed to their ability to adjust issue framing to appeal to the public (Basu 2004; Kozolanka 2007).

Despite protests and voiced discontent in 1998 and during the first term of the Harris government, the Tories were successful during the 1999 election, winning fifty-nine seats,[4] and giving Harris the distinction of being the first Ontario premier to win back-to-back majorities since 1967. Just under 58 per cent of eligible voters participated (Elections Ontario n.d.). Some speculate that the success stemmed from the perception that the Harris government was able to deliver – despite the consequences or outcomes of policies. A political staffer suggested this perception was not an accident:

One, very simple [rationale prevailed] – putting a tick in the box was absolutely critical. Mike Harris, rightly or wrongly had a pretty strong brand with people. When I knocked on doors, 99 people would say that, 'I hate the fact that he amalgamated Toronto, I hate the fact that he did this or that. But this guy did what he said he would do and I love him for that and that is why I am going to vote for him again.'

   The level of cynicism within the general public with politicians is still rampant. But, for a very short period of time, here came along a guy who said something and did it. That was a pretty compelling driving force in terms of holding political staff, Ministers, and the entire public service to account. Getting it done and saying that it was done, the fulfilling of the promise was very, very important. I know that on one level, it was a very simple trite analysis but it really was the prevailing philosophy of the day. (Will, political staffer)

Some suggest that part of the Harris government's ability to appeal to public sensibilities stemmed from effective use of advertising and media to frame and shape issues. Kirsten Kozolanka's research examines the Harris government's public relations tactics. In her analysis of the Common Sense Revolution, she argues that 'the neo-liberal project developed its communications capacity to facilitate the task of gaining public consent, it used increasingly sophisticated professionalized public relations strategies borrowed from the private sector' (2007, 17).

Indeed, the Harris government spent significant amounts of money on polling and advertising. For instance, Kozolanka reports that in 1997 the government spent $3.5 million on advertising and $0.2 million for polling for Bill 160 alone. Moreover, media coverage of Harris government initiatives, in Kozolanka's extensive analysis, tended to strengthen government positions, since the media were slow to pick up on issues significant to the public in favour of addressing government media released. This speaks to Mark Purcell's (2009) assertion of the neoliberal capacity to co-opt and incorporate democratic resistance (in this case, through public dissatisfaction communicated in the Harris government advertising) to achieve its own ends.

As well, Kozolanka found that the media lacked 'preparedness' and 'resources' to provide alternative sources and frames, usually deferring to the government as the source of authority. This speaks to the importance of framing dynamics (Schneider and Ingram 1997) in describing how policy actors interpret issues, events, and information. Borrowing from Robert Benford and David Snow's synthesis of the framing literature related to social movements, participants act as 'signifying agents actively engaged in the production and maintenance of meaning for constituents, antagonists, and bystanders or observers. They are deeply embroiled, along with the media, local governments, and the state, in what has been referred to as "the politics of signification"' (Benford and Snow 2000, 611).

As such, citizens and participants in the policy process become involved in framing policy problems and solutions. In the critical-democratic ideal, the framing and construction of such issues includes official and unofficial venues where actors deliberate the policy problem at hand (in this case, curriculum policy). These may include the media, forums organized by governmental institutions or non-profit organizations, and citizen actions and ingenuity. Within a critical-democratic environment, there ought to be opportunities for citizens share their perspectives, ideally in agonistic exchanges that allow them to come to understanding of the position of 'the other,' without the goal of consensus. A variety of perspectives and voices ought to be included in the media. Finally, concerted efforts to include perspectives from traditionally marginalized groups in this process of social construction are crucial to critical democracy.

Evidence reveals that the media adopted the Harris government's language and ideology when framing education reform. Minister Snobelen's infamous 'crisis' of educational problems that could be solved only by Common Sense reforms framed the issue in the language of the market.[5] In the words of political staffer Will, a 'tick in a box' upon completion of a given solution (or reform) was politically important. Such oversimplification of 'solutions' prevailed. The government successfully communicated message via paid commercials and advertisements (described in the case study), as well as popular news media, perpetuating market analogies. The language of the market used by Minister Snobelen – 'customer' and 'business' – should not be central to discourse in the public sphere (see, for example, Henig 1995; Caldwell 1999; Apple 2004), because it undermines commitment to the public good.

At the same time, evidence suggests that many Ontarians agreed that the education system could benefit from improvements, though not all agreed with the framing and proposed strategies of the Harris government.[6] However, no concrete evidence[7] of alternative framing emerged in the public sphere. At best, citizens attempted to resist and critique Common Sense educational solutions through protest (for example, protests against Bill 160, the teachers' work stoppage of 1998) and published dissent, but no wide-reaching alternative framing of issues emerged. Some isolated and less well-publicized critiques appeared, especially in teacher federation correspondence and publications with smaller circulations aimed at limited audiences (for example, *This Magazine, Our Schools / Our Selves*, and *Orbit*). An environment that failed to provide public space for anyone to challenge the government's construction of issues further compromised the situation. The critical-democratic ideal requires opportunities for citizens to express a variety of points of view (including dissent), rather than government-dominated construction of issues described here. The absence of opportunities for a more inclusive approach to the social construction of issues guiding

Ontario's curriculum policy reform suggests a shortfall of critical democracy in the public sphere.

Concluding Comments

The tumultuous and volatile period of Ontario's political history was characterized by an unprecedented acceptance of neoliberal and neoconservative reforms. The Harris Tories employed a number of tools, including use of the media and advertising, to quickly enact a number of their Common Sense Revolution campaign promises within a highly politicized environment. These reforms, as a whole, worked against social justice through their framing, program cuts, and changes to policy production and enactment. Despite widespread public resistance in the form of massive public protest, this government reigned for two consecutive majority terms. Upon reflection, 'the *Common Sense Revolution* has affected the civil discourse of Canada's most populous province. A society that has governed itself by seeking to accommodate conflicting interests has been transformed into one where interests hurl themselves against one another until the most powerful prevails. Such a confrontational method has made possible enormous changes, that in many cases, were arguably long overdue. It has also left the citizenry raw and bruised and surly towards one another' (Ibbitson 1997, 285).

These divisive consequences eliminated the possibility for critical democracy to flourish. While the government accomplished tremendous changes to public policy, both the aggressive political processes they employed and the content of the policies themselves failed to address social justice and equity. Indeed, as I argued in this chapter, their ideology, language, cuts to programs, and changes to processes failed to address race, reified white privilege, and positioned the 'other' in a damaging light. This chapter sets the political tone for the educational restructuring in Ontario that follows in the next section of the case study.

3 Restructuring Education

Curriculum questions presuppose and anticipate a political debate in which questions about the kind of curriculum that would promote a desirable form of social life are openly acknowledged and consciously addressed.

– Wilfred Carr 1998, 326

Contemporary education reforms are an evolution of education systems over time. In the previous chapter, I discussed how strong neoliberal and neoconservative forces dominated politics and policy leading up to Ontario's education reform. These macro forces affected the way in which educational issues and problems are shaped and addressed. Swift and significant changes to education and curriculum policy followed through Ontario school reform (OSR) under the Common Sense Revolution. OSR included a new approach to funding and major changes to policies governing school board organization, curriculum, student assessment, and teacher working conditions. Curriculum policy formulated between 1996 and 2000 included significant reduction in the number of secondary school courses offered (reduced from 1400 to approximately 200 in thirteen subject disciplines), more prescriptive and comprehensive learning expectations for each course and subject area in K–12 education, and a standardized structure for assessment and for organization of expectations.

This chapter describes how educational problems were framed as crises during the Common Sense Revolution and places this framing in a broader historical context, which begins this chapter. I provide an overview of some of the major educational changes in twentieth-century Ontario in order to historically situate the nature and scope of the reforms studied.

Education Reform in Ontario during
the Twentieth Century

Education in Canada has always been a provincial jurisdiction, as outlined by the British North America Act of 1897, and later in the Constitution Act of 1982.[1] Ontario's formal school system took shape in the mid-nineteenth century when elementary schools were first centralized under the School Acts of 1846 and 1847, creating a province-wide Board of Education. These also established early school finance policies that led to free elementary schooling for all (Curtis, Livingston, and Smaller 1992; Manzer 1994; Prentice 2004). In the twenty years that followed, school attendance increased, leading to the organization of students into classes of uniform achievement (Curtis, Livingston, and Smaller 1992). The School Act of 1871 established publicly funded secondary schools upon pressure from the middle class (Curtis, Livingston, and Smaller 1992; Manzer 1994).

Presently, Canadian provincial and territorial Ministries of Education oversee education policy and legislation, while local or district school boards administer educational programs. Matters of school curriculum are overseen at the provincial and territorial level. While there are variations in structure and terminology, schooling in most provinces (including Ontario) is divided into elementary and secondary levels of education. Elementary education, also referred to primary/junior (P/J), spans kindergarten through grade eight, while secondary – also referred to as intermediate/senior(I/S) – spans grades nine through twelve presently, but included grade thirteen and Ontario Academic Credit (OAC) courses[2] in past years. The minister of education serves as the political head of the Ministry of Education, with a group of public servants[3] to carry out the ministry's work.

Pertinent legislation appears in Ontario's Education Act, and Regulations within the Act (which have the force of law) provide legal authority for governance. However, the ministry also creates 'policy documents,' which, while not legislation, provide directives to boards and educators. Curriculum policy documents fall into this category. Unlike legislation, policy documents need not be approved by the Legislative Assembly of Ontario.

Teaching federations have historically played an important role in Ontario education. In 1944, the Teaching Profession Act created the Ontario Teachers Federation (OTF), largely in response to 'agitation' caused by teacher unions (Gidney 1999). The OTF became an umbrella organization for its affiliates – a structure that continues today. At the present time, the affiliate federations are Elementary Teachers' Federation of Ontario, Ontario Secondary School Teachers' Federation, Ontario English Catholic Teachers' Association, and Association des enseignantes et des enseignants franco-ontariens. All teachers in public and separate boards are members of an OTF affiliate. In addition to the present-day collective bargaining function of the affiliates, they also play a role as secondary policy actors, engaging in the political area through public policy statements and voicing their reactions on behalf of membership publicly.

Education reform has been a constant in Ontario since the beginning of the century. As Robert Gidney points out, 'There was no shortage of proposals of change' since the early 1900s (1999, 30). While specifics are too numerous to detail here, Gidney suggests three central ideas that guided education reform in North America during this century. First, urbanization and industrialization called for a new and more relevant curriculum. Second, developments in psychology changed the way that classroom pedagogy and learning are conceptualized. Finally, a 'widening of democracy' (30) called for extended education for all children, and what he refers to as 'democratization of school itself.'[4]

Throughout the twentieth century, there have been constant tensions between 'conservative' or traditionalist education agendas and 'progressive' or Deweyan education agendas in Ontario (Manzer 1994; Gidney 1999; Lemisko and Clausen 2006). The former advocate a 'back to basics' or '3 Rs' approach, while the latter concern themselves more with development of the whole child and a concern with pedagogy (especially child-centred pedagogy) as much as content. In his analysis of progressive 'frames' ('progressive platitudes, language and goals,' which appear in education policy documents' [Davies 2002, 269]) in Ontario education commission reports between 1950 and 1995, progressive ideals were reworked such that they became vague and reflected contingent meanings that did not necessarily translate into the adoption of a progressive educational stance in schools (Davies 2002). Progressivism shaped education throughout Canada during the mid-century (Patterson 1987; Manzer 1994, 2003). While Robert Gidney acknowledges that the language of progressivism appears in many education policy documents from the 1950s on, his perception is that progressive education practices were not enacted in classrooms: 'Progressivism made far less headway in Canada, and especially in Ontario; still, it provoked equally fierce opposition in newspapers, magazines, and speeches from both educators and the laity' (1999, 35).

Despite the progressive language in policies, practice in classrooms as well as local and district board priorities embodied a more conservative approach to education (Gidney 1999; Lemisko and Clausen 2006). Some attribute the lack of progressive practice (and indeed rather late inclusion of progressive ideas in education policy relative to other countries) to Ontario's overt acknowledgment of Great Britain's traditionalist influence on the province's educational system. Several reasons have been proposed for teachers' lack of enactment of progressive policies during the middle of the twentieth century. Teachers' failure to employ progressive pedagogies is attributed to lack of understanding and refusal to teach while using anything but traditional methods, and evidence of a 'lack of courage' among young teachers (Patterson 1987; Lemisko and Clausen 2006, 1111).

A number of seminal reports and positions documents framed the educational landscape and shaped policies themselves. First, the *Hope Report* of 1950, the result of a Royal Commission on Learning, recommended (among many other things) compulsory schooling for children aged six to sixteen, with kindergarten programs in every school board. It also recommended the abolishment of province-wide exams and grade thirteen, as well as the addition of special education. The recommendations were largely ignored, since the report was considered controversial. Key features of the *Hope Report* include holistic education, relevance, promotion of a social-conservative agenda, and streaming (Davies 2002).

The Robarts Plan of 1960 was concerned with 'education for all' – not just those going on to post-secondary schools – to increase the graduation rates. It introduced streaming of students into various branches, as well as a variety of different courses that students could select all the way up to grade twelve. The resulting policy, *HS1*, laid out the secondary school graduation requirements, for the first time allowing flexibility in course selection. This ushered in the development of provincial curriculum 'guidelines' to direct course content and suggest teaching materials and methods, though these documents were not particularly prescriptive (Gidney 1999; Anderson and Ben Jaafar 2003).

In 1968, the publication of the *Hall-Dennis Report* (under the official title *Living and Learning*) was met with great interest – in fact, the report sold 60,000 copies within sixteen months of publication (Gidney 1999). The report offered 258 recommendations for education reform, and in the decades that followed its publication, it 'attained almost mythic status, praised or blamed for changing the face of public education in Ontario' (Gidney 1999, 75) and strong 'impact on official educational ideology in Ontario' (Manzer 1994, 222). While many of its recommendations were ignored, Ontario adapted some of its progressive principles such as student-centred pedagogies, which shifted the role of the teacher from directing students to guiding them. Like the *Hope Report*, *Hall-Dennis* also called for a holistic model of education but also included what Scott Davies classifies as an 'equity agenda' (2002, 276). Notably, this report recommended decentralization of decision-making to increase school board autonomy (Manzer 1994). The *Hall-Dennis Report* states that 'each school board should establish its own priorities and exercise real autonomy. Only on such a principle can diversity be encouraged in cultural, architectural, curricular, and organizational matters' (in Manzer 1994, 194).

By the 1980s, discontent with Ontario's education system became evident. Diverse groups of educational stakeholders, ranging from teacher unions to the private sector were questioning educational quality (Gidney 1999). A call for 'back to basics' education and standardization were emerging. To address this, the Secondary Education Review Project was struck and released its report in 1981. This report laid the groundwork for policy reforms including new graduation requirements, replacing *HS1* with more standardization through compulsory courses in *Ontario Schools: Intermediate and Senior* (*OSIS*). The ministry developed new curriculum guidelines between 1982 and 1987 to support *OSIS*.

In 1987, the ministry commissioned an inquiry into Ontario's secondary school dropout rate headed by George Radwanski (Manzer 1994; Gidney 1999). The resulting report, *The Ontario Study of the Relevance of Education, and the Issue of Dropouts* (commonly known as the *Radwanski Report*), concluded that the education system failed to address economic shifts from manufacturing to services, that students lacked engagement, and that they did not graduate with requisite skills and knowledge for the economy. Its recommendations contrasted with those of *Hall-Dennis* – including implementation of early childhood education, standardized testing, de-streaming, outcomes-based curriculum, and a common core curriculum to replace the credit system (Manzer 1994). The ministry enacted several of these recommendations, including de-streaming up to grade nine and a common curriculum (Gidney 1999). Tensions emerged during legislative committee hearings between those who favoured education for growth of students as individuals, versus those who were concerned with training students for economic competitiveness (Manzer 1994). According to one observer, 'One side invoked nightmarish visions of schools as assembly lines, producing widgets for the economy, while the other foresaw armies of pseudo-philosophers attempting to discuss the state of humanity but unable to read or write' (Manzer 1994, 239).

Under the leadership of Minister of Education David Cooke, the NDP established a Royal Commission on Learning, which published *For the Love of Learning* in 1995. The initial reaction to the report was positive (Manzer 1994; Gidney 1999). As one newspaper editorial described the report, 'The soft and mushy and warm and fuzzy education system that we have had for the last 25 years has been officially brought to an end' (Gidney 1999, 231). Key recommendations in the report included establishing the College of Teachers as a professional governing body, eliminating OAC, greater emphasis on career preparation in secondary schools, the increased role of information technology, a more standardized curriculum, and literacy and mathematics testing. Though the NDP lost to the Tories shortly after they made commitments to these recommendations, the Harris government picked up where the NDP left off, endorsing a number of recommendations from *For the Love of Learning*. This report, unlike its predecessors, contains an accountability agenda characterized by a return to standardization in curriculum and testing, as well as new governing institutions. As such, *For the Love of Learning* shaped the Tory agenda.

As a whole, this collection of developments illustrates how actual change to policies throughout the twentieth century were incremental, with some (but certainly not all) recommendations making their way into policy, despite occasional recommendations that proposed significant change. As well, tensions between 'progressive' and 'conservative' educational stances persisted (Manzer 1994). Overall, this summary of historic events provides insight into how secondary school reform (SSR) contributes to the overall pattern of educational change in Ontario. Changes championed by the Harris government reflect a pendulum swing to the right of the political spectrum and represent yet another shift in the province's educational landscape.

Setting the Agenda: 'Useful Crises' as Educational Reform Framing

At the heart of the framing during Ontario's school reform during the 1990s were struggles over what, if any, education problems needed to be 'fixed.' The framing of education issues occurred in a very public fashion, largely by political leaders' statements reported in the media, and responses from others (ranging from special interest groups to teacher federations to individuals) in equally public forums. Public framing of these issues began in 1995, apparently unintentionally. A former teacher himself, Premier Harris was often accused of unduly attacking the teaching profession. His appointment of John Snobelen as minister of education caused a great deal of controversy. Snobelen, MPP for Mississauga West, never completed high school. This controversy escalated when a videotape of Snobelen addressing senior bureaucrats was leaked in which the minister explained how he would 'invent a crisis' to garner support for education reform (Brennan 1995). As he said to ministry staff, 'Creating a useful crisis is part of what this will be about. So the first bunch of communications that the public might hear might be more negative than I would be inclined to talk about otherwise ... Yeah, we need to invent a crisis, and that's not just an act of courage, there's some skill involved' (Brennan 1995). Not surprisingly, this revelation caused both concern and cynicism within the education community. The manufactured crisis set a negative tone within the province, despite an apology that followed two days later. Moreover, there was speculation that Harris and Snobelen were planning a major confrontation with teachers in the province, using the media to villainize teachers and their federations (Lupton 1997; Gidney 1999). This environment of animosity between teachers and the provincial government set a tone for policy formulation.

Despite public outcry in the education community calling for Snobelen's resignation, school reform was undertaken, with Snobelen remaining at the helm until 1997, when David Johnson was appointed minister of education. There was widespread speculation that Minister Johnson was appointed in anticipation of further conflicts with teachers, since Johnson was considered a strong negotiator without a history of animosity with teachers. In a front-page story, the *Toronto Star* referred to him as 'Mr Fixit' upon his appointment, in reference to his success in negotiating with doctors in the province to avert labour action (Girard and Ruimy 1997). Within three years of Snobelen's first announcement, Ontario's curriculum was completely rewritten and implementation was well under way. Heather-Jane Robertson quotes Minister Snobelen as saying, 'Power is the rate at which your intentions become reality' (1998, 49). Minister Snobelen discussed curriculum reform during members' statements in the Legislative Assembly in 1997:

A report commissioned for the second national consultation on education in 1996 noted that jurisdictions are reforming education by promoting parental involvement in education; reducing the number of school
boards, while expanding the use of school councils; renewing curriculum
to focus on what students should know or be able to do; providing greater
accountability to parents and the general public by instituting assessment
tools based on a standard curriculum ...

The hallmarks of Ontario's new education system will be high standards and accountability. Our standards will be clear, measurable and
comprehensive in all grades, and the new revised curriculum will be the
same across the province. Our new curriculum for grades 1 to 9 will be
released in the coming months. This rigorous and demanding new curriculum, focusing on language, math, science and technology, is the first
stage in building a complete curriculum that provides a solid foundation
in the basics. (Legislative Assembly, *Debates and Proceedings* [21 January
1997], p. 1540)

The minister's remarks highlight the perceived need for standardization through centralized curriculum development.

While aspects of reform – especially new funding – were contested
in the Legislative Assembly, the political opposition did not contest
centralized curriculum reform. For instance, in 1997 Liberal member Lyn McLeod said, 'There is a role for the province in education.
I happen to think there is a greater role for Ontario in education than
perhaps the province has taken in the last few years. I think it's important for the Ministry of Education, the provincial government, to take
a larger role in looking at curriculum, that there is perhaps too much
duplication, too much repetition and, yes, perhaps too much unnecessary use of resources in rewriting the curriculum documents board by
board by board. I think you could have more standardized curriculum
material prepared by the provincial government, with input from the
professionals in the field, and still leave some local flexibility for curriculum that responds to local needs' (Legislative Assembly, *Debates and
Proceedings* [21 January 1997], p. 1710). McLeod's statement is consistent
with results of research by Livingstone, Hart, and Davie (1996), which
suggests that less than one-third of Ontarians wanted government-
controlled curricula. Again and again, the issue of the crisis 'manufactured' by John Snobelen was raised. As Curtis, a consultation
participant, summarized his perception of the situation, 'When we first
started, I said, in 1995, when the Conservatives came to power, and the

whole Snobelen idea that you had to convince everyone that the system was broken. Everybody knew that the system was not broken. It was a little like "weapons of mass destruction." It was an effort to really try to bring about a public perception about education, in order to really provide a rationale as to why they were under-funding education' (Curtis, consultation participant).

The minister went even further, setting the tone of the reforms to come at the Ontario Public School Teachers' Federation annual convention in August 1995, framing education in the language of business: 'In primary and secondary education, the client is the student and the customer is the taxpayer and parent ... I believe a ministry of education that is clear about the business it is in, that is clear about who the customer is and who the clients are, that has a defined service product and a commitment to deliver it, would be a much different organization' (Snobelen 1995). 'Customers,' he explained, were complaining about the current state of the education system, and changes had to be made to remedy those complaints. He went on to allude to increased accountability for teachers, whom he defined as 'front-line service providers,' clearly understanding that his plan would encounter resistance: 'Now, if front-line service providers are placed at the top of the organization chart, it isn't all happiness and roses. It means increased responsibility and increased accountability. And increased accountability means you cannot hide ... Change is rarely well-received by the status quo. It tears at the heart of a fiction we call security' (1995).

This series of events framed the issue: the school system was 'broken' and could be 'fixed' through sweeping reforms, including a new and better curriculum policy. These repairs, the framing continues, would address the 'needs and wants' of education's 'customers.' As such, this view of education and its 'customers' shapes what sorts of solutions are offered to the policy problem at hand. Customers want specific learning outcomes, as well as standardized learning so that each student graduates with the same knowledge and skills, and accountability is placed on the education system to ensure that kind of consistency. The agenda for curriculum reform was set.

The Grand Scale of Common Sense Revolution Education Reform

Certainly, Ontario's curriculum changes directly affected a large number of citizens, given that during the 2000/1 school year (the first year in which full implementation of the SSR curriculum policy took effect) the Ministry of Education reported that there were nearly 709,000 secondary school students and over 34,000 secondary school teachers in 830 publicly funded schools. At a very general level, two characteristics of the SSR process stand out. First and most notably, the ministry relied heavily on outsourcing for the majority of policy work, given the tight timelines and lack of internal, bureaucratic capacity. Second, the ministry incorporated extensive consultation in an attempt to represent the perspectives of many stakeholders. This attempt addresses a major principles that drives public policy – to ensure that diverse public needs are met by stakeholder involvement. On the surface, these aspects of Ontario's policy process appear potentially democratic.

For the Love of Learning, which I described earlier, released shortly before the Harris government's election, shaped SSR and represented a pendulum swing to the right of the political spectrum. Moreover, the scope, tone, and speed of reforms introduced by the Harris government under the Common Sense Revolution were unprecedented. The environment surrounding educational reforms – including curriculum policy formulation – was nothing less than tumultuous, characterized by conflict with teachers. There was also a fundamental shift in framing educational issues, with the introduction of business metaphors in which education was a 'business' whose 'customers' were parents and students, reflecting the ideological position of the government in power.

The Common Sense Revolution, though encompassing dozens of public policy areas, called for significant reform to education. While this research is concerned solely with the curriculum policy formulation, education reform as a whole provides broader context for understanding curriculum policy outcomes. Thus, salient education reform areas enacted under the Harris government and relevant to this research include:

- Introduction of student literacy and math testing through establishment of the Education Quality and Accountability Office through Bill 30 in 1996.
- Elementary program reform (with new policy documents released in 1997), which resulted in more specific and more 'rigorous' outcomes-based curriculum policy documents for grades one through eight, purported to align with secondary school reforms that followed.

- Secondary school reform, which encompassed policy initiatives
  enacted first in 1998. Changes to *OSIS* practices included the elimination of the fifth year of high school (OAC), a reduction from
  1400 secondary school courses offered to approximately 200 in
  thirteen subject disciplines, a more rigorous, outcomes-based curriculum for K–12 education with prescriptive policy documents,
  more standardized graduation requirements with changes to
  compulsory courses, the integration of a compulsory 'community service' component to graduation requirements, and the re-
  introduction of streaming, replacing basic, general, and advanced
  streams with academic and applied in grades nine and ten, and
  university, college, and workplace streams in grades eleven and
  twelve.
- Elimination of the Anti-Racism Secretariat and its counterpart at
  the Ministry of Education (Bedard and Lawton 2000; Carr 2006),[5]
  and subsequent deletion of references to pro-equity goals from curriculum policy. Carr notes that 'a substantial amount of promising
  social justice work [originating in the Ministry of Education's Anti-
  Racism, Equity and Access Branch] was simply left unfinished or
  sent to the archives when the Conservatives took power' and eliminated that branch (2006).
- Cuts to school board operating budgets, and a new, provincially
  centralized finance structure for education through Bill 160, the
  Education Quality Improvement Act in 1997, based on recommendations by the Education Improvement Commission (EIC)
  established through Bill 104. In addition, Bill 160 changed teachers'
  working conditions (reduced preparation time, increased length
  of school year, fewer professional development days, and changes
  to class size). As well, it called for administrators (principals and
  vice-principals) to be removed from federations. The subsequent
  introduction of Bill 74, the Education Accountability Act, in 2000
  extended and strengthened provincial powers introduced in Bill
  160. By 1999, education spending was reduced by $1 billion from
  the previous year's budget.
- Establishment of the Ontario College of Teachers (OCT), a self-
  regulatory professional body responsible for teacher certification,
  through Bill 31, the Ontario College of Teachers Act in 1996, which
  effectively transferred the oversight of certain professional matters
  (such as discipline, certification, and continuing education) from the
  ministry and federations to the OCT. By 2000, the Ontario Teacher

Qualifying Test for new graduates from initial teacher education programs was implemented, with a plan for ongoing teacher testing tied to recertification in future years.[6]

- Amalgamation of school boards through Bill 104, the Fewer School Boards Act in 1997, reduced the number of boards from 124 to 72. While the intention of this legislation was to reduce costs and eliminate duplication of services, critics argued that it reduced local power in matters of school governance (Anderson and Ben Jaafar 2003).
- Establishment of Parent Councils to participate in oversight at the school level.

This brief summary highlights how education reform as a whole during the late 1990s was all-encompassing, reflecting change to all aspects of Ontario's K–12 education system. Curriculum policy formulation is one piece of these broader reforms to education – though curriculum policy change is affected by broader systemic changes under SSR. Remarkably, these SSR changes (in addition to changes to other public policy domains outside of education) occurred over an extremely short time, demonstrating the political will and power of the Harris government to see its agenda through. The creation of arms-length organizations (EIC, EQAO, OCT) provided institutionalized sources of credibility for the government's position through third-party testimony.

All policy actors interviewed for this research concur that the highly politicized and contentious environment surrounding education reforms, and their consequences. In addition to the tensions between the premier, minister, and educators, there was a sense that the general public had lost confidence in teachers. Two representative positions emerged from interviews with policy actors:

> I'm a former secondary school person. I know that [teachers] had lost public support. We had lost it. I think I can give you all kinds of reasons why, but I don't think we were knowledgeable about how deep the resentment was, and how much public support we had lost ... [A]s a principal at the secondary school level, or superintendent, when you met parents or members of the public, particularly parents, they'd be nice because their kids were in your school. When I came here, people could tell you what they feel without having to fear repercussions. I was ... astonished, I was moved, very moved, by the depth of their fed-upped-ness. They were fed up with

secondary school teachers [stemming from perceptions of] lack of caring, lack of willingness ... total resistance to any suggestion of how you could do things better, or that we were the least bit accountable for student success. (Erica, bureaucrat)

One of the big problems with the teaching profession and Mike Harris – and this is an aside from the main issue but it has bearing on the whole process – Mike Harris decided to take on the whole profession, particularly focusing on the unions. It had exactly the opposite effect of what he wanted. When Mike Harris was elected, I would say that there was quite a big gap between the unions (the teachers' federations) and the average classroom teacher. It wouldn't have taken much to have driven a huge wedge between them and to have won the teachers over independently of the unions, isolated the unions.

Mike Harris politically should have done [that], instead of which, the way he went about operating, he and his ministers of education – Snobelen in particular – drove the entire teaching profession into the arms of their unions. So if Mike Harris had said, 'Today's Tuesday,' the unions would have said, 'No it isn't,' just as a matter of course.

So every teacher in the province began to develop this culture that everything that comes out of this government has to be bad ... There were lots of ideas that were out there that Mike Harris implemented, they weren't his ideas. Now, the profession got to dislike them because Mike Harris had come up with them, not because they were bad ideas. (Robert, project manager)

These quotations describe two important consequences of the political environment. First, the government successfully manufactured a crisis in education – but the crisis resulted in decreasing support for teachers. This is particularly interesting in light of findings by Livingstone, Hart, and Davie that, in 1996, public satisfaction with Ontario schools had been steadily increasing to over 50 per cent since 1988, when satisfaction had been at only 30 per cent. Second, teachers banded together through their federations in response to animosity created. This 'us and them' mentality permeated the atmosphere. In one form, a perception emerged among writers that they were 'protecting' their subjects. As well, policy actors – especially writers and bureaucrats – felt that they had to resort to subversive tactics to ensure their voices were heard. I describe these consequences in more detail in the next chapter.

An Absence of Universally Accepted Direction

Michael Apple states that problems in schools were caused by 'competing social visions' (1996, 97), and he criticizes the status quo for failing to situate curriculum and school reform within a larger social and democratic vision. Education policy involves the re-contextualization of ideas among stakeholders – governments, educators, private research foundations, students, employers, and parents. Through stakeholders' involvement, discourse occurs that has the potential to shape public opinion through debates between groups. These struggles to legitimate a particular social construction of an issue through stakeholder discourse are crucial to critical-democratic policymaking.

For it to succeed, a critical-democratic policy process ought to begin with a discussion of policy formulation goals. In Chantal Mouffe's conception, actors need not agree with the goal, but they must accept it as a temporary resolution after opportunities for deliberation and understanding. Evidence suggests an absence of clear direction from the public in Ontario, which I describe in greater detail in the next chapter, though no apparent discussion occurred in the public sphere. While policy actors directly involved in the process report understanding what the official goals were, they did not necessarily agree.

The official procedural goal of the policy formulation process put forth by the ministry and the political leadership is straightforward: to create highly standardized and prescriptive, yet value-neutral curriculum policy documents using a 'template' within an aggressive timeline. This goal reflects the neoliberal and neoconservative agendas described in chapter 2. The Ministry of Education's statement of education goals contributes to better understanding of this procedural goal. On their website at the time of reform, the ministry stated,

- Ontario students receive the best education in Canada. Ontario's public education system will strive for excellence in the following ways:
  - Students will have access to top quality education, characterized by high standards, clearly stated expectations and frequent, straightforward evaluation;
  - Students will have the right to learn in a safe and respectful environment;
  - The school system will prepare students for higher education, for entering the workforce and for assuming the responsibilities of citizenship;

- Teachers will have full opportunities to be the best qualified and the most highly skilled in Canada; and
- Parents will have a strong voice in the education of their children.

Not surprisingly, the ministry's mission statement, like its reach and mandate, was broad. It began with an overarching commitment that 'Ontario students receive the best education in Canada' and went on to identify five ways in which this goal would be achieved. The third point, 'the school system will prepare students for higher education, for entering the workforce and for assuming the responsibilities of citizenship,' articulated a dual conception of purpose: instrumentalist and ideological.

The instrumental purpose is concerned with preparation for further education and employment. The second, ideological purpose is concerned with citizenship by way of its emphasis on moral and societal learning.[7] Given the historical context of policy development in Ontario, the articulation of these educational aims was probably not a coincidence, since the political leadership was extremely cognizant of public opinion – see, for example, 2001 poll results reported by Julie Smyth (2001), which are consistent with the ministry's direction – and strived to align policy with the stated preferences of constituents, often relying on survey and research data.

The diversity of content goals presents an excellent opportunity for deliberation, debate, and learning among policy actors – especially given the absence of a 'clear direction' from public input cited in research commissioned by the ministry and carried out by Praxis Consulting. Had a venue or forum been available for these discussions to take place, policy actors might have learned from one another and taken different approaches to their individual roles in the process. The absence of opportunities for citizens to be involved in such interchanges represents a missed opportunity for the type of agonistic dialogue called for in a critical-democratic policy process.

Tory Policy Goals: Speed, Standardization, and Value-Neutrality

Goals are the intentional aspects of policy designs emerging from perceptions of conditions measured against a preferred situation – and therefore 'reveal a great deal about conceptions of the state of democracy in a society' (Schneider and Ingram 1997, 82). Which goals are chosen result in advantages for some and disadvantages for others, and thus are related to democratic concerns of justice. They may be broadly framed in terms of fairness or equity, or narrowly formed to address only certain groups. According to Anne Schneider and Helen Ingram (1997), policy best serves democracy when goals reflect a balance among democratic values, or when they focus on one or more aspects of democracy deficient in the societal context, reflecting the public interest over private interests.

Bureaucrat Marcellas outlined the situation preceding curriculum reform. He explained that once the Harris government took office, the policy directions laid out by the previous NDP government remained the same[8] – while the 'outcomes' sought were similar, the 'style of implementation' and policy formulation process were very different. In particular, the Harris government focused on 'internal design' as well as the design of the approach to consultation. According to Marcellas, the Harris government eliminated some steps and tended to move from an 'educator control' towards a 'public input' model. However, he remarks that teachers tended to use the public consultations to convey their perspectives.

All policy actors interviewed understood and complied with the procedural goal of completing the policy formulation within stated timelines. However, not all policy actors shared the official content goals and ideas about educational purpose. As I will show later on, many writing team members felt that they were guardians of their subjects and believed that the official policy goals could destroy their subjects. Thus, their individual goals were preservation of certain aspects of their subjects. Consultation participants reported a variety of personal goals – ranging from 'making sure that there was content – meat and potatoes in this curriculum' (Alison, consultation participant) to social justice goals, like Curtis's. However, no substantive discussion took place over these competing goals.

Policy actors concurred about the official content goals of curriculum policy formulation. The first goal was to establish standardized learning expectations for all students in the province. As Janelle, a bureaucrat, framed it, 'What we knew is [that] the curriculum that existed before this gave no standardized expectations anywhere, it was so open to local interpretation. We wanted to make sure that all kids learned the same things.'

A second goal involved content- or knowledge-based curriculum policy documents in which content is phrased in the form of student expectations. Alison, a consultation participant, made the point of clarifying that in her view, 'knowledge-based curriculum was not just nebulous kind of philosophical ideas, because that's not a curriculum.'

Concluding Comments

While no strangers to educational change, Ontarians experienced an unexpected shift in the approach to large-scale reform. The Harris government's creation of a 'crisis' in education against the backdrop of the Common Sense Revolution shook the educational landscape. Despite an absence of clear direction on educational aims, the government embarked on a series of measures that altered the structure and content of education in the province. Beginning with the controversial introduction of Bill 160 amidst protest, the province was divided. The government proceeded with aggressive reforms characterized by a clear and centrally mandated policy agenda. The directions set forth, and the approach to swift policy formulation and implementation, clearly contradicted the inclusive approach consistent with the critical-democratic ideal. Moreover, given the intimate relationship between education and democracy, values – especially social justice – must become central aims of education and curriculum policy development if the democratic ideal is to be realized. This sets the stage for an investigation into the details of the secondary school curriculum policy formulation described in the next three chapters.

4 Hidden Privatization in the Institutional Culture: Policy Actors or 'Hired Guns'?

Depending on the choice of policy design elements and the way they fit together, government can appear fair or unfair, logical and straightforward or illogical with hidden agendas, helpful or antagonistic, and an important aspect of life or irrelevant.
        – Anne Schneider and Helen Ingram 1997, 79

Curriculum questions presuppose and anticipate a political debate in which questions about the kind of curriculum that would promote a desirable form of social life are openly acknowledged and consciously addressed.
        – Wilfred Carr 1998, 326

The Harris government is widely recognized for achieving ambitious policy goals in Ontario during the 1990s – but not without trade-offs, particularly with respect to democracy. In order to produce curriculum policy quickly and within certain parameters, the Ministry of Education undertook some unusual – and perhaps innovative – strategies. Perhaps the most striking feature of the ministry's approach to Ontario's curriculum reform was its use of 'hidden privatization' in the form of outsourcing production of policy texts. This chapter describes the process and features of the privatized process, while paying particular attention to how the institutional culture promoted and rationalized outsourcing to perform tasks traditionally carried out by bureaucrats and members of the education community. I describe and analyse this outsourcing with respect to background research and the production of policy texts.

At first blush, contracting non-government players to produce policy texts may not appear problematic, but this practice carries 'ethical dangers, and many examples of tactical and opportunistic behaviours are already apparent in schools and among parents within such systems' where educational services are privatized (Ball and Youdell 2007, 56). Like the Common Sense Revolution's preference for quantitative measures over qualitative, these common arguments for privatization are over-simplified and fail to recognize more complex criteria (Hefetz and Warner 2004), including equity, fairness, and the nature of public goods themselves (see, for example, Ball and Youdell 2007).

This chapter illustrates how hidden privatization can result in 'quick fixes' carried out by 'hired guns,' in the words of policy actors. While privatization undoubtedly led to efficiency, writers' perspectives point to problematic aspects when the process is measured against the critical-democratic ideal. When curriculum policy development is viewed as a political process, writers' experiences illustrate how hidden privatization in the form of policy outsourcing becomes problematic. Most administrative arrangements, which are presumably short, do not permit contractors to engage in and fully respond to all stages in the process, particularly in debate, discussion, and consultation, which are necessary conditions for democratic deliberations. The role of the writer as contractor (and not citizen) contributes to greater politicization of curriculum policy, since the policy actor loses the opportunity to provide input as a citizen. Coupled with emphasis by New Public Management (NPM) on efficiency, critical reflection and dialogue are eliminated, as described by the writers interviewed for this research. Moreover, a process in the spirit of democracy is compromised when such limitations are placed on who can participate.

Ministry Institutional Culture: Efficiency through New Public Management

Undoubtedly, the culture, rules, history, and accepted practices of governing institutions influence the level of democratization in policy formulation. Institutions reflect and contain values, norms, and ways of operating that define their culture (Schneider and Ingram 1997). Institutions are 'persistent patterns of relationships and interactions, including legislatures, courts, administrative agencies, nongovernmental organizations, and the like' (76). Traditional conceptions of institutions imply an ascribed role in society. Because public policy is developed within institutional settings, the characteristics of institutions and the systemic frameworks they create are always imprinted on policies themselves (Schneider and Ingram 1997). Most importantly, the institutions play a key role in establishing the power relations within policy formulation or are the outcomes of these relations. In Ontario, governmental ministries set the rules for policy formulation. They determine inclusion in the process, what roles individuals and groups play, and the criteria for discussion and decision-making. These rules and procedures reflect values, norms, and ways of operating that define institutional culture. David Tyack explains that in the twentieth century, elected leaders tended to believe that 'professional experts' knew what was best for children, and this belief resulted in a trend towards centralized education policy (1999).

'No form of institutionalization will accommodate such democratic struggle from the margins' (Glynos 2003, 190), since governing institutions such as the Ministry of Education tend to reproduce dominant structures. Because the critical-democratic ideal calls for many, varied forums for deliberation to accommodate discourse, it is nearly impossible for any one institution to house these struggles (Glynos 2003). However, 'to make room for dissent and foster the institutions in which it can be manifested is vital for democracy' (Mouffe 2000c, 150). In this case, the Ministry of Education acted as the formal institution to initiate and oversee the formulation of curriculum policy. In this section, I analyse the ministry's institutional culture, accountability mechanisms, and finally the distribution of power and ensuing politicization.

The institutional culture reflects the values, norms, and methods of operation within institutions involved in policy formulation. For the purpose of analysis, I examine the degree to which the institutional culture of the ministry acknowledges and includes social justice in their practices and goals, the degree to which it involves a cross-section of citizens in policy formulation, and how they articulate goals and accountabilities. Criteria central to a critical-democratic institutional culture include:

- Institutional values that are consistent with the critical-democratic ideal, including a strong commitment to social justice and a sincere interest in creating opportunities for agonistic exchanges
- Internal processes and values that privilege input from a reasonable cross-section of citizens over political will
- Flexibility in institutional structure and roles, so that the bureaucrat facilitates citizen learning and engagement, rather than acting as a researcher to provide 'neutral' advice to elected officials

In stark contrast to the critical-democratic ideal, NPM approaches to public administration gained popularity in the United States, the United Kingdom, and Canada (at the federal level) during the 1980s with a move towards smaller governments and less bureaucracy, driven by business models (Perl and White 2002; Saint-Martin 1998). Often associated with neoliberalism, NPM applies models of business management to the public sector, with considerable emphasis on efficiency and private-sector management styles by shifting bureaucrats' roles from 'administrators and custodians of resources to being managers' (Parker and Gould 1999, 110; deLeon and deLeon 2002). Within NPM, citizens are viewed as consumers of government products and services (consistent with the neoliberal conception of democracy and at odds with critical democracy), representing a move away from traditional bureaucracy, towards a corporate model (Saint-Martin 1998; Gualmini 2008). Thus, governments abandon traditional practices of a large public service, accountability to the government, and hierarchical centralization in favour of decentralization and outsourcing, and emphasize quality 'customer' service as the principal accountability (Saint-Martin 1998; Box 1999; Perl and White 2002; Gualmini 2008). Outsourcing is the engagement of 'external analytical capacity by state actors to perform all or part of the strategic, research, assessment, or evaluative tasks that comprise the functions of policy analysis' (Perl and White 2001, 51).

In applying business models consistent with NPM, governments increasingly rely on privatization. Broadly speaking, privatization is a social process by which services traditionally carried out by governments are devolved to the private sector. This includes the contracting of 'quasi-public goods or services to private entities in accordance with government regulations and specifications,' which are 'ultimately designed to reduce the direct and indirect role of the state' while enabling 'private agents to respond optimally to changing market opportunities and challenges' (Ramírez 2003, 263). Consistent with the rise of NPM, privatization flourished in developed countries during the 1980s, especially the United Kingdom and United States, taking a variety of forms, including sale of public goods, contracting out service delivery, and a variety of other indirect techniques, each targeted toward achieving different objectives (Berg and Berg 1997). The 'success' of privatization is extremely difficult to measure – moreover, the criteria by which such initiatives are judged can vary.

Arguments in favour of privatizing public goods and services within NPM tend to focus on two areas: efficiency and an opposition to growth of the public sector. The first – efficiency – is based on the assumption that the private sector is better able to manage tasks and finances and to use public tax dollars more effectively. The presumption is that private firms are efficient because of economies of scale, higher labour productivity, and fewer legal constraints than those under which governments operate. The second operates under an ideological belief in 'small government,' which is elaborated in the Common Sense Revolution and is consistent with the neoliberal stance. Governments are perceived to be monopolies with a history of unresponsiveness to citizens' needs (Sclar 2000). However, the literature cites a lack of definitive evidence to support the success of privatization, particularly when it is measured against qualitative and/or democratic criteria (see, for example, Birdsall and Nellis 2002). Nevertheless, as Linda and Peter deLeon point out, NPM discourses remain prominent in the public management literature, with surprisingly little attention being given to democracy and democratization in the field (deLeon and deLeon 2002).

Privatization of Policy Production

Privatization initiatives in education have been well documented in the literature (see, for example, Ball and Youdell 2007; Ball 2009; Burch 2009), though most of the literature has focused on the privatization of educational service delivery (e.g., charter schools, private schools, and various forms of partial service delivery). Indeed, private firms 'have long acted as suppliers to education and will continue to do so' (Burch 2009, 136). Despite a substantial body of research and literature documenting and critiquing privatization in education, little investigation has been conducted on the privatization of policy formulation in education. Policy text production and research to inform policy decisions are increasingly conducted by private-sector organizations and represent a hidden form of privatization (Ball 2009). The literature does recognize that privatization occurs in education policy production, though this phenomenon is not well documented. For example, 'It is not simply education and education services that are subject to forms of privatization: education policy itself – through advice, consultation, research, evaluation and forms of influence – is being privatized. Private sector organizations and NGOs are increasingly involved in both policy development and policy implementation' (Ball and Youdell 2007, 59).

Canada is no stranger to the hidden privatization of policy outsourcing: federally, a 647 per cent increase in expenditures on policy outsourcing in the twenty-year period ending in 2000/1 is documented, from $239 million to $1.55 billion annually (Perl and White 2002). This represents a nearly three-fold increase as a proportion of total government spending at a time when the federal government reduced its workforce. The types of consultants that take on policy work come in several forms: large, multinational firms (e.g., KPMG); individuals (e.g., academics, professionals, or retired public servants); and a 'third sector' of non-profit organizations with specific research or policy agendas (e.g., Conference Board of Canada) (Perl and White 2002). Outsourced consultants perform a number of tasks for governments that had been traditionally carried out by public servants, such as pure research, analysis of existing policies, and creation of policy or program evaluation. Outsourcing of one or more of these policy functions can affect the capacity of the state or public service, and the policy process based on the administrative arrangement of the contract. Whereas the outsourcing of public service delivery is fairly well known, outsourcing of policy functions is not widely discussed and few findings are available. Reasons for outsourcing public policy may include the expansion of the knowledge base beyond the existing public service and facilitation of politicized decision-making.

Evidence confirms that the Ontario Public Service (OPS) as a whole adopted an NPM approach to public sector work (Bedard and Lawton 2000; White 2000). Burak's (2000) claim, consistent with the neoliberal NPM stance, is that one of the Ontario government's main challenges in the twenty-first century is that 'most taxpayers and certainly all businesses expect that Governments will be run efficiently.' The OPS decreased from 81,000 to 61,000 full-time equivalents (FTE) (White 2002), and spending on outside consultants increased from $271 million in 1998, to $662 million in 2002 (Mallan 2002). In a controversial finding, some bureaucrats left their permanent positions and returned immediately as consultants at triple their salaries; in some cases duplicate contracts were issued and paid for the same work, suggesting poor management of external capacity and misuse of funds (Mallan 2002).

Time is one of the most valuable commodities in the NPM paradigm – one that the Ministry of Education struggled with during SSR, since 'the short and unpredictable tenure of most government causes them to expect quick and obvious changes within their time in office' (Earl et al. 2002, 29). Developing and implementing policy in short order is thus key to political leaders – and NPM is a means to achieve it. Ontario's curriculum policy formulation reflects NPM through its outsourcing of policy writing. Though the expense may have been higher than other approaches, such as utilizing internal capacity (approximately $16 million for secondary school curriculum policy production, with full development and implementation of the K–12 curriculum between 1996 and 2003 estimated to cost $488 million, according to the provincial auditor of Ontario), outsourcing expedited the process.

Ontario's curriculum policy process reveals how outsourcing affects capacity and process through contracted policy writing. Outsourcing allowed the Ministry of Education to complete massive curriculum policy reform in a short time by providing additional 'capacity.' Certainly, policy outsourcing might make sense for certain situations in which there is no in-house expertise, and the policy work is limited in duration, with no need to employ policy analysts for the long term (as was the case in Ontario). Indeed, some of the writers and bureaucrats interviewed feel that outsourcing was an effective solution for this particular policy task, when judged by the narrow criteria of efficiency. However, as the following sections illustrate, outsourcing poses problems when analysed in light of a critical-democratic ideal.

Bureaucrats and Policy Actors: Speaking Truth to Power?

A number of individuals in bureaucratic capacities, working for the Ministry of Education, played a role in curriculum policy formulation and in doing so, embedded certain values and practices in the institutional culture. Bureaucrats are individuals working for the ministry in different capacities and are considered public servants. By virtue of their training, experience, and commitment to nonpartisan values, public servants have played an important role in policy analysis. Historically, a significant part of their role has been 'speaking truth to power' (Wildavsky 1979). However, public servants today hold a variety of stances – from maintaining political neutrality to pursuing specific agendas (Radin 2000). Moreover, some governments shifted their expectations of public servants towards politicized agents expected to carry out government agendas, rather than to provide a variety of nonpartisan policy options representing a wide spectrum of perspectives to an articulated problem (Bedard and Lawton 2000).

In Ontario Management Board of Cabinet issued a Directive on Accountability in 1997 to hold both public servants and external service providers more clearly accountable for their actions. The directive's principles state, 'Public servants uphold the public trust and provide the highest level of quality service, consistent with their oath of allegiance and oath of secrecy as stated in the *Public Service Act.'* Public servants in Ontario are required to take an Oath of Public Service. By virtue of their training, experience, and commitment to a common set of nonpartisan values, public servants have played an important role in policy development (promoted by managers and supervisors). Paul Carr, a Ministry of Education bureaucrat prior to and during the time of the policy process studied, observes, 'My experience is that reference to ideology was systemically discouraged; there was a certain pride in feigning that public servants are "neutral," and that regardless of the orientation of the government, public servants were there to implement policies, not develop them' (Carr 2006).

Indeed, one bureaucrat with extensive ministry experience acknowledged that since the NDP government's leadership in 1990, the role of the bureaucrat in presenting a range of non-partisan options based on research has diminished, and public servants are increasingly expected to carry out political agendas without questioning them (see, for example, White 1997c). The role of research to inform policy shifted to the hands of the political advisors for the party in power. In my own professional experience, many bureaucrats perceive this phenomenon as de-professionalization that diminishes the ability of the public service to offer 'value' to political decision-makers.

Moreover, since the bulk of the policy work for curriculum formulation was contracted out to writing teams, bureaucrats' manage a process rather than being directly involved in policymaking. A popular OPS analogy is that the bureaucrat 'steers' the process, while contracted writers 'row' by conducting research and writing curriculum policy.

Interviews with policy actors reveal overt politicization of curriculum policy formulation arising out of the ministry's institutional culture during the late 1990s. James, a participant in stakeholder consultations, said that the task of curriculum reform was 'based on an entirely straightforward concept of accountability' in that producing a new set of more prescriptive curriculum policy documents would fulfil the government's commitment. He added, 'My description of the process would be, taken the ideological predispositions, the government knew they had constituents among quality education,' and this was an 'easy win' to please this group. That is to say, producing new and prescriptive curriculum policy documents would please the quality education constituency represented by groups such as the Organization for

Quality Education. James described the policy process as 'a broad front without political oversight.'

Contrary to James's perception, others felt that the process was highly politicized, with unprecedented levels of involvement from political staff in curriculum policy content. Another consultation participant, Danielle, remarked, 'It's outrageous. You see, I don't think, and from what I've read, that politics has been tied to curriculum ever before like it was this time. I don't know a time when it has. It has never been tied so intimately with the politics of the current government.'

Political staffer Will revealed that Danielle was correct in her perception about the politicization:

> It would have been very, very easy for the politicians to let that first draft go. They could have spun it, they could have characterized it as new. It was certainly different from the common curriculum, and it would have been a check in the box. Yet a whole bunch of people got really invested in actually taking a hard, hard look at it. Some would argue it was undue political interference. I am going to suggest that it was really a good exercise – a marriage between politics and curriculum development. I think there was a lot of politics associated with it but it's small p and big P . . .
>
> But as political staffers, rightly or wrongly, we were pretty hands-on in taking a look at the content of the document as well. My role was, for a lack of a better term, to play air-traffic controller with a bunch of different interests. I guess the other set of interests were the stakeholders. The stakeholders would often liaise directly with the ministry staff, but of course they went right up to the food chain in wanting access to minister's representatives in order to, for a lack of a better term, keep the public servants in line. All of these disparate pieces of the equation would aggrandize all that I had done, but at one point or another intersect with my role as the person advising the minister on education policy. (Will, political staffer)

These remarks are consistent with Graham White's claim that, beginning with the NDP's tenure in 1990 through 1995, the government 'politicized the public service to an unprecedented and dangerous degree' (White 1997c, 147). Under Premier Harris, decision-making occurred under 'tight political control by the premier and a small, highly-trusted staff in the premier's office,' weakening the capacity of ministries to facilitate their own policies (Wolfe 1997, 161). Premier Harris believed that 'the most important public consultation took place before the election, [and] fearing that ministers would be sabotaged by bureaucrats, the Premier requested that [deputy ministers] report to his office directly. Thus, ministers [were] often kept in the dark, making them little more than salespeople for initiatives cobbled together by the Premier's office' (Crittenden 2002, 57).

Ambitious Timeframes as a Central Feature of the Process

Perhaps the most obvious concern voiced by policy actors about the process is aggressive and ambitious timelines reflected in the appendix – completion and enactment of policy texts in under two years. Bureaucrat Marcellas interviewed for this research remarked that while the educational system felt 'rushed' with the timelines for policy formulation and implementation, parents did not. Janelle, another bureaucrat, added, 'There are lots of things I would have changed – the fundamental one being the timelines, and I think everyone knew that was an issue.' Though timelines were considered problematic by most, not all policy actors interviewed disliked them. Drew, a writer, appreciated the timelines to an extent: 'I could be of two minds about that. In part, I like to work fast. Personally, I like to engage in a project, and go at it full blast.'

Privatization as the Outsourcing of Two Functions

As I alluded to earlier, two functions of the policy process were outsourced to private entities: the contracting of background research, and the production of policy text by writers obtained through tender.

Contracting Background Research

Prior to the actual production of secondary school curriculum policy texts,[1] the government undertook several research initiatives and public consultations. The ministry contracted two private consulting groups to conduct this research. Praxis Consulting, a private Canadian company, carried out research that led to the development of a 'course menu' outlining the organization of subject disciplines, and courses within each discipline. To gather data for their report, *What People Said about High School Reform* (July 1997), they distributed three 'background discussion documents' to schools and public libraries across Ontario, as well as directly to 'identified stakeholder organizations and individuals.' The documents were 'Ontario Secondary Schools (1998) Detailed Discussion Document,' 'Choices into Action: Guidance and Career Education Policy Grades 1 to 12,' and 'Excellence in Education: High School Reform.'

Each of these documents included a 'response document' in the form of a questionnaire to be completed and returned. Additionally, a document titled 'Understanding and Participating in Curriculum Change' (Ministry of Education 1996) – available online and distributed – provided extremely concrete strategies, including a proposed timeline, and readers were asked to respond to specific questions. Rather than a more open-ended document with a menu of options, it provided arguments for the positions already preferred by the ministry and/or government. The ministry received over 28,000 responses, including documents, letters, and essays. In their report, Praxis describes public response as 'modest or highly conditional support' (unconditional agreement ranged from 6 per cent to 18 per cent on any given question) for the proposed reforms. Praxis explains that this means that respondents agreed with a particular proposed item, but had some concerns. The report concludes,

- Citizens made tremendous efforts to alert the ministry to their concerns.
- A 'large number of respondents' added 'conditions' to their support of aspects of proposed reforms.
- Disagreement resulted in an overall 'absence of clear direction from the public.'

A second private consulting group, Gregg, Kelly, Sullivan & Woolsten-croft: The Strategic Counsel Inc., prepared a second report, *Report to the Ministry of Education and Training [sic] on the Secondary School Reform Meetings* (September 1997), which summarizes two days of meetings involving fifty-five stakeholder groups with 115 representatives. This report addresses five broad areas: cooperative education /work experience / school-to-work programs; teacher advisors; testing (literacy and grade twelve exit exams); compulsory courses; and streaming. According to the report, participants worked in tables of ten, facilitated by a staffer from the consulting group. The report indicates that the goal of this particular research was to seek input on the broad areas, not to find compromise or consensus. Similar to the findings in the Praxis report, little agreement was reached on many topics – an absence of 'clear cut' direction for those leading the reform. Specific ideas for course progression and course menus are also investigated in the report. One consultation participant, James, attended these early consultation sessions and remarked, 'When the secondary came about, we were contacted again, went through the same process where we were assigned to subjects and sat in a room with a facilitator. I always cringe – here we go with this facilitator. I always cringe when that happens, because the facilitator becomes the filter for what is said in the room, and they get to interpret what you say.'

While bureaucrats interviewed emphasized the need to engage consulting firms for these consultations because of a lack of ministry staff to complete the task within the time allotted, James's remarks underscore the perceived problems with the use of an external facilitator, who, in his mind, filters the content of discussions. While certainly if a ministry bureaucrat were to facilitate, her role would also be to filter, the difference is that a bureaucrat might apply different criteria and a broader mandate. Without a clear sense or understanding of how consultants were instructed and managed, I cannot draw definitive conclusions. However, both Praxis Consulting and Strategic Counsel took this work on in order to yield a profit, and this could result in an ethical conflict. In one sense, the engagement of private firms in the policy process contradicts the neoliberal call for transparency in government. However, 'the more economic incentive there is, the greater the tendency for for-profit firms to want to keep their finances and operations out of public view. When firms are privately held, they disclose very little to the public' (Burch 2009, 103). Thus, the public good of educational decision-making becomes tied to a private commodity of lucrative consulting contracts. The alarming result is that 'distinctions between advice, support and lobbying for work are sometimes hard to see,' and there is evidence of opportunistic behaviour resulting from such arrangements (Ball and Youdell 2007, 56). As well, and as I described earlier, the focus remains on cost and efficiency, rather than accountability to public goals such as of access, equity, participation, and quality in education (Ball and Youdell 2007; Burch 2009).

Contracting Writers

The ministry relied on outsourced writing teams to produce the bulk of policy text, though it maintained some oversight during the writing, in terms of deliverables submitted. The actual structure and process of writing teams varied from subject to subject, but the ministry provided requirements for each team. First, ways to differentiate between student learning expectations in the different streams (academic and applied for grades nine and ten; workplace, college, and university for grades eleven and twelve) was an important area of communication. Nearly all writers commented that the instructions, particularly for academic and applied streams, changed several times during the process, leading writers to conclude that, in the beginning, the ministry might not have been certain of the distinctions between streams. However, interviews reveal that some members of policy writing teams felt those distinctions were never made perfectly clear.

Second, the ministry defined a very specific format for courses (referred to by some as a 'template'), which required that each course contain three to five *strands*, each representing a unit or theme of study. Each strand contained five *overall expectations*. Each overall expectation represented a *sub-organizer* within the strand, appearing as a heading. Each *sub-organizer* contained three to five *specific expectations*. At some point during the writing, teams received lists of verbs to be used for overall and specific expectations.

Obtaining external knowledge and capacity among members of the writing team had several advantages. First, very specific expertise is required in preparing curriculum policy – expertise in both pedagogy and subject matter. Second, a shrinking OPS meant that there may not have been enough, or the right kind of, public servants to carry out a complex policy task. The widely accepted NPM paradigm suggests that the size of governments in Canada and the United States will continue to decrease, and this will result in greater reliance on non-bureaucratic individuals and organizations to perform what has traditionally been OPS work (Zussman 2000). Indeed, the NDP education critic pointed out, 'They [the Tories] have gutted the central Ministry of Education. That was part of their first round of cuts in order to try and make up the dollars they need for the tax cut. There's hardly anybody left to develop curriculum in the Queen's Park Ministry of Education ... So if they're going to save this $16.7 million in educational curriculum support at the school board level, who is going to be left to develop any kind of curriculum in this province? The minister likes to talk about how this is going to improve quality and improve standards and give consistency' (Legislative Assembly, *Debates and Proceedings* [21 January 1997], p. 1610). Finally, the ministry, driven by the politicians' agenda, ambitiously planned to complete the policy cycle in an extremely short time, thus requiring added capacity.

During the writing stage, the Ministry of Education had some over-sight over deliverables submitted.[2] However, the actual structure and process of writing teams varied from subject to subject. To recruit curriculum policy writers, the ministry undertook formal tendering (referred to as a Request for Proposal or RFP) in January 1998, seeking contractors to write the curriculum policy documents. MERX, an elec-tronic database that provides subscriber access to RFPs from the pub-lic and private sector, was used. Ministry staff created detailed RFPs for each subject grouping and posted them to MERX. In this respect, tendering through MERX offered transparency, since RFPs could be viewed by any interested individual or party.

However, as a private-sector enterprise, owned by Bank of Montreal at the time of this policy formulation, MERX contributed to govern-ment privatization. Revenues from the cost of viewing ministry pro-posals went to MERX. Because the system is subscriber-based, the cost of viewing the RFPs for all thirteen subject areas was over $300. The expense, coupled with only several weeks allotted to prepare and submit a proposal (see table 4.1), excluded small players from partici-pating in the tendering. Moreover, bidders had to show evidence of financial resources, including a letter of credit of at least 10 per cent of the contract, as well as at least $1 million in general liability insurance. While the cost of submitting a proposal was arguably high, speculation was that remuneration was upwards of $500,000 for the 'larger sub-jects' (Ibbitson 1998), which required substantial resources for anyone bidding in light of the letter of credit. As a result, tensions emerged between and open and transparent process and the ability to include a variety of potential participants in the process.

Larry O'Farrell (2001) and John Fielding (2002), both successful in their bids during this RFP process, discuss the challenges facing those attempting to establish proposals. O'Farrell and several individuals partnered with Excalibur, a private-sector firm that had experience in proposal-writing. As Ibbitson (1998) points out, 'There is no such thing as a private-sector curriculum development industry in Canada. No government has ever made such a request before' – thus the job of responding to the RFP was new territory for all involved. O'Farrell (2001, 2) describes the complexity of the RFP as 'extraordinary, and rather intimidating.'

No comprehensive list of successful bidders is available through the Ontario archives, but public information and accounts of policy actors

Table 4.1   RFP timelines

14 January 1998	RFP for the development of course policy documents was published by the Ministry of Education
25 February 1998	RFP closing date
23–31 March 1998	Interviews between shortlisted project managers and Ministry of Education staff
14–28 April 1998	Contract signing of successful parties
12 June1998	First deliverable (overview, streaming and courses, course organization and expectations)
29 July 1998	Second deliverable (revisions to first deliverable; remaining sections)
14 September 1998	Third deliverable (revised version of second deliverable; remaining sections including sub-organizers and specific expectations)
30 November 1998	Final deliverable (final draft of document)

involved in the process provide insight into some of the successful bidding organizations. In addition to the partnership with Excalibur, some of the known organizations who submitted successful bids included a consortium of school boards who called themselves the Public School Board Writing Partnership, the Canadian Foundation for Economic Education, and the Fields Institute for Research in the Mathematical Sciences. Details of others are sketchy. For instance, for the science curriculum writing team, one individual interviewed recalled only some details about the private sector firm that was successful in the bidding process: 'I was contacted by a private company who had decided they wanted to bid on this, or they were exploring the possibility of doing a bid. I can't even remember their name. It was a consulting firm ... [I]t was a huge amount of work, particularly the requirements that they had called for in the bid were things that most teachers could not have put together by themselves.' Indeed, the requirements of the RFP were both rigorous and specific. Development team requirements articulated in the RFP for composition of team members included:

• Minimum of 50 per cent Ontario secondary school teachers
• Minimum of one college educator
• Minimum of one university educator
• Minimum of one workplace representative

- Representation from northern/southern, separate/public, rural/urban
- Minimum one writer with ability to integrate technology
- Minimum one bilingual writer
- Minimum one member with experience in anti-discrimination education
- Designated, experienced professional writer

Leaders and project managers of writing teams describe the challenge of finding individuals who met the criteria to include in proposals within those timelines. The requirement that an extensive proposal be developed at this time of year appears to have eliminated many educational stakeholders from bidding, in addition to the cost (O'Farrell 2001).

Writing teams were organized by subject, with team members representing disciplines within the subject. One or more project managers led each team, oversaw the process, and interacted directly with ministry staff. Project managers were also responsible for managing their project's budget – a sum agreed upon in the successful RFP bid. Writers for specific course policies reported to those project managers, carried out the tasks associated with preparing curriculum policy drafts text, and usually had little or no access to ministry staff. The design was articulated by writing teams in their proposals (details of proposal process appear in the next section). Some teams, such as English, worked collaboratively in large groups to ensure parallelism and continuity in their courses. Others, such as the Arts, worked in small teams with groups of writing representing sub-disciplines (dance, music, etc.). In some instances, single writers worked independently on a single course. This section discusses individual policy actors' accounts of how they came to be·involved.

Writers were often handpicked for participation. Thus Ontarians experienced an absence of opportunities to volunteer to participate in policy production. As bureaucrat Janelle described the situation, 'Look at who had to be on the team – it had to be Ontario people. Theoretically, could a company from the States have applied? Yes, but they would not have been granted the contract, because we wouldn't have seen sufficient evidence of Ontario ... We worked and worked – that's why the RFP was so huge – we worked and worked to make sure that we were stipulating all the things we would actually need, and introduced a lot of new elements, like, you know, the core team had to be this, but then that was that other – the people who had to be advisors to the team. Spec[ial] ed[ucation] had to be ... somebody had to have that knowledge. So we were bringing in a much broader group of perspectives to look at each draft than a small group of teachers would have.'

Bureaucrats interviewed pointed out that historically, teachers have been brought into the Ministry of Education to participate in policy writing. However, tendering was an entirely new feature. SSR was the first instance of a corporate model of educator representation. Tendering limited applicants to organized consortia with the means to afford a MERX subscription, sufficient liability insurance, and the capacity to write effective proposals for large-scale consulting projects. This process prevented individual teachers from applying. Moreover, though there were different approaches to the recruitment of individual writers, at least a portion were approached by groups who submitted proposals – thus eliminating opportunities to 'volunteer' or apply to participate. Coupled with the aggressive timelines of the RFP, these constraints significantly limited who might be able to participate as writers and led to participation of individuals who knew the right people – compromising the potential for the process to yield qualified experts via open application.

Interview responses confirmed that most individuals were simply approached by someone to participate, much like my own experience. However, some project managers sought 'applicants' from subject associations. While these do not represent all writers' experiences, they provide an account of the process, which suggests that selection was arbitrary and based largely on 'who you know,' giving an advantage to elites and insiders. By contrast, a critical-democratic process would offer more equitable and open opportunities, and ensure that individuals from the margins would be included.

Consequences of Privatization: 'Hired Guns'

While further details of the policy production process are described in chapters 5 and 6, a brief overview of the consequences of policy outsourcing is called for here. The institutional culture governed the rules and tools of the process – and thus shaped the way in which policy actors were able to carry out their roles. Under NPM, the contracting process led some members of the policy writing team to express how they felt like 'hired guns' paid to carry out a directive, as opposed to contributors. Consider these two accounts, representative of several writers' perceptions:

> [The project manager] would say, 'Yes, the bottom line is they're the ones who wrote the contract, they're the ones that hired you, and you're just writers.'
>
> And that kept coming back, now that I think of it, more and more that you have been hired to write a curriculum: 'Here are the guidelines, do it. We're not here to argue points. We're here to write curriculum, so do it.' And if they choose the structure of it, well, that's part of the contract that you sign. Okay, so you're the boss, I'll do what you tell me to do. I'll throw my two cents worth if I can, but ultimately they were writing the cheques. (Hardy, writer)

> Whenever there were problems they hadn't spotted, they would never have a discussion with us. We were always treated as the servants of the process. The people who understood the details – it was like, parent knew best, and they'll tell the children what they decided. They will never have a discussion. We were never treated like adults, or even people who had more expertise than they did. (Robert, project manager)

This perceived treatment left writers feeling de-professionalized and may have been a contributing factor to some of their attempts at 'subversive' tactics, described in sections that follow. In addition, Tory political opponents voiced public criticism over the contracting-out of policy formulation. For example, Liberal member Lyn McLeod said, 'I get concerned about their curriculum initiatives being applauded when I know that the process, this contracted-out process, for writing the secondary school curriculum is in total and absolute chaos' (Legislative Assembly, *Debates and Proceedings* [29 April 1998], p. 1920).

While undoubtedly technical or subject-matter expertise is required for writing teams, a critical-democratic ideal would require a strong equity component or criteria for selection in addition to a criterion of expertise. The somewhat arbitrary process of selection described by policy actors interviewed also calls into question whether those selecting writers applied objective criteria to ensure 'experts' in the field were considered. The criteria for inclusiveness and meaningful deliberation were not realized for those engaged in the process as a result of the procedural constraints. Instead, the prominent policy roles were exclusive to high-status elites who had adequate connections to groups or professional roles to allow them to participate. This lack of inclusiveness conflicts with critical democracy in the selection.

Quiet Resistance: Hired Gun, or Subject Steward?

Despite the sense of their role as 'hired guns,' some writers noted a sub-versive aspect to their role through their attempts to 'save' their subject, given the political constraints. For example:

> To a large extent the members of our writing team saw themselves as the protectors of quality arts education against a government that was likely to value science and technology more than artistic expression, to value preparation for employment more than preparation for life, and to value conformity more than individuality . . . I feel that from time to time we did lose a battle with bureaucracy. (O'Farrell 2001)

> There was really a sense that we were up against a Goliath and that we somehow had to save our subject by writing something that was good, even though it was in this format that didn't match it very well. (Drew, project manager)

In spite of their attempts to 'save' their subject areas, some openly admitted that they were relieved when authors' named did not appear on the final policy documents. Policy actors also expressed a concern about colleagues' negative reaction to them for having participated:

> I think we were afraid that we were going to be seen as the tools of this government who was lambasting the profession. I certainly didn't want to be associated with that. Once that's gone out, now I'm quite proud to say I was part of the changes that have taken place, and being involved in the profiles. At that time, I thought, 'Oh, boy.' . . . I know when I was sitting in on sessions where people didn't know I was involved in any of this stuff, I had to bite my tongue, because I kept hearing, 'Who wrote this stuff? Did they bring in teachers, or is this the bureaucrats in Queen's Park?' (Hardy, writer)

> Teachers said, 'Why are you helping these people?'
> I said . . . 'You should be glad I'm there, because it could be a lot worse than it was going to be. It might not be that you and I want it, but at least we have some influence about what it will look like. And we can make our case – because eventually they will find someone to do it.' (Scott, writer)

This sense of stewardship suggests that while they recognized they were contractors, writers perceived themselves has having a richer role in lending their expertise to the subject area in order to achieve a more personal goal. Had there been greater opportunity for agonistic exchange in the spirit of critical-democratic policymaking, a variety of policy actors could have better understood individual perspectives and might have reduced some of the problematic procedural aspects that emerged, which I discuss in the next chapters.

'Rules' and 'Tools' Used to Manage Contractors

The choice of rules and tools to structure policy production has implications for democratic messages and values. Moreover, the choice reflects assumptions and biases about the policy process itself. Rules refer to the actual parameters of the policy formulation process (such as timeframe, roles assigned, how individuals came to be involved, level and format for deliberation, and the process for coming to an acceptable decision), while tools are those elements that cause actors to engage in activities or behaviours to solve problems or achieve goals. In general, four categories of tools are traditionally available to influence responses to policy during its enactment (Schneider and Ingram 1997). First, authority tools use authoritative measures to direct activity. Their use to direct the policy process undercuts democratic values, teaching 'uncivic' lessons. Second, inducements or sanctions use tangible payoffs (rewards, consequences) to influence policy actors' behaviour and actions. Their use assumes that individuals are self-interested actors who require extrinsic motivation. Third, capacity-building tools provide training, technical assistance, or information needed to take policy-relevant action. While capacity-building aims to remove impediments or empower through knowledge, it reinforces hierarchies, since those designing the training, assistance, or information yield power in dissemination. Finally, hortatory tools are proclamations, speeches, or public relations campaigns through which governments or other institutions exhort people to take action. Like capacity-building tools, traditionally hortatory tools function in a top-down fashion, reifying power in the hands of a few to shape and disseminate messages.

To an extent, conventional rules and tools may make critical-democratic participation in policy processes impossible, since they reinforce and reify institutional structures, whereas critical-democratic participation requires institutional resistance. A critical-democratic policy process would rely on 'reformulated' capacity-building and

hortatory tools – which must redefined in a way that encourages agonistic exchange, while allowing and encouraging participants to question the status quo and, in Aaron Wildavsky's conception, speak truth
to power (1979). There are several criteria to evaluate the degree to
which rules and tools address the critical-democratic ideal of agonistic
exchanges:

- Participants 'express their [opposing] perspectives in their own
  terms, albeit within the bounds of civility' (Goi 2005, 60).
- Participants respect rules of civility, which include listening to others and refraining from 'polarizing rhetoric' (71).
- Participants respect the agonal context, so that the other is viewed
  as an adversary, not an enemy.
- For at least a portion of the process, participants refrain from arguments intended to persuade – rather, the goal is to understand one
  another's point of view, not change it, where the goal is to reach
  understanding, not agreement.
- Participants agree to a process for moving forward with a particular policy direction through a process such a voting, which represents a provisional agreement as envisioned by Chantal Mouffe
  (2000b, 2000c).
- There must be opportunities for participants to learn about the policy issue beyond individual knowledge, and acknowledge broader
  research, positions and arguments.
- Reasonable timeframes balance the need for resolution with citizen
  education and ample opportunities for meaningful agonistic exchange.

In Ontario, fragmentation as the first salient feature of the process
emerged as the most prominent authoritative tool in the policy process. Fragmentation takes the form of tightly controlled channels of
communication and piecemeal (rather than holistic) work: writing
team project managers communicated directly with bureaucrats and
passed information along (rather than allowing for discussion and an
understanding of reasons).

Political staff had no contact with writing team members to speak of,
so messages from political staff to writers were filtered first through
bureaucrats, then through project managers. These chains of com-
mand reflect a Fordist[3] production model of curriculum policy formulation consistent with neoliberal and neoconservative ideals, rather
than a participatory model in the spirit of critical democracy. The

absence of direct communication also eliminated any real possibility to hear others' points of view or to engage in agonistic exchange.
Bureaucrats' roles as information gatekeepers contributed to a power
imbalance and politicization also described earlier in this chapter.

Curtis observed, 'Part of what made it problematic was you never
got all the pieces presented to you at the same time. So you never really
were sure how this particular initiative or change would impact other
parts of programming or delivery.' Similarly, members of writing teams
were not necessarily apprised of consultations, or were given very limited information about them. For instance,

> I remember hearing that they had gone through this process of getting
> feedback from various stakeholders, [but] they didn't tell us much because
> that would taint what we were going to do. (Hardy, writer)

> I don't know whether that was because of the timelines, or because
> everything had happened prior, but I think they chose to do it in a dif-
> ferent way, basically take what I wrote, and they [the project manager]
> would . . . or whoever would meet with a variety of groups. I think he was
> getting input from various Aboriginal groups, civil rights groups – there
> were a range of folks who were on the radar. I don't know how often they
> met, I don't know how much input, I certainly didn't get as much . . . as I
> anticipated. [This] course, for example, its very nature is to reflect multiple
> perspectives and ensure the various voices are somehow infused. So that
> was a bit of a concern. (Justin, writer)

This lack of awareness among writers reflects my own experience.
Essentially, as writing team members, individuals were aware only of
their own work (or their team's work), without broader understandings of how or why suggestions and changes were made to draft policy
texts, or how ultimate decisions came about. This kind of fragmentation
placed power in the hands of ministry staff, who acted as gatekeepers.
Bureaucrats effectively controlled who received what information and
kept policy actors in other roles from fully understanding the broader
context of the process, as well as others' perspectives.

There are some reports that bureaucrats attempted to withhold
information from political staff, including the minister, during curriculum policy formulation: '"There is absolutely no doubt, they [the
bureaucrats] dragged their heels," says a former senior official in the
government. Ministry staff went so far as to withhold information from
Snobelen that would help his cause' (Ibbitson 1997, 279).

Second, and related to the first feature (fragmentation), outsourcing serves as tool through sanctions and inducements. Writing teams were rewarded with payment if they fulfilled their contractual obligations and faced sanctions if they failed to meet deliverables. This tool ensured writers' roles remained limited, eliminating the possibility of full participation in the process, as I described in the previous section. Notably absent from process is deliberate use of capacity tools, which, in the critical-democratic ideal, are crucial to building citizen capacity in deliberation, and learning about policy issues (discussed in greater detail in the next section). First, the Ministry used authoritative tools to create fear of removal from the process, as described in the case study, to ensure compliance among policy actors – a strategy that undercuts critical-democratic ideals.

Third, government utilized hortatory tools, largely through the media, to garner support and shape issues related to policy formulation. In the critical-democratic ideal, as I described, hortatory tools would be widely distributed, allowing policy actors to participate in this process. Finally, the ambitious curriculum policy formulation timelines, a 'rule' in the process, shaped the process and policy actors' roles. The aggressive timelines limited opportunities for participants to expand or change their roles, or to engage innovation. Rather, writing-team members described how they worked feverishly (often at the expense of collaboration) to meet deadlines, so those who attended stakeholder consultations had limited time during meetings to dialogue with others. Particularly in subject areas with many courses, writers were assigned to courses and worked simultaneously to complete the curriculum learning expectations, resulting in few opportunities to communicate with others on their own teams. The activities omitted in order to adhere to the timelines would have contributed to more robust participation (and deliberation) and would have contributed to achieving a critical-democratic process. I explore this in more detail in the next chapter.

Fragmentation and aggressive timelines (discussed earlier in this chapter) eliminated not only opportunities for considered and reflective writing, but more importantly shut down opportunities for the exchange of ideas – important within essentially any conception of democracy, but especially for realization of the critical-democratic ideal, which requires agonistic exchanges, particularly where parties have differences of opinion. Writers' experiences highlighted how undemocratic approaches to policy work can lead to undemocratic actions. When unable to actively voice their dissent or work through disagreement, they turned to subversive behaviour. When those in power sought to achieve their goals, they turned to secretive tactics, which led to conspiracy theories. Trust among policy actors was compromised and in some cases eliminated.

Concluding Comments

While it is widely recognized that 'ideologies of neo-liberalism are remaking education policy to fit the needs of the market' (Burch 2009, 136) through privatization of education services, Ontario's policy production illustrates how those very ideologies shaped the way in which policy was produced. Overall, the government and Ministry of Education closely controlled the curriculum policy process, applied market principles through hidden privatization, and thereby limited opportunities for participation in policy production. However, 'the governance of education is not just another educational market' (Burch 2009, 136). By applying a privatization model to the production of policy, we see how democratic shortfalls can occur. While we cannot attribute the problems entirely to privatization – it is a necessary but not sufficient condition for an undemocratic process – this research reveals how neoliberal values and an NPM environment within government led to an absence of inclusiveness, of critical reflection, and of civic skills among policy actors.

Decision-making under tight political control weakened the voices and roles of policy actors (bureaucrats, writers, and consultation participants) involved. Within the NPM paradigm, efficiency was emphasized. Efficiency took the form of extremely short timeframes to complete curriculum policy text – a concern voiced by policy actors interviewed. As one bureaucrat remarked, 'There are lots of things I would have changed – the fundamental one being the timelines, and I think everyone knew that was an issue.'

This NPM approach to public sector work, and quite specifically the privatization of policy creation, is in direct opposition of the critical-democratic ideal. Heavy reliance on outsourcing to create policy is potentially very dangerous terrain. Perhaps most obviously, a profit motive for conducting policy research and drafting policy texts can compromise both the process and output. If the policy actor's motive is to remain profitable, this can (and perhaps does) subordinate a primary concern for the public good. Whereas policy ought to address the needs of people – and in a critical democracy, with particular attention to the needs of oppressed, excluded, and marginalized groups – hiring contractors detracts from the possibility of inclusiveness.

While, from a critical-democratic perspective, this NPM approach to privatizing policy functions is problematic, certainly analysis using neoliberal criteria might yield a different conclusion. To be sure, the Ministry of Education was able to meet unthinkable time constraints in the production of policy texts; as well, the privatization undertaken allowed the ministry to compensate for a lack of internal capacity that resulted at least in part from the NPM smaller government. However, these gains were minor, when examined against qualitative measures of democratic policy and governance and building not only a democratic government, but a democratic education system.

Time constraints and a complicated bidding process further limit opportunities for participation by a broad cross-section of citizens, particularly those from the margins who might be able to offer insight into equity and social justice.

5   Policy Writers, Power, and Politicization: Were the Books Already Cooked?

A well-functioning democracy calls for a vibrant clash of democratic political positions.
– Chantal Mouffe 2000b, 104

Making and implementing curriculum are 'not just technical and administrative tasks, but are political as well' (Werner 1991, 113). Curriculum formulation is political in that, as Walter Werner points out, its salient features include struggles of values and feasibility among citizens and stakeholders. These struggles involve the use of power, either to influence or to mandate decisions. Formulation of critical-democratic curriculum policy must include discussion and debate and ought to take place in an active political arena as envisioned by Aaron Wildavsky in which a 'vibrant clash of democratic political positions' are voiced (Mouffe 2000b, 104).

While, as I concluded in chapter 4, privatized policy production undertaken by the Ministry of Education was undoubtedly efficient, writers' accounts point to problematic aspects when viewed from a democratic perspective. When curriculum policy development is viewed as a political process characterized by dispute and negotiation in the critical-democratic ideal, writers' experiences illustrate how hidden privatization in the form of policy outsourcing becomes problematic. Most administrative arrangements, which are presumably short, do not permit contractors to engage in and fully respond to all stages in the process, particularly in issues of debate, discussion, and consultation, which are necessary conditions for critical-democratic deliberations. The role of the writer as contractor (and not citizen) contributes to greater politicization of curriculum policy, since the policy actor loses the opportunity to provide input as a citizen. Coupled with NPM's emphasis on efficiency, critical reflection and dialogue are eliminated, as described by the writers interviewed for this research. Moreover, a process in the spirit of critical democracy is compromised when such limitations are placed on who can participate. When he becomes a contractor, the role of the policy writer shifts – some describe their role as 'hired guns' to write curriculum without the ability to question or provide input.

Because of Ontario's fragmented process, curriculum policy writers missed opportunities to hear the views of consultation participations over values and feasibility. Dialogue among writers to address conflicts within teams was minimal because they raced to complete their work within aggressive deadlines. Moreover, consultation participants reported that opportunities for 'open' dialogue during sessions were limited. In this chapter, I provide further analysis about the politicization and power, manufactured consent, and subversion.

Power and Politicization: Were 'the Books Already Cooked'?

Distribution of power is closely tied to the institutional structures governing policy production. Politicization occurs when consensus or negotiation among groups is resolved through the use of power when decisions are made 'that resolve the struggle over value differences' (Werner 1991, 107). As Benjamin Levin (2005) astutely points out, politics will always result in winners and losers in the process of producing policy.

The literature reveals the challenge of capturing the roles of power and resistance within the micro-and macro-political contexts of policy processes using traditional approaches to policy analysis (see, for example, Crawford 2001; Rorison 2002). These power relations are a key area of exploration within the critical-democratic framework presented here, particularly in the degree to which participants challenge them. Within the critical-democratic ideal, first power and politicization must be openly acknowledged (Mouffe 2000b, 2000c, 2005). Criteria include:

- The extent to which the institutions openly and explicitly acknowledge power and its distribution. Ideally, power would be openly acknowledged, and where it is (or needs) to be exercised, institutions are transparent in their use of power.
- The degree to which institutions are perceived to and actually share power with citizens involved in the policy process (for example, avoiding real or perceived manufactured consent).

- How value conflicts among policy actors are overcome to arrive at a final solution. In a truly agonistic exchange consistent with the critical-democratic ideal, citizens would agree to a temporary resolution to the issue. A mechanism for arriving at such resolution would need to be put in place, which may include a politicized decision, or a system of voting.

Power in policymaking cannot be eliminated. Thus, the issue becomes 'how to constitute forms of power more compatible with democratic values' rather than to eliminate it (Mouffe 2000b, 100). Within this ideal, a shift in power allows outcomes to be shaped by input from those involved in deliberations. I analyse additional procedural impediments to open and agonistic exchange related to power in this section. Within the critical-democratic ideal, power and politicization must be openly acknowledged (Mouffe 2000b, 2000c, 2005). All policy actors were aware that there were centres of power, though they disagreed about (or did not know) where they were. For instance, some representatives from parents' groups involved in consultations indicated that the educator groups held more power than they in decision-making. Others believed the bureaucrats held the power to make decisions and grant access to the policy process. Still others felt that the elected officials unilaterally made decisions. The lack of certainly about power structures led, at least in part, to rumours. As such, open acknowledgment of power as envisioned by Mouffe was not evident in Ontario's policy process.

When there are no opportunities for dialogue, the danger arises that one party could impose its views and shape policy documents to reflect its values about content and beliefs (as described by Werner 1991). There is reason to believe that this happened in Ontario. In particular, student learning expectations in draft policy texts appeared and disappeared without explanation. Rumours abounded regarding who was making decisions, and few policy actors understood why some decisions were made. These allegedly mysterious decisions and changes highlighted the level of politicization. According to Walter Werner, politicization occurs when consensus or negotiation among groups is resolved through the use of power when decisions are made 'that resolve the struggle over value differences' (Werner 1991, 107).

Writers' perceptions of how and whose power shaped policy texts varied. Some claimed they flew 'under the radar' (their words) and had autonomy to shape their policy texts. Others involved in subjects perceived to have higher political priority (such as English, mathematics, and history) reported they were closely monitored and their draft documents were often challenged or simply changed. This surveillance of writers, coupled with mysterious 'revisions' by either ministry bureaucrats and/or elected officials, illustrate how power was exerted to shape policy without apparent consideration of policy actors' perspectives.

The sources of power and ultimate decision-making remained unclear to many policy actors. Certainly, in some cases, political leaders made decisions without consultation. In other cases, bureaucrats appear to have made decisions. In still others, members of writing teams made decisions using their personal power. Ideally, in a critical-democratic process, power should be brought to the fore and made visible in democratic politics, rather than attempting to minimize or erase it (Mouffe 2000b).

A unique theme that emerged from policy actor interviews was the degree to which policy writers felt that they had freedom to conceptualize policy texts and shape them. Some members of writing teams felt they were able to write with less scrutiny because they perceived their subjects/courses to be 'under the radar' politically. This point was confirmed by James, who attended a number of consultations. He reported that mathematics and English were the most politicized by parents and the media. One writer working on history curriculum policy said, 'History was of less concern by way of parents.' Other writers describe their perceptions this way:

> In fact, in some respects we felt that maybe we were under the radar a bit and were able to do a few more things, because the timeline was shorter and people weren't watching as closely ... I think by the time the final draft was done, it was a very short period before it was released. I'm not sure it went through the same levels of review, particularly at the Cabinet level, that some of the documents had. (Justin, writer)

> I would say, overall, our feeling about it was, about the whole experience – my feeling was that we were not politicized the way that some of the subjects were. It's probably because we were [this subject area], and people tend to thing of the [this subject] as being secondary somehow – not as crucial to their political will, or whatever. But, in fact, the [this subject] can be very powerful, but they don't know that. It can be a very powerful element for presenting certain points of view in the curriculum, but people don't realize that ... I felt we escaped some of the politicization. (Drew, project manager)

We started getting feedback when the first draft came in, and then it became very clear which groups were having a lot of say, and it became fairly clear to us fairly early in the process that this is a really hot political subject. If I remember correctly, [the project manager] had kept telling us that this was one of the Premier's Office and I don't remember hearing that from other subject areas. So we knew we were under the spotlight, and when comments would come back to us, it didn't take long to figure out, OK, somebody's got their ear up there, so we would have to change. (Hardy, writer)

James also recalled an absence of research – and saw this as problematic. The same issue was raised by Alison, another consultation participant. According to James, in one of the only instances where research was brought into the discussion for physical education curriculum policy, a stakeholder found and brought in a study that showed that instruction on drugs actually increases the likelihood that students will take drugs. James said, 'Empirical research rarely entered the discussion to "win the day."' This is puzzling, since the first stage in the official policy process (see appendix) included background research for each subject area. As well, the documents from Praxis and Strategic Counsel provide the results of larger-scale consultations on curriculum policy. However, when asked, writers and consultation participants did not recall reviewing copies of any of these documents.

Potted Plants and Flies on the Wall: Silencing Writing Team Members

This political nature of curriculum policy calls for a unique approach to its production. Michael Apple's vision is for a 'free, contributive, and common process of participation in the creation of meanings and values' (1993, 238) that incorporates the voices of a variety of groups, perspectives, and ideologies. Along those lines, Aaron Wildavsky calls for an active and sustainable political arena, which must exist so that democratic principles drive debates over curriculum policy. This would allow debate over values and feasibility, and reduce politicization. In an ideal critical democratic arena, actors representing the diversity of the community would participate in vibrant dialogue.

While the Ontario government offered feedback sessions to discuss draft curriculum policy texts, they hardly conformed to the critical-democratic ideal, which would include open debate. Writing team representatives who attended consultations reported that they were 'muzzled.' In some cases, they were told outright by the bureaucrats or staffers who invited them to participate not to speak in meetings. This theme came up many times and provides an interesting level of insight.

> We were told ... I was told by [the project manager], 'You are just to be a potted plant. You don't speak unless spoken to, unless they ask you to answer a question, you don't get to speak. This isn't the platform.' And then after these meetings, we would get these required revisions. (Scott, writer)

> I remember going to that meeting but we were told not to say anything, we were just to listen – which was frustrating to no end because they would mention something and I couldn't give a rationale for it, and I'd try but [the project manager] would pull me back every once in awhile because I would get frustrated, the context, criticize us all you want but give us a chance to put context, so I thought a bit of a straitjacket. The ministry people were watching us pretty closely. Boy, I tell you, they had us on a tight rein ... Well, I did talk some, I wasn't totally silent, but they were pretty strict on the timeline. We were sending confidentiality agreements all over the place, so we didn't say much about anything. I didn't want to get kicked off the team, to be quite honest. I put a lot of effort into this and I wanted to see the end result. (Hardy, writer)

> We weren't allowed to talk at all during the meetings. It was odd, and it was actually kind of amusing, because my co-manager is the most gregarious person in the world, and for him to sit still for ten minutes without talking is a miraculous feat. But to do that for two or three hours is unheard of. We took along our laptop computers, and we would type things. We were actually given a summary, in a way there was no need for us to be there ... What was a surprise was that we couldn't speak at all, we didn't make a presentation, and we couldn't answer questions. I guess they didn't want us to get into an argument with stakeholder groups.
>
> The stakeholders spoke, the ministry people made a record and then presented the record to us later. So, actually, in a way there was no need for us to be there ... It was a very odd experience. It wasn't an exchange; it was just people made presentations and listened, we typed on our laptop computers, the ministry people typed on their laptop computers, and you were sent a report on which we had already started to act because we had our own notes. (Drew, project manager)

Consultation participant James confirmed that individuals involved felt that they were not permitted to speak to one another. For example, during the development of the science curriculum, one person on the bureaucratic side said, 'We have to communicate offline about this.' He perceived that neither could reveal that they had been communicating, and that this bureaucrat believed 'she would be in trouble' if others in the ministry found out that they had been speaking to one another.

Even within teams, and among peers, members were silenced. One might expect that writing team members would engage in professional dialogue, and perhaps even conflict within the group, in devising curriculum policy texts. When asked about this, many writers admitted that, in an effort to complete tasks within aggressive timelines, they glossed over conflict. As Scott described his team's approach, 'When we would get to a point of contention, I would listen to all sides, and then I would start typing, and that would be the end of that.' By reducing policy actors' roles to 'potted plants,' the critical democratic ideal is compromised, since the possibility of a vibrant exchange of ideas and perspectives is eliminated.

Rumours and Conspiracy Theories Abound

When a process lacks the transparency associated with democratic policy production, a number of problems can arise. In Ontario, questions about the legitimacy of the writing process arose out of a preponderance of rumours and conspiracy theories that writers offered in the course of their interviews. A number of policy actors raise the issue of rumours and 'conspiracy theories' that they believed might explain aspects of the policy that they did not understand. The first group of rumours concerned who might be chosen to write the curriculum when word of the upcoming RFP was leaked. Scott, a writer interviewed for this research, as well as Fielding (2002) and O'Farrell (2001), explicitly brought this up: 'Who would do this? Of course, the rotten Americans were immediately suspect.'

A second set of rumours concerned perceived content 'rules.' Fielding (2002), a project manager for a writing team, described how 'rumours swirled' (his words) among his writers around content issues, such as a directive to downplay things such as Aboriginal issues, gender issues, and the labour movement.

Early in the writing process rumours swirled that we were to downplay Aboriginal issues, women's history, and the labour movement. Our history writers asked me if they should comply with this perceived directive. My response was that I had never been given a memo stating this; therefore, it was simply a rumour. Also I didn't think we should put ourselves in the position of self censoring in anticipation of what the Minister or Premier would accept. In September, the shoe dropped, we received feedback from OMET[1] that we could not use the word 'contribution' in connection with Aboriginal people, the Women's movement and labour unions. They also wanted some expectations that spoke to the importance of business. They specifically wanted this expectation – 'describe the founding of the Canadian Manufacturing Association and assess its "contribution" to the Canadian economy.' I explained that the CMA was founded in the 19th century and this should be taught in the grade eight course. I was informed we didn't have a choice, it was going in. I contacted our OMET liaison person and she conceded that she had received a memo months ago explaining how Aboriginal, women's and Labour history were to be addressed, but she had not passed it along because she knew that it would not be well received by our team. At this point I threatened to go to the media with this issue. After what I am sure was some hectic scrambling and a few days delay it was decided we could use the word 'contribution' to describe the women's movement and Aboriginal peoples. The word 'contribution,' however, was deleted from our expectations referring to labour unions during the final OMET edit. We never did see the last draft before it went to the printers.

The third set of rumours surrounded mysterious changes to policy document drafts (also appearing in the Fielding's account above). Writers and project managers had many 'theories' about how and why changes appeared – largely political – but rarely had concrete substantiation. For example, Hardy, a writer, explained, 'Well, I can't be a 100 per cent sure: rumours were saying this was going to the Premier's Office and that somebody up there was taking a look.' Similarly, Robert, a project manager for a writing team, rationalized the unexplained changes: 'When I raised questions about the changes, we were just told implement them – the fact that it was the Premier's office, I got from the back door, from my contacts. They wouldn't openly say where it came from – they tried to maintain a sort of solidarity.'

When asked about such issues, bureaucrats provided varying perceptions about the role of the minister's and premier's offices. For instance, one bureaucrat explains, 'We got feedback from the minister, from the premier – from the minister's office, the premier's office. They were sending it out to other people and getting feedback, and sending it back to us. They have every right to do that ... I certainly felt, with Snobelen, that he was listening, and considering ... Given the government of the day, I think the relationships were remarkably cordial. They had a lot of respect for the people who were running this. I felt that they treated us with reasonable respect all the way through' (Janelle, bureaucrat).

John Ibbitson's account supports the writers' perceptions: 'Snobelen's staff, though devoid of pedagogical training, went so far as to start writing the [curriculum] guidelines themselves. The situation eased as senior staff [who were] more sympathetic to the Tories' philosophy gradually replaced their more obstructionist predecessors' (Ibbitson 1997, 280).

This very issue was debated in the Legislative Assembly on 7 October 1998 when NDP Member Howard Hampton questioned the minister of education on curriculum deletions, based on a memorandum the opposition obtained:

Mr Hampton: To the Minister of Education. You will remember that many of us were very shocked when you indicated that you were going to contract out the development of Ontario's new secondary school curriculum, that teachers who are actually in the classroom would not be developing it. You tried to mollify us and say, 'Don't worry, teachers who are in the classroom will be involved.' We were worried that many important curriculum issues would be left out in this new contracting out of curriculum. You said, 'Don't worry, it'll be OK.'

Minister, can you tell us why, then, you have directed the curriculum project managers to change the grade 9 and 10 curriculum policy documents by deleting 'education about discrimination and anti-discrimination,' deleting 'education about native people,' and deleting 'education about violence prevention'? Why have you instructed that these things should be deleted from the curriculum?

Hon David Johnson (Minister of Education and Training): I made no such instruction.

Mr Hampton: I'm amazed that this government wants to control everything, but then when they get caught at it, they say, 'It wasn't us.' This is a Ministry of Education and Training memorandum to project managers of curriculum from Karen Allan regarding program planning. It says:

Part 1: Delete cross-curricular considerations – education with respect to anti-racism; education with respect to anti-discrimination – delete violence prevention; delete education about native people.

Why would one of your officials be sending out this kind of directive to the people who are working on the curriculum? Minister, don't you think these things are important in our high school curriculum? Don't you think these things ought to be addressed? The last time I checked, this city is one of the most multicultural cities in the world. The last time I checked, some of these issues are very serious. Why are you deleting them?

Hon David Johnson: The curriculum is being developed by teams of teachers. At least half of the composition of the teams has to be teachers from Ontario, a representative from the college, a representative from the university, a representative from the workplace. These highly trained, highly experienced teams are consulting with people across Ontario, making various drafts, and based on various inputs they have at various points in time, they will make changes to the curriculum as they deem suitable. Certainly the kinds of issues that the opposition member has raised are important issues, and I can only conclude that the experienced teams such as have been involved would have those topics suitably incorporated into the curriculum.

Mr Hampton: Minister, you can try to spin a good line. This is the reality of your government: You disbanded the anti-discrimination and equal opportunity branch soon after you became the government, you held back the release of an anti-hate guidebook for teachers and principals that was drafted for you by B'Nai Brith, then you send out this September 14 memo saying that all these other things are going to be deleted from the curriculum. Now you're trying to say it will somehow be added on.

These are important issues. You don't sort of add them on to the curriculum. They aren't extras that you put in at the end. These are issues that have to be integrated into the classroom on a daily basis by teachers. They have to be part of the curriculum if that's going to happen. Why have you done this, Minister? Why did you not release the booklet from B'Nai Brith? Why have you deleted education on anti-discrimination? Why have you deleted from the curriculum the issues dealing with anti-violence? Why are you taking all of these important issues out of the curriculum? Don't they matter in Conservative Ontario?

Hon David Johnson: This makes for wonderful spin in the House, but the member opposite knows full well I have deleted nothing. (Legislative Assembly, *Debates and Proceedings* [23 April 1997])

A similar issue was raised in the Legislature about the removal and absence of environmentally focused expectations and courses just weeks following this instance. Despite the minister's denial, the evidence gathered from policy actors suggests that the memorandum cited by Mr Hampton appears to be correct, and a degree of politicization on removing specific topics from curriculum policy likely occurred. This level of politicization, in itself, is anti-democratic. More importantly, the substance of these mandates – the elimination of anti-racism, Aboriginal, and anti-violence content – contravenes the critical-democratic goal of social justice.

Resistance and Subversive Activities: An Undemocratic Reaction to an Undemocratic Process

Not surprisingly, policy actors occasionally engaged in resistance and subversion. Some felt they had resort to subversive tactics to achieve their ends if they felt resistance would be futile. A critical-democratic process would have allowed for open discussion of policy actors' concerns. Though reported mainly by writers, bureaucrats recounted examples both on and off the record when interviewed. Will, a political staffer, confirmed that he 'got a lot of institutional resistance from the senior public servants.' Drew, a project manager for a writing team, explicitly identified his perception that members of his team were engaging in subversive tactics: 'I think a general consensus that [the direction prescribed by the government] wasn't the best way to conceive this program, but if we didn't do it, who was going to do it? And it might be much, much worse. There was, I would say, a genuine feeling of being subversive in our group' (Drew, writing team member).

To prepare for, or perhaps combat, resistance and subversion, Will explained that a public servant acted as a 'mole in the ministry' on their behalf. 'She would come up and say to us, "I am not sure if you are aware of this but they're going off on a crazy tangent, not planning to tell you about it, so be aware of it."' Project manager Mike recounted an incident where another member of his team, knowing he was not to speak at a consultation meeting, called several of individuals who were to attend that meeting in advance to convey his perspective. Others, such as Robert, lived by the rule, 'It's always easier to ask forgiveness than permission. Particularly at the ministry, if you ask permission, you're most of the time going to be told no.' These responses illustrate that while some policy actors engaged in subversive tactics to communicate with other policy actors or to otherwise achieve certain ends, the success of these efforts was mixed, largely as the result of the power and control of the ministry to make final decisions and to revise policy texts.

Chantal Mouffe's conception of agonism – a central feature of a critical-democratic policy process – calls for the 'expression of dissent and institutions through which conflicts can be manifested' (Mouffe 2000c, 149). In Ontario, forums for those expressions of dissent simply did not exist. Interaction is a necessary component for this type of dissent, but the fragmentation and tightly controlled communication channels kept interaction and dissent to a bare minimum in Ontario. While some writers engaged in subversion as a type of dissent, none challenged the 'official framing' in any explicit ways. As I described in the case study, the government was aware of this and engaged a public servant to act as a 'mole in the ministry' on their behalf to combat subversive efforts. From the critical-democratic perspective, the lack of opportunities and time to engage in framing or reframing of issues is problematic. Moreover, the fact that policy actors felt that they had to resort to subversion to assert their positions suggests a lack of opportunities for democratic dialogue – let alone agonistic deliberation. Subversion is not consistent with the critical-democratic ideal. Rather, critical democracy calls for open resistance and dissent, which takes place within agonistic exchanges among policy actors. As such, the subversive response among Ontario policy actors may be an undemocratic form of resistance in reaction to an undemocratic process that failed to offer them different (and more constructive) means to voice their disagreement.

Concluding Comments

Policy writers' perceptions of the process point to an absence of critical-democratic procedure and values, undercut by a highly politicized process that lacked transparency. Because Ministry of Education officials controlled, and to some degree filtered, the information passed from one group to another, policy actors lacked opportunities for debate, discussion, and deliberation. In some cases policy actors were not exposed to the perspectives of others and were uncertain about how decisions were made. Consequently, writers frequently speculated about politicization through conspiracy theories. This politicization limited the weight of policy actors' input into the final policy texts. Policy actors had conflicting perceptions of the weight given to others' perspectives and/ or suggestions in the process, especially related to progressive versus conservative educational agendas. Some policy actors described situations in which writers were explicitly told they were not to speak during feedback meetings with stakeholders; in other cases consultation participants felt they were implicitly obliged to withhold their points of view. These rules of deliberation, in many cases, shut down the opportunity for an exchange of ideas. However, the data gathered confirmed cases of politicization in which the premier's or minister's office made decisions, added, and/or deleted policy content.

6 Citizen (Dis)Engagement in Selection and Consultations

One of the reasons that the traditional system of governance [in Ontario] has endured for as long as it has, despite decades of growing disillusionment, is that those who hold the levers of power are disinclined to see their positions challenged or their power and prerogatives diminished. One of the reasons why increasing numbers of citizens appear to be prepared to disengage from our traditional political system is that their relationship to it is increasingly marked by a sense of impotence or lack of power. If politics is about making the crucial collective choices of a society, then political power is the energy source that permits these choices to be made definitively . . . Difficulties with representative democracy, then, both create and are the result of public disaffection from conventional politics . . . Democratic reform, if it is worthy of the name, is all about power – about relocating power from politicians and elites to citizens. If reformers are not prepared to live with the often untidy consequences of that, then their initiatives are likely to be greeted by citizens with the cynicism they deserve.
– David Cameron et al. 2003, 97–8

The curriculum attracted passionate people who freed up their time to make this time. This is a credit to both public servants and the stakeholders. People dropped everything. I remember our first meeting was put together with a two-week notice and we had, I think a 95 per cent uptake on the invite to participate. We tapped into a lot of passion and that ultimately fuelled our turnaround.
– Will, political staffer

As I discussed at the start of this book, attention to 'democracy' and citizen participation abounds in popular discourses. Civic engagement is a necessary component of critical democracy. To be sure, the nature of public involvement must be 'thick' and inclusive in order to conform to the critical-democratic ideal. Ontario's curriculum policy reform process included several forums and structures for citizen involvement – undoubtedly a move towards some degree of democracy in the process. However, as I illustrate in this chapter, the degree to which opportunities to participate were open to all remains in question, and the opportunities for truly open exchanges of ideas were limited. Those who were in the privileged position to be fully engaged in the process reported tremendous learning in civic skills.

The sheer numbers of individuals involved in producing Ontario's curriculum policy – and particularly those consulted during the contracted background research – suggest at least an attempt by the government to democratize the process via broad citizen input. However, when viewed in its totality, an elitist approach to inclusion in the process characterizes the selection of policy actors, and the substance of their participation is nothing less than thin. In addition to the tendering process, policy actors revealed that invitations to participate depended on 'who you know,' resulting in educational or political elites being 'hand picked' to participate in writing teams and in stakeholder consultations. RFP criteria required that writing teams had to possess substantial financial assets – not to mention skill in proposal-writing – to be considered. Ontarians interested in participation faced a marked absence of significant 'open' opportunities to come forward. This limited who could participate in the process as writer.

Democracy and Civic Engagement in Ontario

A great deal of popular and academic literature in recent years concerns itself with an alleged decline in civic engagement. Despite uncertainty about Ontario's level from an empirical standpoint, largely due to a lack of comprehensive data (Cameron 2002), several measures suggest a decline in civic engagement at the provincial level during the latter part of the twentieth century (Morton 1997; Cameron 2002). David Cameron cautions that this disengagement from political institutions does not necessarily mean a lack of interest in politics – rather, he postulates it is 'an indication of discontent with the way in which traditional public institutions are operating' (Cameron 2002, 44; Dahlgren 2007).

Two measures provide some insight into this matter: attachment and voter turnout. However, the indicators available to measure civic engagement presented here are thin and more consistent with representative democracy than critical democracy. Nevertheless, they provide a useful starting point for my description and analysis of engagement in Ontario's curriculum policy process. First, attachment as a measure of civic engagement reflects the degree to which citizens feel part of and committed to their community. David Cameron reports, 'Attachment of Ontarians to their province has been declining in the 1990s (81% in 1995 to 64% in 1998), while the attachment to Canada has been high and stable (89% in 1994 and 87% in 1998). Thus the political community and government with which people in Ontario are more inclined to engage are Canada and the federal government, not Ontario and Queen's Park' (2002, 4). An apparent apathy in political matters is reflected in provincial election participation. Ontario voter turnout in provincial elections since 1867 has ranged from a high of 74.4 per cent of eligible voters in 1898 to a low of 58 per cent in 1981 (Elections Ontario n.d.). Moreover, Ontario's participation in elections has been consistently lower than that of other Canadian provinces (Cameron 2002). By contrast, overall participation in elections worldwide rose between 1945 and 1990, with a slight decline during the 1990s (Cameron 2002).

David Cameron and his colleagues (2003) call attention to problems associated with weakness of the role of Ontario members of Parliament (MPPs) as a problematic aspect of governance, and express concern about the lack of opportunities and roles for citizens to actively participate in Ontario's democratic processes. Because power is concentrated in the hands of the Executive (the Premier and Cabinet), MPPs have little voice. The result is that MPPs are unable to represent their constituents, and decisions are made by an elite few – a situation not unique to Ontario. Beyond electoral participation, the Ontario government has provided some opportunities for involvement through stakeholder 'consultations' and feedback, though as the case study will reveal, access tends to be limited to a chosen few, though arguably the level of involvement was higher than in previous decades.

By the late 1980s, parent activism emerged through special interests groups, most notably the Quality Education Network (QEN) and the Organization for Quality Education (OQE), both considered right-wing (Gidney 1999). Later, during the 1990s, People for Education (P4E) was formed, offering a left-of-centre perspective. These organizations engaged in a variety of activities, including lobbying and independent research, to support their positions and to voice opposition to the actions of existing structures and institutions described in the next section. While extreme in their politics stances, these organizations and the public support for them suggest more than a passing interest in political participation among Ontarians.

Policy Actors and Their Selection

A critical-democratic policy process relies on the inclusion of citizens – and particularly those from groups traditionally marginalized (López 2003; Gillborn 2005) – in policy formulation. As Gillborn (2005) argues, understanding who drives education policy is crucial to unmasking privilege. To achieve a critical-democratic ideal, those in power must ensure that those often excluded from political processes are given an opportunity for meaningful involvement: 'Although citizens will express them in a variety of forms and activities, all members of a vibrant democratic body would share a sense of ownership in their common world, and an ethos of care for a radically pluralistic public sphere. But it is only through the practice of agonal engagement that citizens can sustain the belief in the importance of participation, remain vigilant against potential injustices, actively engage their fellow citizens, and retain the passion and desire to appear before one another in speech and action' (Goi 2005, 81). Thus, we must question how policy actors were selected, which individuals or groups were included, and what measures were taken to ensure inclusiveness of diverse players. One consequence of highly institutionalized policymaking environments is the 'over-representation of high-status members of the population' (Glynos 2003, 190). This is substantiated by empirical evidence that suggests participatory, discussion-based forums are no more successful than conventional strategies to engage minority and low-income citizens (Kohn 2000). Criteria for critical-democratic policy actor inclusion include:

- Openness and transparency of policy actor recruitment.
- Degree and/or number of opportunities for interested citizens to participate.
- Degree to which recruitment makes an effort to include those from marginalized groups in society. Inclusion of citizens from the margins would vary, depending on the local context. Strategies to involve them are highly dependent on who is marginalized, to what degree, and what kinds of supports they require in order to participate (e.g., technology, interpreters/translators, time, flexibility, education, etc.).

- Outreach mechanisms to ensure that those from traditionally marginalized groups are encouraged to participate.

Critical-democratic deliberation is not measured by numbers of
participants, but rather by inclusion of a cross-section of individuals
representing marginalized groups, and by the quality of deliberation
that would allow for agonistic exchange as envisioned by Mouffe. For
Ontario's feedback opportunities to reflect critical-democratic ideals,
several conditions must be met. First, criteria to ensure inclusiveness
must be applied to ensure that citizens beyond high-status members
of the community are included. This requires analysis of the sorts of
groups that are in the margins, and concerted efforts to engage those
groups and/or individuals. Second, there must be opportunities for
meaningful deliberation – whether in person or another format, such as
online. Participation, in the critical-democratic ideal, requires agonistic
forms of exchange, as I described in chapter 1, and due consideration
of perspectives must be offered. In this section, I analyse two aspects of
policy actor involvement salient to critical democracy: elitism in selection, and the quality of opportunities for input.

Policy actors described ways in which they, as well as others, were
selected for inclusion. Overall, an elitist approach emerges – inclusion,
for a variety of reasons, depended on 'who you know' and often resulted
in educational or political elites receiving invitations to participate.
Without a doubt, policy actors selected to join writing teams and
consultations were 'hand-picked' by those in positions to make the
choices – exacerbating elitism while reifying privilege as 'a system of
favors, courtesies, exchanges, and tacit agreements that enable whites
and their friends to get ahead' (Delgado 2011, 1286). Thus, Ontarians
faced a marked absence of significant 'open' opportunities to come forward with an interest to participate, and those already privileged were
more likely to be involved. A summary of the policy actors who participated in the process studied here appears in table 6.1.

In addition, the ministry held consultations in the form of presentations
to a variety of stakeholder groups between 20 September and 20 December 1996, prior to the commencement of the curriculum writing.
These consultations were to inform course menus, graduation requirements, and streaming. Composition and locations included:[1]

- 144 teacher federation district office presentations, with 7,500 participants attending

Table 6.1 Policy actors involved

Policy actor	Explanation	Role
Elected political leadership and their political staffers	Political staffers provided advice and recommendations to elected officials	Set policy agenda, vision Set timelines for development and implementation Attended some consultation sessions Provided feedback and made revisions to policy texts
Bureaucrats	One secondary curriculum work team (SCWT) was established per subject Made up of ministry staff from the Curriculum Branch, SCWTs guided policy development	Managed all aspects of policy process Provided direction to contractors and stakeholders Negotiated or traded off competing interests and vision
Contracted policy writing teams	Teams were contracted for each subject discipline through a Request for Proposal (RFP) tender The project manager was the only member who liaised directly with the ministry	Contracted policy writers developed the actual policy based on the guidelines provided by the ministry within a budget and timeframes outlined in successful RFP proposal Feedback and recommendations were to be incorporated
Consultation participants	Organized into groups for each subject area, and stakeholders participated in consultations Members of the community from a database representing 250 organizations and 700 individuals maintained by the ministry	Feedback was gathered during the process (when deliverables were submitted) from stakeholders in the database through face-to-face meetings and written responses Selected stakeholders validated the final policy documents through face-to-face meetings and written responses

- Ministers' meetings with an external advisory group and with the Ontario Teachers' Federation (OTF)
- Public meetings with 992 citizens in Kingston, Barrie, London, Waterdown, North Bay, North York, Scarborough, and Ottawa
- Group consultation meetings with 131 'provincial organizations,' including school board / administrator organizations, teachers organizations, students organizations, parents organizations, faculties, labour organizations, business organizations, special education groups, community interest groups, and trustee groups[2]

On the basis of these three consultation documents (the Praxis Group report, *What People Said about High School Reform;* The Strategic Counsel Inc. *Report to the Ministry of Education and Training [sic] on the Secondary School Reform Meetings,* and the ministry's internal report on consultations summarized above), it is evident that the Ontario government, through the Ministry of Education, made a concerted effort to consult with citizens. Notably absent from the documentation and from the archives is a clear explanation of how individuals and groups came to participate in consultations. While Praxis explains that background discussion documents were distributed to schools and libraries (and presumably those who responded came upon those documents one way or another), how participants were identified to participate in face-to-face presentations and consultations remains unclear.

In Ontario, public consultations have become a consistent and important feature of policy development since the Harris government introduced them in 1995. Consultations involve bringing together stakeholders from the community, and obtaining either their input or feedback on a particular issue or policy. The intent is to incorporate stakeholder views into policy development, thus attempting to ensure that their needs and views are considered. One bureaucrat described the consultations for SSR curriculum policy as a new approach to large-scale consultations: 'We've never had this open a process, where everybody saw every draft and could comment on every draft, and where the people gathered around the table was not a homogeneous grouping. There were workplace people, and college people, and university people. And they all speak different languages, so there was a lot of mediating of those languages' (Janelle, bureaucrat). Though this approach to large-scale consultation for curriculum policy was new to Ontario at the time, the Royal Commission on Learning under the previous

NDP administration also included large-scale public involvement for broader educational reform issues.

All individuals involved in consultations were officially representing a larger group – and the ministry emphasized that this process was not open to anyone as an individual citizen. Rather, consultation participants represented 'provincial interests,' excluding individuals and local/municipal organizations. Consequently, stakeholder groups represented included parent organizations, Ontario teachers' subject associations, bodies representing higher education such as the Council of Ontario Universities (COU), and teacher federations.

Early in the course my research, I spoke to the director of a local education organization (representing Toronto), who expressed frustration in her attempts to participate in consultations. She and her organization were excluded because they did not represent a provincial focus. Janelle, a Ministry of Education bureaucrat, explained,

> You couldn't get on, unless the minister put you on. You couldn't get on as an individual. You had to represent a provincial body.
>
> We sent out an invitation to all subject associations and all provincial associations. Anyone who had a provincial association that I could find got an invitation . . .
>
> But if they're not a provincial association – and that was my criterion – if they don't represent provincial interests, we didn't want that. There were lots of people who said they wanted to participate, and the response was, 'If you are a provincial association, then there's legitimate access.' If not, they could still send me information [feedback, their perspectives] if they wanted, and I still read everything I got . . .
>
> There was no formal weighting of, well, 'You're one association, so I'll weight you less than these others.' Aside from the meeting that they attended, I had meetings with each of the key stakeholder groups before those review meetings. So there would be a representative from, say, the college system on each review team, but I met, before those review meetings, with ACAATO, with COU, with the minister's special education advisory council, with the federations – key stakeholder groups, for their overall perspective. Not discipline-specific, but overall. That also had to be brought into play . . .
>
> First, nobody was there as an individual – they were all there representing an organization. I think people forgot that from time to time, and got onto their own particular issues that weren't representative of their associations. (Janelle, bureaucrat)

Regardless of the role, elitism characterized Ontario's policy actor selection process – a feature at odds with critical-democratic ideals. The ministry invited writers and consultation participants to apply, attend, or otherwise participate in the policy process. Ministry bureaucrats argued that allowing 'just anyone' to participate might not represent the provincial interest – though by limiting the definition of 'provincial interest' it appears to exclude those who do not hold positions of power in provincial organizations. As well, bureaucrats emphasized that all Ontarians had the opportunity to review draft documents and provide feedback in writing. However, one wonders how marginalized individuals and groups find themselves part of the process.

By hand-picking writers and consultation participants, and holding them to conform to a particular vision of education while expecting them to produce curriculum within extremely short timelines, the government eliminated the possibility of full consideration of divergent perspectives that would address social justice in the curriculum when coupled with the troubling political stance described earlier in chapter 2.

Arenas for Discourse and Citizen Engagement: Government-Controlled Public Forums

Highly controlled 'official' arenas dominated discourse during Ontario's curriculum policy formulation, with limits on who was invited to participate. At the outset, the provision of arenas for discourse is a necessary but insufficient component for critical democracy; the quality of deliberation within such arenas for discourse is equally crucial. As a way of life that goes beyond the narrow conception of democracy as a form of government, critical democracy relies on an active citizenry to offer input into government decisions through meaningful, agonistic participation, when power is placed in the hands of citizens, and active involvement becomes part of everyday life.

Perhaps the most obvious arena for public discourse in Ontario's curriculum policy formulation was consultation meetings. Indeed, citizens had to meet criteria to be invited to formally participate in curriculum policy reform consultations – though opportunities were available for anyone to provide input in writing, should they wish to draft letters to the ministry or minister. Those selected to participate in consultations had to represent provincial interests recognized by the ministry and had to be formally invited to participate. Consequently, opportunities for meaningful participation (that is, participating in face-to-face and preferably agonistic exchanges) were limited to those in positions of power within certain types of organizations.

Citizen involvement in the policy process is particularly relevant here, since it is one of the principal methods used to democratize the policy process. Though a fair amount of literature has emerged on this topic as an integral part of the policy process, Wolf (1999, 20) characterizes it as 'thin,' in that it provides neither insight into effective processes nor empirical data about outcomes. Genuine citizen/ stakeholder involvement makes an important contribution to democratic life through empowerment, collective decision-making, education of participants, and general development of skills, which would allow them to participate in policymaking and is therefore consistent with the critical-democratic ideal. The focus of inclusion and learning opportunities, of course, are unique to each jurisdiction, as well as to the policy area. Criteria to evaluate the degree of citizen engagement include:

- Commitment to reciprocity, so that the right of participation is connected to citizens' responsibly to be duly informed through educative opportunities (discussed later)
- Meaningful participation, such that citizens have access to information and perspectives to reflect upon their own views, and that their views are given due consideration in policy decisions and/or solutions

Similarly, the opportunity to participate as a member of a writing team was limited. Moreover, the ministry limited and controlled communication among writers and consultation participants. From a critical-democratic perspective, limited opportunity for citizen participation in discussions surrounding policy formulation is problematic. Because of these limits, voices of those excluded from the process are silenced. Moreover, ministry control over interactions among policy actors eliminated the possibility of agonistic exchanges and consequently the opportunity to enhance knowledge and understanding.

'Thin' Opportunities for Input and Participation

To approach a critical-democratic ideal (issues of inclusion aside), forums of deliberation must allow participants a voice through ample opportunities for meaningful communication, and rival positions must be taken seriously. In Ontario, the process limited opportunities for discussion, and when those opportunities were presented, time constraints and tightly controlled channels of communication disallowed articulation of points of view, let alone a means for those positions to be given due consideration. The conceptual framework raises several specific questions about policy actors' experiences: To what extent did they experience agonistic exchanges or deliberation? How did they view their opponents – as enemies, or as adversaries 'whose ideas we struggle with but whose right to defend those ideas we will not put into question' (Mouffe 2000c, 149)? Did policy actors acknowledge power and exclusion?

First, I touch on the quality of participation offered by written responses. There were somewhat open opportunities for citizen input. Recall that Praxis Consulting received over 28,000 responses, including response documents, letters, essays, and other forms of response. The Strategic Counsel engaged 115 people representing fifty-five stakeholder groups for their *Report to the Ministry of Education and Training on the Secondary School Reform Meetings*. The ministry held presentations for stakeholder groups between September and December 1996 with over eight thousand individuals. Bureaucrat Janelle reported that the ministry received over one thousand written responses. From the perspective of involvement, these numbers are impressive and suggest that the government and the Ministry of Education made some attempt to involve citizens in policy formulation through written feedback. As I describe in the next section, while these numbers appear impressive, the quality of participation requires examination.

These opportunities for written feedback were by no means 'thick' or inclusive, falling short of the critical-democratic ideal. The 'one-way' communication of writing a response letter does not allow citizens the crucial opportunity to understand the position taken in policy solutions that would be achieved through a two-way agonistic exchange. At the same time, the written responses failed to provide decision-makers and other policy actors the opportunity to understand the writer's position.

However, the quality of interaction among policy actors offers another aspect for analysis salient to a critical-democratic policy process: evidence of agonistic exchanges among policy actors. The quality of participation with respect to agonism appears to have varied, depending on the policy actor's role. Writers, for the most part, did not attend consultations, and when they did, they were not allowed to speak. This eliminated the possibility of their full participation in the process, let alone substantive and agonistic exchanges with others. Within their own teams, aggressive timelines prevented writers from engaging in agonistic exchange.

The process of coming to respect a rival is a necessary (but insufficient) component of Mouffe's agonistic conception of democratic dialogue, which calls on policy actors to view the rival in an agnostic fashion: 'a legitimate enemy, one with whom we have some common ground' (Mouffe 2000b, 102). Those from the education sector (teachers, educators, advocates) tended to view elected officials, and to a lesser degree, bureaucrats, antagonistically, accusing them of making uninformed decisions against policy actors' wills. The fact that many policy actors did not have the opportunity to meet the opponents in question may have contributed to their antagonistic stance. This stance was unproductive and undermines attempts at (critical) democratic dialogue.

Conversely, consultation participants tended to view their opponents in a more favourable light. Certainly, some constituents representing parents' groups acknowledged that they learned a great deal from speaking with representatives from the education sector who 'were on the other end of the political spectrum.' For example, one consultation participant recalled that he expected to meet 'tub thumpers' but was surprised to learn that his opponents were 'reasonable people.' This example is consistent with observations in the literature about how stereotypes lead to a dangerous suppression of rival positions (see, for example, Lugg 1998; Robertson 1998), thus undermining the critical-democratic ideal. Some of the common and unproductive stereotypes in educational discourse include situations in which 'traditionalists have argued that "tenured radicals" and other left wingers have hijacked the curriculum, turning it into a vehicle for the promotion of revolutionary ideas ... Most of the undesirable developments in education, curricula and social policy have been seen as emanating from "left wing" sources, and constant jabs at the language and practices of the left have been made' (Roberts 1998, 35, 44). Critical-democratic forums for deliberation are crucial to overcome such stereotypes and for an open discussion of alternatives. This type of dismissive attitude to rival positions in the Ontario process was moderated, once there was engagement in face-to-face discussion. This suggests that venues for public deliberation can overcome this sort of de-humanization of opponents or rivals in the process.

The ministry took a different approach to involve stakeholders in consultations. Clearly the ministry limited participation to those who were officially invited. Most policy actors described some degree of 'balance' in the perspectives represented. Despite that, not all policy actors concurred. Others felt that groups who shared what they perceived to be 'right-wing' views of the Tory government were overrepresented: 'When we used to go down to the ministry, I was always quite surprised by how they set the table, by who they invited . . . You'd be sitting there with representatives from parent groups, who you knew, they were on record, whether you went to their website or publicly, that they basically believed everything the government was saying about teachers and about skills. They were quite supportive of what's going on. So you're trying to address the issue, at the same time, you know you're being broadsided by these groups' (Curtis, consultation participant).

Discussion about consultative feedback would not be complete without mention of written feedback received. In addition to the consultation meetings, Eric – a bureaucrat involved in the process – explained, 'We had over one thousand people responding to each draft. So there was a lot of input, all of which was considered . . . All was given consideration. In the context of every piece of input, decisions were made.'

Fear of Removal from the Process

Policy actors expressed a sense of privilege about their inclusion in the process – and a perceived threat that they could be cut out of it at any time. Those who did not carry out the tasks and produce outcomes as intended were removed and/or replaced. Bureaucrat Janelle described several instances of writing teams being 'disbanded' by the ministry, either when the policy document was not sufficient, or when members of the writing team could not conduct themselves appropriately during consultations. Inappropriate conduct included expressing anger through yelling or disrespectful comments (such as insults) directed at others in the group. When this happened, ad hoc teams were struck, usually identified and contracted by the ministry, to rewrite courses within the time remaining. Such was the case with the two International Business course policy documents on which I worked. Similarly, according to a bureaucrat, misbehaviour might lead to removal from consultations: 'My fear for them [a particularly vocal organization], always, was I put you on the list, but you can be taken off.'

A representative from that very organization, Danielle, actually did feel pushed out after her organization held a press conference criticizing the process. She said, 'When you had little conversations with people before and after, and sometimes during, those sessions, you sensed that there was similar unhappiness with the process from these people ... They felt that they had to participate, because they couldn't not participate, and in part to keep up their relationship with the ministry.' The significance of this authoritative tool is that it reinforced the power imbalance by creating a fear of reprimand through removal. Its strength and effectiveness lay in policy actors' perceptions of this consequence, suggesting that the balance of power was skewed and that those who held the power, intentionally or not, conveyed the notion that those who did not obey would experience negative consequences.

Without a doubt, the opportunity to deliberate issues face-to-face provides policy actors with the potential for agonistic exchanges with others and is crucial to a critical-democratic policy process. Earlier, I described impediments to the quality of deliberation, including power, politicization, and manufactured consent. The aspects of the process I described in this chapter minimized, and in some cases eliminated, the possibility of meaningful participation, which is necessary for a robust, critical-democratic process.

Formal Deliberation Venues: Neutralizing Dissenting Voices

The ministry held a series of formal 'feedback sessions,' which served as consultations specific to curriculum policy texts at several points in 1998. Stakeholder groups, organized by subject area, attended these sessions and provided feedback on draft documents in a group setting. Erica described attending the first session, as she began her bureaucratic role: 'In July, I came to some of the very first set feedback meetings they had for the first draft. It was on a Saturday or Sunday. It was an all-day meeting on the second floor of the Ministry ... You had this curriculum document in this room, that curriculum document in that room, and that was the day, over that weekend ... There were huge decisions made.'

Many consultation participants felt that they had insufficient time for dialogue and deliberation at these sessions. Since the agenda of these sessions was limited to feedback on documents, not generation of ideas or debate, and since they were controlled by ministry representatives, there was no room for participant-generated topics for debate or discussion. Only one policy actor, James, commented on the size of groups. He felt that the groups consulted for the secondary school curriculum policy documents were too large. He recalled that 'dissenting voices' in the large groups tended to result in the group 'neutralizing itself.' Thus, in his view, meaningful feedback in the spirit of critical democracy did not happen. Moreover, as I described in the previous chapter, writers as policy actors were forbidden from actively participating in consultations.

Absence of Conflicts, Dialogue, and Debate

Many prominent theorists including Michael Apple, Walter Werner, and Stephen Ball contend that arriving at curriculum policy is the result of negotiations and trade-offs between those in positions of power. Likewise, the critical-democratic ideal would encourage meaningful, agonistic discussion among individuals and groups as envisioned by Chantal Mouffe in order to arrive at policy decisions. Virtually all policy actors felt that others involved in the process were 'well-intentioned' – a phrase that appeared in several interviews. By 'well-intentioned,' policy actors referred to a concern for the welfare of students and a commitment to some greater good. Consultation participant Alison believed that conflicts arose when policy actors had different ideas about how to arrive at their ultimate goal of student success: 'We all want to see students be successful – it's just that the route we take to get there, we're going to differ on how we get there. I think that's where any disagreements would have arisen.' Nevertheless, Alison pointed out that some had their own agendas, which seemingly conflicted with her perception of well-intentioned policy actors. 'It came that everyone is there on their own agenda. If they've got, let's say it's the teacher librarians' association, the person obviously has an agenda that they want to see preserved in the curriculum. Our organization is very big on content, knowledge, measurable outcomes – the old standards, very traditional; probably what the education community would consider very traditional goals of the curriculum.'

Having said that, not all perceived conflict across all groups. For instance, James recalled that sessions were 'cordial,' with some disagreement, but no real conflict in his own subject grouping. He was aware of some conflict in the Mathematics group, which was dealt with through changes to a document (presumably rather than full discussion

and consensus or compromise): 'The general tone at consultation sessions was cordial. There was disagreement on many issues, but little or
no strong conflict in the sessions I attended. But I do know that there
were strong disagreements in other groups, e.g., Mathematics. There
were strong objections raised to the changes proposed . . . All disagreements were recorded, and editing changes were made to the document
for review at the next meeting' (James, consultation participant).

The degree to which conflicts were permitted to occur during consultation sessions varied, depending on policy actor perception.
Consultation participant Alison remarked, 'It got to be pretty heated,'
while bureaucrat Erica recalled, 'The development of that curriculum, I
would describe as "bloody." It was a bloody process.'

Echoing the province's century-long tensions between conservative
and progressive education philosophies described in the previous chapter, policy actors present at consultations described many different topics that caused group conflict. Alison suggested that it was not 'what'
went into the curriculum that was contested, but 'how' it was presented:
'Were we going to be knowledge, content, standards, outcomes, measurable? Everything had to be tested. These guys were scientists and math-
ematicians so they wanted a way to measure achievement and make
sure it was high standards, rich knowledge-base curriculum and not so
much this process where kids would – this constructivism. That's the key
word that I would say, because that seems to be pervasive in modern-
day North American curriculum, this concept of constructivism. From
our point of view, we think that's terrible. It's not what leads to a good
curriculum that would give you a good outcome . . . It really became the
process versus content argument' (Alison, consultation participant).

Alison also felt that common ground on such debates was impossible: 'There's such a polarization that you can't have consensus. You
can't have constructivism and outcomes-based – they're at odds with
each other.' She reported that political staffer Will played the role of
a 'diplomat, because there were times when some of these guys were,
"I'm leaving! That's it!"' Will often spoke *in camera* to those policy actors
and convinced them to stay and participate: 'That's where a lot of the
real nitty-gritty got hashed out. It wasn't so much the concern about
what went into the curriculum, because that got sorted out pretty well
and everybody kind of agreed that certain things, and you could get
really picky on, oh, you have to make sure differential, this equation
has to be studied at this point in the year. It wasn't that picky, but broad
concepts to make sure that they study frog anatomy or something at

grade ten, or learn about photosynthesis at this point, so that those kinds of concepts they would definitely decide what grade they would go in' (Alison, consultation participant).

Will confirmed this account and provided greater justification for his role in managing 'misbehaviour':

> We were pretty clear in making sure that the ground rules of the engagement and discussion was civility. I got phone calls from public servants saying that this person was just absolutely rude to one of my staff and I said earlier, a lot of time was spent keeping people in line. We wouldn't condone that type of behaviour . . .
>
> What probably the public servants weren't privy to were the hours of meetings with those stakeholders in a room telling them to cool their jets. Nobody from the public service saw the crap that the political staff took [from stakeholders] for not telling the public servants to do this and this and this. So a lot of work I and others did was to bring the stakeholders to the side of what the public servants were trying to do. Our point was to produce a document that met with the approval of what I'll call the established public education stakeholder community and the disfranchised public education stakeholder community. (Will, political staffer)

Scott and Alison both felt that the degree to which views were seriously considered varied:

> No, there were no attempts to find common ground. They would tell us what they thought of what we had written. They would tell us what they thought was missing, and they would tell us what they thought needed changing. People from the ministry would be taking notes . . . There were people from the premier's office there taking notes on the feedback . . . There were some people they listened to, and some people they didn't listen to. I listened to them all, I would periodically try to talk to them during the break.
>
> In actual fact, the process that was developed was a good process. The way that it worked out in practice was that some people were listened to and some people weren't. In the end, once I saw who got the contracts and how they scrounged around to find real expertise in the province, I thought those contracts were quite efficient. (Scott, writer)

All stakeholders came with their own agendas, as I did myself. Input that we gave was as valuable as the people listening to us. If they shared the philosophy, then that got in there. If they really didn't like it, it didn't get in there. The only way to go around a lot of that was to go directly to government policy people. (Alison, consultation participant)

Both Will and Alison acknowledged how bureaucratic or political forces stepped in to address situations, resolve conflicts, or make decisions where consensus was not reached:

There was always the pressure on us to always come up with consensus, so what usually happened, people would just give in. The less aggressive people would just say, 'OK, it's not that important,' or 'I'm too tired,' or they wear you down. And you say 'That's enough, I can't do this.' Or they drop out of the process. (Alison, consultation participant)

Periodically, when rubber hit the road and there were some passionate disagreements in the secondary school reform initiative, that was the point at which the political staff ultimately had to get engaged. (Will, political staffer)

I think it ended up that you just give in, because even if you disagree – and that was the thing, too – even if there were things we were very clear about and emphatic that we didn't want to see or we did want to see in the curriculum, somebody else made the final decision in the end, anyways. You kind of felt like no matter who really worked at that – and it was really, like, for some people I know in other groups, let's say the English – it really became, 'I'll give you Shakespeare if you give me Atwood.'

It almost ended up being like labour negotiations. This is what people were bargaining for that they wanted to see in the curriculum. (Alison, consultation participant)

However, many perceived that, despite good intentions, 'Out of conflict, out of disagreement, you can sometimes grow a much better product. And you have to seek points of others, to different ideas. When you want the best decisions, you bring the most disparate points of view to the table, and you don't let them get away. And that's what happened during that process, because there were very disparate points of view coming together and attacking that first draft. They had the first draft, and they said this about it, they said that about it. The poor writers had to have the best egos' (Erica, bureaucrat).

These quotations show the varied perceptions that emerged about the degree to which policy actors perceived conflict was encouraged or discouraged, as well as the extent to which they believed consensus was sought. Most considered the idea of discussing areas of conflict or disagreement to be desirable, but the degree to which this actually occurred in official arenas for discourse remains disputed. That dispute in perception, itself, suggests that the process fell short of the critical democratic ideal.

Lack of Time for Meaningful Dialogue

The absence of conflicts and dialogue might have been be a direct result of aggressive and unforgiving schedules for completion, which I described in chapter 4, but there would need to have been opportunities for more meaningful deliberation in order to address the democratic ideal. As Carr points out, 'The debates about the curriculum that occur in a democracy at any given time will reveal both how that democracy interprets itself, and how that interpretation is being challenged and revised in order to bring into being a more genuinely democratic form of life than that which currently exists' (1998, 324).

As Carr suggests, an examining dialogue and debate over curriculum provides insight into the presence of democratic ideals and how they operate in practice. Indeed, changes to curriculum policy – a part of broader education reforms – cannot be fully understood unless they are examined in a wider context (Carr 1998). Rather, curriculum policy formulation is intertwined with other aspects of the societal context, including democratic, political, industrial, and cultural processes. Such deliberative opportunities require individuals to engage in agonistic debate and discussion with others; arenas for discourse need to be made available, and citizens would require support to develop the skills and dispositions necessary to engage in agonistic exchanges.

Consultation participants described a lack of time for meaningful discussion. Several mentioned colleagues who had dropped out after feeling tired and 'burned out.' For example:

> I was frustrated, and for the most part, I gave up on the ministry and got on with the job. We did a competent job, but not a great job. The timelines were far too short. There wasn't ... I would have liked to have had the opportunity to have consulted with draft copies of the curriculum ourselves before they went to the ministry.

The ministry later had a consultation, but it was a very contrived one, and very politically controlled by Harris' departments. (Robert, project manager)

But we got to a certain point – not quite finished – where we were really fed up with it, with this feeling that we were being pushed, pushed, pushed through it. And that it did feel like a sausage factory, in a way, on really short timelines, and we felt that we couldn't condone it or feel that we could sign our names to it. (Danielle, consultation participant)

The working tables themselves, the specific working tables, the subject area groups, it was a very interesting group of people. I was quite fascinated with the group of people who were at my table, because they represented many different groups – they represented teachers with specialties, they represented universities, they represented faculties of education, and teachers' groups ... And there was also a very right-wing group represented, which was quite obsessed with phonics, so I was balanced off. But the discussions were quite interesting when they were allowed to take place. They really didn't seem to go very far [because there was insufficient time]. (Danielle, consultation participant)

Thus, the features of the process defined by the Ministry of Education minimized possibilities for truly democratic dialogue. Unless the institutional culture prioritizes and mandates time for discussion, the critical-democratic ideal in policy production cannot be realized. Instead, as Danielle points out with her sausage-production metaphor, a corporate production-model consistent with NPM values persisted.

Perceived Manufactured Consent versus Perceived Transparency

While consultations were an important stage in policy formulation, the degree to which they were 'legitimate' remains uncertain. In a culture of manufactured consent, consultations 'masquerade as partnership' (Looney 2001, 156) to serve those in power, while marginalizing the voices of dissent or conflict. With the exception of the ministry bureaucrats interviewed, policy actors expressed a general perception that the consultations relied on 'manufactured consent' some or all of the time. As such, the ministry appears to have made attempts to impose policy directions on policy actors. Indeed, the political staffer interviewed admitted, 'There is the appearance of being consultative and truly being consultative. And every government, including the one I was participating in, is guilty of that.'

This perception that outcomes had already been decided upon led some policy actors to believe that their opinions were not taken seriously. While it is impossible be certain if those perceptions are accurate (though Will's remark suggests that they were), the fact that the perceptions arose suggests a less-than-ideal forum for deliberation. As well, better understanding of how decisions were made after deliberation would assist policy actors in understanding why some groups were thought to have disproportionate input into the process. In the critical-democratic ideal, consultations would be a venue for exchange of ideas, not an attempt at persuasion, as a culture of manufactured consent implies. The goal of agonistic exchanges among policy actors would be compromise as 'temporary respite from ongoing confrontation' (Mouffe 2000b, 102). Thus, while not every individual's or group's view would be reflected in policy outcomes, they ought to share a mutual understanding of how and why those decisions were made.

Bureaucrats all viewed the consultation process itself as transparent and legitimate. Writing team members and consultation participants tended to perceive manufactured consent. Some perceived that either politicians or bureaucrats had decided what would be included in policy documents, and that consultations were not actually spaces for deliberation, but rather attempts to manufacture consent among those present. Some representative points of view of this perception include:

> In the plenary groups, I remember a feeling of growing dissatisfaction, the sense that we were being managed and that there really wasn't a true consultation. I think it was much more for appearance than for real input. (Danielle, consultation participant)

> They would argue that they were very consultative in the process, but you had the feeling that the books were already cooked on this one. And it was simply going through the motions to a large degree. We really didn't have any opportunities to shape the look of the process. The government had, I think, announced and signalled where it wanted to go, and it was just a question of getting the ship turned in that direction.
>
> Again, the feeling always was you could voice your concerns, but it didn't mean that they necessarily went anywhere . . . But the realities were that there was never any kind of guarantee that anything that you brought forward would really go anywhere. (Curtis, consultation participant)

I think it was political side of the ministry putting pressure on the bureau-cracy to ensure that their political ends were met. They had set up a num-ber of opportunities for other stakeholders to provide input, but in the end I don't think they listened. Or they listened selectively to stakeholder groups. But I think in the end, it was a political decision, what was in and what was out. (Mike, project manager)

I thought, we're not being listened to at all. At that time, I found it dupli-citous – 'You have a role, we want to hear what you're saying, but we're really not going to write it down, basically. We're not going to listen, we're going to do this, and it's just for show.' (Danielle, consultation participant)

One of the things that they did very well, depending on what it is that you're trying to achieve, they did do a great deal of divide and conquer. They would seldom have forums where all the various stakeholders were together. They would pick and choose the constituencies that they wanted to work with. It was quite clear to all of us that the parent groups had the ear of the premier and the Cabinet ... I think, to what they thought the politi-cal gain would be by choosing features of secondary schools that would be much closer to what parents wanted. (Curtis, consultation participant)

Policy actors placed considerable blame on various parties for unsat-isfactory processes and outcomes. Writers and consultation partici-pants felt that the political leadership drove the details of curriculum policy content:

Part of the problem was the ministry bureaucrats got put down so often by political people above them, that they gave up and said, 'We're going to do what we're told.' And that's what they did. There was less and less long-term thinking. Everything was just political reaction. And the politicians didn't know how long it would take to do things. That's what happens when politicians try to micro-manage – or worse, not just politicians but political officers try to micro-manage complex processes, and that's what I think was a problem. (Robert, project manager)

Some expressed concern that the decisions made by the political leadership reflected more concern about votes than about what was best for students and teachers:

Again, it was quite clear that when it moved away from what you might call the practitioner's conversation into political conversation, that was what was going to make it ... I feel that that the political conversation had much more to do with, when they asked if this would work, would they get political gain out of reconstituting secondary schools in this particular way? Would it make the parents happy? Then you had the taxpayer question: would people feel that their money was being invested efficiently in what was going on in secondary schools?

You were sort of reminded of these various kinds of agendas, more than I ever remember previous governments ever having to worry about in quite the same way. (Curtis, consultation participant)

At the same time, others felt that the process was very transparent. Consultation participant James perceived that 'the feedback was usually taken seriously.' He believed that, overall, decisions were made in a transparent way. He gave one example of when, during a Saturday meeting of stakeholders, the deputy minister came in and 'negotiated,' saying, 'Could you live with this? Could you live with that?'

However, many of those present did not have the opportunity to articulate their views. James also believed that 'the politicians were dependent on the responses from officials,' perceiving that it was 'clearly the civil service.' In his view, the government became 'tied up in Bill 160' and other issues, diverting their full attention from curriculum.

Both the Strategic Counsel report and the Praxis report describe respondents' views on educational purpose. In their report, Praxis note that respondents were concerned about too narrow an educational purpose. One question asked respondents to select one of two statements to represent the goal of education: 'skills, knowledge and work habits they need to find or create gainful and satisfying employment' or 'fulfil their personal potential, develop life skills ... and become good citizens' (7). These respondents felt that selecting one was an 'unnecessary dichotomy' and that both should exist in balance.

When investigating the issue courses and their content, the Strategic Counsel reports that 'participants felt that the "big themes" such as critical thinking, life skills, and planning should also be woven into each subject' (32). Both reports apparently resulted in little consensus, though evidence that respondents desired a 'liberal' curriculum is evident. Moreover, one would imagine that these findings, which clearly point to curriculum policy choices, would thus be relevant to the curriculum policy formulation process.

The ministry struck a committee called the Secondary School Reform Advisory Group to 'provide ongoing input to the Ministry in the reform process' (OECTA 1998, 5). Membership in this committee

Table 6:2 OECTA account of recommendations versus announcements

What the SSR Advisory Group recommended	What the ministry announced
Total number of compulsory credits should not exceed half the total number of courses required to graduate (15 of 30)	18 compulsory credits
Secondary school curriculum should be developed with the integral involvement of Ontario secondary school educators and representatives from colleges, the workplace (employers and employer organizations), and universities	RFP process included members on the policy development writing teams, but no integral group with representatives of educators, colleges, universities, and the workplace (employers and employer organizations) to oversee curriculum development
Performance-based diagnostic test focusing on literacy and numeracy should be administered during grade nine in order to put appropriate remedial/enrichment programs in place	Literacy test will be administered in grade ten. The results will be used for remediation if necessary; students must pass the test in order to graduate
Organization of program and instruction should focus on ensuring student success, increasing the rate of student retention, facilitating student focus on their post-secondary destination, and improving the rate of completion of secondary school within four years	Courses will be streamed in all grades (nine through twelve), without definition of the streaming or how courses will look Policy development teams will have access to the Expert Panel paper and Synthesis paper to guide their writing
• A core of fundamental learning expectations should be identified for each grade nine and ten course (e.g., 70% of content)	
• Remediation as well as enrichment should be provided	
• Utilize flexible groupings of students and timetables	
• Successful completion of grade ten should make a student eligible to proceed to any grade eleven course	
Secondary school curriculum should follow logically from elementary school curriculum	RFP process makes no reference to the elementary school curriculum, and the elementary school curriculum will not be complete at the time of writing

Source: OECTA 1998, 6

included directors of education, representatives from student associations and teacher federation affiliates, principals, college and university
representatives, the Organization for Quality Education, and members
of the business community. According a report from OECTA (1998),
the ministry's decisions regarding whom to contract for curriculum
writing, details about the number and types of compulsory credits,
and issues of streaming were ignored in the final policy decision, as
reflected in table 6.2.

While this reflects but one perspective, and it is unclear how the
government's decisions at this phase of the process were made, OECTA's
report suggests that a degree of politicization occurred.

Perceived Weight of Opinions Taken Seriously

Policy actors expressed conflicting perceptions about how seriously
their (and others') voices were taken during consultations. To an
extent, this contradicts the notion of manufactured consent, since if
consultations were purely 'for show,' as one participant put it, then no
policy actors' perspectives would be taken seriously.

Some of those present at consultations, especially bureaucrats,
insisted that all voices received equal and due consideration. However,
others acknowledged that all were heard, but some were given greater
consideration. Stakeholders as well as writing team members tended
to feel that the 'other' was being taken more seriously than they. Many
expressed a sense that some groups' perspectives received greater
'weighting' in the policy decisions. Scott observed, 'You could tell by
when they picked up the pen and started writing, and when they put
down the pen, and when they wrote and when they didn't write.' While
bureaucrats might disagree, Will concurred with many stakeholders:
'[The political staffers] weren't satisfied that the stakeholders had been
given as much opportunity to participate or in another way – certain
well-established stakeholders were given a voice while other stakeholders were given a diminished, often marginal opportunity to participate. And it was our view that in order to be in a position to stand
by the reform, it was important that the document have an opportunity
to be subject of discussion among a variety of different stakeholders'
(Will, political staffer).

What is interesting is that each group felt that their opponent received
more consideration: conservative groups felt that those with progressive agendas were listened to while the conservative perspective was

ignored (and vice versa), while parent groups felt teacher groups were being listened to at their expense (and vice versa).

Writer Justin suggested that some were 'heard' because they were more skilful in participating in the political process than others: 'It is a political document, and some people know how to engage in that process better than others, and some have more privilege than others.' When asked what led to strength in a stakeholder's position (that is, what factors led their feedback to be taken seriously), one bureaucrat responded, 'It would certainly have had to do with how articulate they were, how well-informed they were. They certainly had their ducks in a row. They weren't coming in shooting from the hip. They had information, they had a constituency that they went and consulted with their constituency and brought forward points they wanted to raise' (Erica, bureaucrat).

The issue of including special interest groups in consultations and feedback also arose. Some groups were mentioned several times by policy actors – particularly the Dominion Institute, the Canadian Manufacturers' Association, and the Canadian Jewish Congress. Writing team members felt that some of these groups had disproportionate input into curriculum policy expectations, though bureaucrats tended to emphasize the organizations' provincial mandates to justify their inclusion. Some policy actors provided examples, such as,

> For example, the Canadian Jewish Congress went through the curriculum and suggested expectations to be added, references to the Holocaust. And we made sure the balances wasn't just – and I don't mean 'just' – but the Armenian holocaust, and holocaust and genocide in the world. It was the Canadian Jewish Congress who brought attention to that, and we hadn't had a reference to that because it hadn't emerged from the writers. How could they not have that? And they were one of the groups that sat in on every curriculum policy document so that you could get that sort of perspective.
>
> So if you had the labour unions, then you had to have a balance from the perspective of the Canadian Manufacturer's Association or the Chambers of Commerce, or something where you have the employers' perspective. That was something that we were reading the curriculum, to make sure you had these lenses in, but that you had all elements of society – that they could find themselves reflected. For instance in the business, we had Canadian Investors have a look at the document. They wanted references to things like investing and preparing for the future, retirement. When I

was in school, nobody asked me if I knew about investing or retirement. (Erica, bureaucrat)

A high degree of politicization, as I described in the previous chapter, limited the weight of policy actors' input into the final policy texts. Policy actors had conflicting perceptions over the weight given to others' perspectives and/or suggestions in the process, especially on progressive versus conservative educational agendas. Some policy actors described situations in which writers were explicitly told they were not to speak during feedback meetings with stakeholders; in other cases consultation participants felt they were implicitly obliged to withhold their points of view. Overall, opportunities to exchange of ideas that would be necessary for critical-democratic policymaking were eliminated.

Positive Impacts on Policy Actors

Despite the democratic shortfalls in participant selection and policy production, the process yielded some important, unintended benefits. Through their participation, policy actors reported significant democratic learning that arose out of their involvement, and particularly from their direct interaction with other policy actors. These were direct benefits to the cultivation of democracy, and were consistent with the critical-democratic ideal, though in this case, only elites with access to participation enjoyed this outcome.

Building Civic Capacity and Civic Learning

A critical-democratic policy process that includes deliberation, Shawn Rosenberg (2005) suggests, should have several impacts on policy actors relevant to critical democracy:

- Exposure to new information that results in education about the policy issue through deliberation and formalized learning opportunities discussed earlier
- Awareness of other views and experiences of others in the community through agonistic exchanges
- A venue for 'testing' views to get greater clarity and commitment
- Increased sense of political agency and increased likelihood of future participation
- Greater sense of community or belonging

As these criteria suggest, learning is a critical participant outcome. Thus, participation becomes an experience in civic education, in which policy actors learn not only about procedural aspects of government, but also about the policy issue at hand, as well as the perspectives of other members of the community. Agonistic exchange, central to the critical-democratic ideal, is an important venue in which learning takes place. Policy actors learn from one another via dialogue and debate about perspectives and the policy issue at hand. Ideally, the formal institution responsible for the policy process would also provide opportunities and/or resources to contribute to participant learning. This might include readings or seminars about the policy issue, information about the political process, and assistance to develop the deliberative and communication skills that allow policy actors to express themselves and actively listen to one another.

Policy actors described how negotiating the waters of public dialogue and debate during consultations required a particular skill set. All emphasized the importance of disagreement and dialogue to achieve better curriculum policy decisions. While quite a few policy actors indicated that they learned a great deal from the process, many suggested room for formal learning to improve their skills for deliberative policy-formulation. One writer remarked that the experience was the best professional development he had, and several said that their participation helped them learn about how government works.

Some also described how they overcame stereotypes about rival groups (that is, those that hold different ideological positions) and were surprised about passion and intelligence voiced by their rivals – a key feature of agonistic exchanges. Building greater capacity through policy actor engagement is a positive, yet unintended outcome of the process. To be able to participate in agonistic deliberation, policy actors and citizens require a set of dispositions, including the ability to listen, giving due consideration to rival positions, critically evaluating information, and of course asserting their own views.

However, greater transparency in the process, as well as more deliberative opportunities to work with rivals, would certainly have contributed to even greater capacity-building. Policy actors' perceptions about learning suggested that more opportunities for a greater number of citizens to participate could lead to enhanced understanding through agonistic exchange. In the critical-democratic ideal, there would be formalized learning opportunities to prepare citizens for this type of agonistic participation in a public policy process, as well as opportunities to come together with rivals whom they might not encounter in their everyday lives. Much of literature on democracy and participatory policy emphasizes the skills and dispositions citizens must possess to effectively participate in meaningful deliberation. I asked policy actors in the consultations, as well as bureaucrats, what opportunities those involved in consultations had to learn from one another. The response was mixed. While some felt that they had exposure to other perspectives and new information, others did not.

Bureaucrat Janelle reflected on the process: 'If I was redoing it, I would try to find a way to spend a lot of time teaching people how to talk to each other,' though she acknowledged, 'There was a lot of good learning that came out of it.' Despite challenges they experienced during deliberation, writers felt that this was the best professional development they had experienced, particularly the 'education' they received about politics: 'And the question is, are we doing the politics well? Do we understand the politics that others are doing with us? Most educators, because they've had no political education, as it were, don't recognize the politics. Or, if they do recognize the politics, they just say it's bad. Whereas, you go back to Aristotle, education has always been political and it always will be. The question is, are the politics being done well or not? During the Harris years, we saw some terrible, badly done politics ... He had some good ideas. But in terms of the process, it was disastrous. It left the education system demoralized for years' (Robert, project manager).

Consultation participant James described it as a 'radicalizing experience' in that most stakeholders had not previously met. He believed other policy actors had been involved in schools as parents, but had little or no exposure to issues of pedagogy or to the politics of education. It was the first time most of them had formal experiences with 'the Establishment' (he used this word, said he didn't like it, though he continued to use it). In his view, 'the Establishment' is generally interested in empirical research and results, and tended to 'avoid specificity.' He described it as a 'delicate process,' and he 'had to be in diplomatic mode' throughout. He had to 'build alliances' to get things done, to try to build consensus. 'People don't check their preferences at the door ... In order to persuade people to leave their "hobby horses." I had to, too.'

James also perceived a democratic motivation among all groups: 'Concern of people participating is not themselves, but more the greater good, especially for the disadvantaged.' He felt that a concern with contributing to a greater good brought policy actors together. However, he felt that the government 'didn't trust the bureaucracy.' While James conveyed these positive comments, he also described some aspects of the process as 'distressing.' When asked what he meant, he referred to conflicts, pettiness, and a lack of open communication. James described the 'dynamic' at meetings as teachers versus quality education advocates (the latter mostly parents). 'The battle lines were drawn very quickly,' he noted. These perceptions suggest that Janelle's wish for education on how to communicate in a deliberative setting might have been beneficial.

When James met representatives from the education sector, he expected 'tub thumpers' (his words) from the unions. He was pleasantly surprised to meet others who were interested in their subjects and 'reasonable people.' He pointed out that not all 'ministry people were cut from one mould.' He recounted that some ministry bureaucrats had agendas that contradicted those of the government, while others were 'like-minded.'

I asked all policy actors if they experienced opportunities to help them learn new things from one another as part of the process. None recalled any. The bureaucrats thought that this was a good idea, but hadn't considered it. A ministry document entitled 'Understanding and Participating in Curriculum Change' (Ministry of Education 1996) suggests that it provided potential policy actors with guidelines, while in fact it proposes curriculum changes and invites readers to provide feedback.

Missed Opportunity: Absence of Policy Learning

While, as I illustrated in the previous section, outcomes included positive aspects of civic learning, policy actors missed out on the opportunity to learn more about policy areas. They described surprisingly few instances of opportunities to learn about the policy area: curriculum. The background research documents prepared by universities and the reports prepared by Praxis and Strategic Counsel appear to have fallen through the cracks. No policy actors recalled seeing them. The opportunity to at least review the information in these documents might have provided opportunities for policy actors to better understand rationales for policy directors, and insight into curricular areas reflected in the policy documents.

A second possibility for learning rested with writers, who presumably had expertise in their subject areas. Consultation participants and political staff missed the opportunity to learn from 'subject experts,' since writers who were fortunate enough to attend meetings were told to remain silent, rather than share rationales or expertise with others. At the most basic level, allowing writers to express expert opinions in consultation dialogues would have contributed to other policy actors' understandings of those subject areas with respect to curriculum and pedagogy.

Third, a range of other possibilities might have been developed and utilized for policy actors to learn. For instance, the ministry might have organized seminars or workshops (either in person or using information and communication technology) with professionals in the education community to contribute to better understanding of curriculum policy, assessment, and/or the approach to streaming (which still remains unclear in policy actors' minds). This missed opportunity for learning about the policy area – whether through something as simple as distribution of background research, or more complex through dialogue among policy actors – detracted from critical-democratic possibilities.

Concluding Comments

Ontario's policy formulation process was also characterized by elitist selection of policy actors and tightly controlled arenas for discourse and deliberations, notwithstanding the sheer numbers of participants who provided feedback, cited by the ministry. But these were not by any means 'thick' nor inclusive democratic opportunities. Inclusive democracy is less concerned about the proportion of citizens who participate, but rather the nature of inclusion and the quality of deliberation. For Ontario's feedback opportunities to be truly democratic, criteria to ensure inclusiveness would have needed to be applied, which would have ensured that selection of policy actors avoided elitism. Moreover, a truly critical-democratic process would have ensured that policy actors represented a wide range of citizens, with attention to the inclusion of those traditionally 'from the margins.'

Despite efforts to include stakeholders in the curriculum policy decisions, Ontario fell short of the critical-democratic ideal in its formulation process. Chantal Mouffe's agonistic democracy, a central component in my elaboration of a critical-democratic policy process, relies upon the domestication of hostility into agonism, where participants view their opponents as adversaries (not enemies). It calls for the 'expression of dissent and institutions through which conflicts can be manifested' (Mouffe 2000c, 149). Ontario's curriculum policy formulation was grounded in neoliberal and neoconservative ideologies with goals and processes that gave little or no explicit consideration of either critical democracy or agonism as features of the process.

While the process reflected a democratic shortfall with respect to inclusion and much of its procedure, it also highlighted the potential benefits of democratic participation. Policy actors raised several interesting and unintended consequences of their participation in the process. Writing team members and consultation participants felt they learned a tremendous amount through participation – ranging from how government works to the points of view of their opponents. However, the interviews pointed to areas for further improvement, especially building trust and equipping policy actors with the skills to participate in deliberations and learn from one another. As well, there were no opportunities to learn more about the policy area.

7 Perceived Policy Outcomes and Their Absence of Democracy

Democratic process makes policies better, and better policies are needed for democracy. For this matter, it is argued, not only has society to be democratic, but the norm of democracy also has to be reflected in policymaking.

– Udaya Wagle 2000, 220

The debates about the curriculum that occur in a democracy at any given time will reveal both how that democracy interprets itself, and how that interpretation is being challenged and revised in order to bring into being a more genuinely democratic form of life than that which currently exists.

– Wilfred Carr 1998, 324

No one ever comes back and says, 'My teacher thinks this is the worst curriculum ever written and couldn't possibly follow it.'

– Drew, writing team member

Curriculum policy reflects the power and social relationships within society, and the fact that an important purpose of knowledge construction is to help people improve that society. Indeed, 'policy texts represent the outcomes of political struggles over meaning' (Taylor 1997, 28). Within the education policy discourse, there are competing concerns – one set for equity, participation, access, and so on; and another for markets, enterprise, and entrepreneurialism (Taylor and Henry 2003). Outcomes of curriculum policy can be viewed from a variety of perspectives: student learning, impacts on teachers and school systems, and broader societal benefits of a trained workforce or educated citizens. The outcomes – particularly the texts themselves – are salient in that public policies 'carry messages. The ways in which various publics are treated by policy – whether their views of problems are recognized as legitimate or ignored; whether they are targeted for burdens or benefits; the rules to which they are subjected such as means testing; and the reception they encounter in interaction with implementing agencies – all teach lessons related to democracy' (Ingram 2000). These outcomes in the form of public policy as well as consequences of the enactment of those policy texts affect individual policy actors, groups involved in the process, and the citizenry to whom the policy applies.

Despite subversion by some policy actors, policy outcomes were weak when viewed from the standpoint of critical democracy in education. Particularly salient aspects included the use of outcomes-based curriculum policy to promote value neutrality, the exclusion of social justice as a goal or area of accountability, and the lack of support for the non-university-bound student. Taken together, these outcome features of the policy texts neither embodied nor promoted democracy in education. Overall, when examined against the ideal of critical democracy, the quality of Ontario's curriculum policy decisions fell short of critical-democratic and social justice aims in education. The official framing of issues, coupled with a highly controlled and prescriptive process, certainly influenced the content of curriculum policy documents. For example, despite policy actors' strong concerns about the streaming model's adequacy to meet student needs, the decision-makers chose to move forward with that model. These two examples suggest that a more democratic policy process might have overcome these two areas of inequity and thus might have led to curriculum policy that would be more likely to reflect critical democracy in education.

A number of researchers report that teachers generally recognized a need for curriculum change or renewal (Earl et al. 2002; Hargreaves et al. 2002; Majhanovich 2002; Anderson and Ben Jaafar 2003; and Ryan and Joong 2005). Drew, a writing team project manager, noted, 'No one ever comes back and says, "My teacher thinks this is the worst curriculum ever written and couldn't possibly follow it."' In fact, many teachers in the aforementioned studies agree with the need for consistency across the province, integration of technology, and streaming in curriculum policy. The Auditor General of Ontario (2003) supports this view, citing the finding that over 40 per cent of teachers interviewed considered the curriculum policy generated an improvement over previous curriculum, and supported the idea of consistency.

Policy actors interviewed and researchers who have since investigated Ontario's curriculum policy outcomes report that these 'positive features' are overshadowed by a number of concerns. Earl and her colleagues' extensive 2002 work reveals several important concerns: (1) unrealistic, 'content-laden' or comprehensive curriculum implemented unrealistic timelines; (2) fewer course options; (3) failure of centralized curriculum policy to meet the needs of diverse students, particularly those with special needs; and (4) a lack of coherence between assessment and reporting. In this chapter, I address several of the more prominent concerns arising from interviews (rather than those appearing in the literature) and triangulate them with other sources where possible.

Policy Texts Produced: Rigid Structure and Format

The final curriculum policy documents were released to teachers and the public in 1999 and 2000, and they reflect a structure and format entirely new to Ontario. Policy actors called attention to the new, expectations-based approach. For instance, Curtis observed, 'This was the first time we had seen language that identifies specific expectations of learning, whether they were overall or specific, which then served almost as program standards in ways that they hadn't done before.' These new policy documents establish a common curriculum for all students in Ontario and follow traditional subject disciplines. Roughly 1,400 courses available under the previous curriculum policy are reduced to 200. Each course is organized into strands (thematic units), which are made up of highly prescriptive learning expectations, in the form of between 80 and 130 student learning expectations. Courses are presented within a rigid template. As well, policy documents rely on what the ministry refers to as a new 'paradigm' of assessment. In addition to fundamental changes in the organization of learning domains, this assessment paradigm introduces the concepts of rubrics and achievement charts for student evaluation, as well as a different approach to student grade calculation.[1]

Given the focus of this research, my investigation addresses policy actors' perceptions of the resulting curriculum policy texts as they relate to critical democracy in education and education for critical democracy. Thus, critical-democratic curriculum decisions would:

- Be considered socially just by policy actors, though perception does not necessarily lead to empirical truth
- Foster social justice in the curriculum based on the criteria articulated above (for examples of social justice pedagogies and content, see Pinto 2005, 2007; Romas 2008; Stocker and Wagner 2008)

- Address (in)equity
- Reflect critical democracy in education and education for democracy within policy texts. This may include classroom activity to promote the civic skills associated with agonistic exchanges, using empowerment instead of instrumentalist goals (e.g., narrowly conceived career preparation) when framing subject matter, or using examples that openly address power, equity, and social justice in traditional subject disciplines such as mathematics

In the subsections that follow, I examine several aspects of the policy texts that emerged from policy actor interviews: a fragmented curriculum lacking continuity, value neutrality, and the absence of a curriculum to address the needs of the non-university-bound student. On the basis of policy actors' assessments of policy texts, I also discuss the absence of social justice and equity reflected in the texts as well as how policy actors conceptualized it.

Fragmented Curriculum Lacking Continuity

Policy actors described a lack of continuity among courses through duplication of content and expectations, as well as gaps across grades in a given subject. One consultation participant[2] described gaps in elementary and secondary mathematics: 'Most of the curriculum documents are acceptable, but one document is particularly problematic. The mathematics courses still need to be re-examined and sequenced properly in conjunction with the elementary curriculum. Many students have difficulty with this subject. More work needs to be done to improve this subject.' Similarly, some Ontario teachers expressed frustration about the 'overlap' of expectations in some courses, causing situations in which two teachers, teaching different courses, address the same course content, causing complaints from students. Conversely, there are gaps where a course requires prerequisite skills or knowledge but the curriculum policy documents do not account for them. For instance, several grade nine courses require students to have keyboarding skills, but the elementary school curriculum fails to include expectations that address keyboarding.

These problems arise, in part, because each subject's curriculum policy was developed independently and concurrently. In fact, writers of one subject's curriculum policy did not have access the work of other writing teams. Similarly, because consultation participants had access only to draft texts of their own subject, and often ministry bureaucrats were assigned to a single subject, these sorts of overlaps and gaps slipped through the cracks. As well, OECTA's (1998) claim that the elementary curriculum was not complete when secondary policy was written may account for gaps between elementary and secondary curriculum.

Value-Neutrality, Streaming, and Career Focus in Policy Texts

Within market democracy as defined in chapter 1, models of economic 'choice' and 'consumption' of services (including education) are often conflated as components of 'citizenship.' Resulting curriculum policy tied to notions of market democracy tends to emphasize student achievement through uniform standards in the form of outcomes-based education (see, for example, Portelli and Solomon 2001; Hyslop-Margison and Sears 2006), which is thought to be value-neutral. Explicit curriculum policy aimed at education *for* democracy and democracy *in* education tend to be minimized within these ideological models. In this section, my analysis focuses on issues raised by policy actors: streaming, career focus, and value-neutrality.

Participants in Lorna Earl's large-scale study expressed concern that Ontario's curriculum developed during the period studied was too focused upon content. Policy actors interviewed concurred, though they raised this concern in conjunction with other issues – namely the exclusion of the 'affective' domain in expectations. As well, some criticized the policy text for failing to address more complex learning. For example, 'That was a big struggle for us, because we knew you're now looking at the lowest level of critical thinking: just memorize it, regurgitate, and forget it as soon as you finish with it. And we thought that and [the project manager of the writing team] to his credit thought it as well . . . I thought they want these kids to take this stuff and just go through. They don't want them to be questioning too much, because then they can be advocating for things. Maybe in hindsight it seemed to have been so, but I could start to feel what was happening: the problems with education And I thought they want these kids to be simply compliant with everything – "Don't rock the boat." We felt these kids need to start rocking the boats, because things aren't looking too good' (Hardy, writer).

Value-Neutrality: Problems with Deciding
What Is Worth Knowing

The notion that curriculum is or ought to be value-neutral has 'made something of a comeback in recent years in many countries' (Roberts 1998, 30). The Ontario government as well as some policy actors embraced the ideal of creating a 'value-neutral' curriculum. Value-neutrality is alluring in that it suggests one can avoid making choices, thus standing above controversy, but choices that involve values cannot be avoided when constructing a curriculum. Values are present within at least three levels of curriculum policy. First, statements about aims of education reflect values. Second, values shape how course subjects are grouped, which courses are offered, and how courses are streamed. Finally, learning expectations convey values within curriculum policy documents.

An educational system – and the curriculum policy stemming from that system – contains presuppositions about its educational aims, and as such, avoiding values in education policy is impossible (see, for example, DeFaveri and Kach 1987). Which subjects are emphasized, included, and excluded have significance. Deciding what is 'worth knowing' or 'most important' are value-laden acts. Items that appear in the explicit curriculum – that is, perspectives, skills, and information that are presented to students in classrooms – privilege certain knowledge, skills, and attitudes while marginalizing the null curriculum (those things omitted). A hidden curriculum thus emerges in the form of the underlying assumptions and values transmitted by the explicit curriculum.

In Ontario, value-neutrality as an aim of curriculum policy formulation is closely tied the outcomes-based education model – that is, student outcomes (called expectations in Ontario's policy texts) are uniform for all students. Outcomes rhetoric tends to equate outcomes-based education with value-neutrality within a 'common sense' rationale: 'The notion that learning outcomes can and should be predicted, and then measured, seems sensible, objective, natural and practical. Gone is the reliance on the teacher's value-laden, unreliable and subjective assessments. Gone too, is the uncomfortable and inefficient heterogeneity of curriculum content, and the unpredictable and circumstantial pedagogy of classroom teachers' (Smyth and Dow 1998, 298). This position is problematic because it suggests that outcomes themselves are value-neutral, when in actuality they are one-sided and interest-serving: 'The views of the Right are depicted as neutral and/or natural, while opposing positions are constructed as "political," defective, and contrary to common sense' (Roberts 1998, 42). This assertion is consistent with the rationale posited by those policy actors in favour of the value-neutral curriculum goal. This position blatantly dismisses the rival position: that education is a political activity and that it cannot be value-neutral. Moreover, the false notion of value-neutrality ignores the issue of equity entirely, trivializing learning by over-emphasizing measurable, brief snippets of information (Wrigley 2003). To achieve alleged neutrality, learning outcomes become highly prescriptive and standardized to ensure consistency and to limit opportunities for teachers and students to interpret them in ways that might compromise standardization. This approach to value-neutrality undermines education *for* democracy, and through its prescriptive nature also undermines democracy *in* education, both consistent with the critical-democratic ideal.

In addition to these problems associated with a so-called value-neutral, standards-based curriculum, some research, such as that of Linda McNeil, has illustrated the 'destructive effects of the move towards standardized and state-mandated curricula,' especially among schools with a high proportion of racial minorities (Apple 2001a, 206). Just as gains were being made in decentring dominant narratives through flexible curriculum, dominance returns through standardization (Apple 2001a).

The Ontario Ministry of Education required an absence of any 'values' in the new curriculum policy texts, which included removal of pedagogies, affective-domain expectations, and expectations that dealt with issues such as equity. All policy actors interviewed pointed out that the resulting policy texts minimize expectations or outcomes pertaining to the affective domain, and eliminate prescribing what pedagogical approaches teachers are to use. However, the degree to which the levels of affective expectations and an absence of pedagogy are acceptable was disputed.

Political staffer Will explained that the rationale was largely to avoid controversy should the policy documents be perceived as 'value-laden.' Many policy actors, such as Janelle, described this approach within the context of previous curricula: 'Earlier curriculum was built on knowledge, skills, and attitudes. Our instructions were to get rid of that attitudes column.' Will explained how policy actors removed values, to create an 'objective' document:

> The decision was: let's keep the content to skills and knowledge and be confident that the teachers would bring to their frontline interaction with their

students the appropriate experience, values, perspective, and subjectivity. We were trying to produce as objective a document as possible – what is not presumptuous of either being pro-conservation or anti-conservation. In some of the studies in the secondary school level, I remember there was an issue about how 'green' we wanted to be. We thought, You know what? How do we pick and choose which of these competing values? The direction was that: let's try to strip the document as much as possible of that. Whether in hindsight that was the right or wrong decision, I am not sure. (Will, political staffer)

Curtis provided examples of the sorts of values or affective components that were excluded: 'We had come through a period with the previous government, with the NDP, where [equity and diversity] were considered key policy pieces and therefore were in all of the documentation. There were content pieces that were completely left out when the policy documents were generated, simply because, you know, they were considered to be ideological positions, and this government decided, "No, we're not going to go there."'

Several stakeholders interviewed were in favour of an ideal of value-neutrality and objectivity in curriculum policy documents. Consultation participant James recalled, 'In general, the process was the government trying to structure the process where it was rich in knowledge, content, and skills, and downplay the affective.' He added, 'Before you can think critically, you need something to be critical about.' He gave the example of studying media literacy, in which students are expected to 'watch TV and look for bias,' but they cannot find bias until they have some foundation skills and knowledge. As such, something like media studies does not belong in the curriculum, in James's opinion.

However, writers tended to dislike the idea of pedagogy in curriculum documents. For instance, Scott voiced his perceptions about the absence of pedagogy and affective expectations, which were representative of other writers' positions on the matter: 'We were told, "There will be no pedagogy in the curriculum documents." We had hoped that there would be front matter in the curriculum documents that would talk about how you would go about teaching. Nope. It's just what the students need to know and be able to do. How the teachers get there is through their professional judgment. They're trained professionals. But we all know that there are degrees of trained professionals out there, and that most jurisdictions include pedagogy as part of their curriculum – how you get students to those levels.'

Consultation participant James made the connection very clear in his understanding of the attempt at neutrality: 'The curriculum policy made it very clear that the curriculum documents were to define what each child would be expected to know and be able to do at the end of every course. These expectations were defined as knowledge and skills. And each of these learning expectations was to be viewed as a content standard. The content was knowledge and/or skills. Each of these learning expectations had to be testable to be truly accountable. The curriculum process in this sense was sound in principle.'

Despite a perception that policy texts are objective and exclude the affective domain, some perceived that, upon enactment, the 'wrong' philosophy emerged in classroom. James offers his comment, representative of other consultation participants: 'The enactment aspect posed problems in several ways. Most notably, the "interpretation" of curriculum policy expectations through Course Profiles developed by the ministry, and by textbook writers/publishers, resulted in a loss of intended meaning.'

Bureaucrat Janelle observed that, despite the aim of value-neutrality, 'there is lots of affective stuff' in the final policy documents. She claimed that 'we embedded the attitudes as knowledge and skills, so that they wouldn't jump out as attitudes,' and thus 'fly under the radar.' This was an example of a subversive tactic to address an issue, to which some objected. The political act of aiming for value-neutrality in itself was simply not possible. More importantly, the significance is that a value-neutral and standardized curriculum ignored the very real issues of inequality in Ontario, thus minimizing the importance of social justice education, with little attention to marginalization, exclusion, and parity. This absence of attention to equity and social justice resulted in a policy text that was in opposition to the critical-democratic ideal.

Career Focus in the Curriculum:
Employment at the Expense of Empowerment?

Another key feature of Ontario's secondary school curriculum identified by policy actors was a preponderance of career-focused expectations that explicitly required students and teachers to tie courses, learning, and individual skills to careers. Benjamin Levin observes, 'The most common rationale advanced for education reforms is economic, particularly in relation to preparation of a workforce and competition with other countries' (Levin 1997, 254).

The use of language and rhetoric consistent with that ideological stance serves as a powerful device for legitimization and persuasion. For instance, a shift from access and inclusion towards a vocational focus to address international competitiveness, standardization, and accountability (e.g., standardized testing) occurred in Ontario (Basu 2004). When a predominant career education privileges the needs of the private sector, business reaps 'direct benefits of public taxation,' because this arrangement funds 'narrow, private aims' that serve the interests of employers, at the expense of other aims (Alemán 2001, 394–5). When market and individual needs (over collective needs) are privileged through the dominant neoliberal and neoconservative framing, equity and diversity are left out of educational discourse and issue framing. This absence of social justice as an aim, or even a part of public discourse, with emphasis on vocational outcomes at its expense, is at odds with the critical-democratic ideal.

The way in which careers are emphasized and discussed in Ontario's policy documents in courses coded as E and C sent the message that students' prospects were limited to certain roles in a certain type of society, thereby running the risk of compromising students' visions for their future roles, and potentially blocking their ability to achieve parity of participation in the workplace. These courses tended to exclude them from some discourses and issues (and even subjects) to which university-bound students were likely to be exposed. Indeed, course choices of non-university-bound students dictated what curriculum they would experience and to what sorts of possible careers they were introduced. But few – if any – non-university-bound students would enrol in U courses. Those who sought school-to-work programs such as apprenticeship or co-op education opportunities had practical workplace experiences, though all courses (including unlikely subject areas such as music and dance) included a career component expressed within their curriculum expectations.

The implicit message sent by the strong career focus was that learning is of value only when it relates to careers – and caused individuals (students, teachers, parents) to believe that the 'only valid questions about education' have to do with workplace preparation (Martin 1985, 6). This implicit message minimized the importance of other aims of education, such as those of citizenship, personal growth, and so on, as I discussed earlier. The concern is not that discussion of careers and workplaces happens (in fact, it probably should), but rather that careers took a front seat and other, important forms of learning were ignored – constituting the null. Some advocated a 'curriculum of life'[3] as a central organizing concept of education in order to include the whole student. Career-focused education undoubtedly has an important role to play in the development of the individual as citizen, but the framing of career-focused education affects how students view their roles as workers and citizens.

The career focus, as practised in this curriculum policy, subordinates an equity/social-justice focus (see, for example, Welch 1998; Bartlett et al. 2002) and is thus significant for three reasons. First, this form of career focus blatantly commodifies education through strong emphasis on career-related outcomes. Second, it creates social reproduction and inequality by reinforcing the status quo via legitimization of the interests of the dominating groups. Finally, it promotes a form of social Darwinism (Apple 1993; Natale 1998).

Ken Osborne contends that 'education in all parts of Canada is being turned into an instrument of economic policy' (1999, 19). It goes without saying that education has always played a role as an economic instrument, though both Ken Osborne and Suzanne Majhanovich suggest that this economic aim of education has been over-emphasized. Indeed, in her analysis of Ontario's curriculum policy, Suzanne Majhanovich identifies the neoliberal underpinnings through 'the language used in educational documents; e.g., the rationale of every course includes a statement as to how the particular subject or course will contribute to helping students success in the global economy and will prepare them for the workforce' (2005, 602).

The sorts of workplace skills prescribed in Ontario curriculum policy (e.g., problem-solving and social interaction) do not give workers more power in the workplace. Rather, they emphasize employability skills and career foci (Hyslop-Margison 2000). These skills teach workers to be 'productive' (but not critically reflective) employees rather than cultivating dispositions such as critical-democratic participation and taking on equity and social justice. This perpetuates an ideology that puts the needs of the private sector above individuals and reinforces power of dominant groups (Hyslop-Margison 2000). Specifically, Emery Hyslop-Margison questions the ethical appropriateness, social impact, and soundness of the concept.

Skills evaluation specifically relating to employability resulting from career-focused education creates an atmosphere of competition among students. This also implies over-emphasis on the importance of education as a tool for success in a career. This type of education policy can be construed as a form of social engineering that merely reinforces neoconservatism and neoliberalism (Hyslop-Margison 2000).

To provide a concrete example, I turn to Ontario's Business Studies curriculum, largely because this is the subject area on which I worked as a policy writer. However, similar career-focused expectations and statements appear in all curriculum policy documents, including the Arts. Business education exemplifies the fragmentation of a subject in a way that fails to address broader contexts of a 'curriculum of life' that neglects the 'whole student.' Because business courses in secondary schools[4] position themselves as career preparation, they tend to present course content from the perspective of the learner as potential manager or employee. Indeed, many Ontario Business Studies courses limit their focus to the types of decisions made by upper-level management, though few of the people taking the courses will ever hold such jobs, and that poses the question of whether it is really career preparation.

In general, all learning materials for these courses present commerce as an extremely positive entity. In a broad societal context, however, business touches citizens in more ways that merely employment – business shapes public policy, use and conservation of the environment, public values around consumerism, and the state of the economy. To function as consumers and as citizens in a complex society, all individuals would benefit from understanding how business works. And yet, in Ontario and elsewhere, we still fail to see Business Studies courses beyond those that limit business to a career. This narrow conception of business courses ignores the complexity of the subject and the impact that business has on the lives of students and communities.

While this discussion highlights some aspects of the null curriculum in contrast to a career focus, I acknowledge that a variety of null curricula dealing with social justice, equity, race, gender, and class are also omitted in favour of value-neutral and instrumentalist student learning expectations. Quite deliberately, as revealed in interviews for this research and documented in previous chapters, perspectives of labour, Aboriginals, anti-racism, and feminism were left out. This absence of multiple perspectives, coupled with an absence of social justice (discussed in greater detail later in this chapter) contributes to the critical-democratic shortfall in outcomes.

Inadequate Streaming Fails to Serve 'Non-University-Bound Students'[5]

Streaming is a long-contested issue in education (see, for example, Manzer 1994, 2003; Osborne 1999). Within the neoliberal and neoconservative frames, educational policies abandon development of the whole person in favour of the development of 'training an efficient workforce, creating a culture of entrepreneurship and enterprise, and fostering a positive view of industry and wealth creation' (Carr and Hartnett 1996, 21). Critics suggest that streaming keeps working-class and minority students out of more challenging programs, resulting in an inferior education for them (see, for example, Curtis, Livingstone, and Smaller 1992; Ireson and Hallam 1999; Oakes 2005).

Streaming usually creates two broad categories of students: those thought to be 'academic' and those considered 'practical' learners. The latter group is often thought to be less intelligent and less interested in school. A number of large-scale reports (see, for example, the 1988 *British Columbia Royal Commission on Education*, the 1993 *New Brunswick Commission on Education*, and Ontario's 1994 *Royal Commission on Learning*) have concluded that streaming disadvantages students not placed in university-streamed or academic courses. Research overwhelmingly suggests that when streaming is used, middle-class students go into the academic (or university-bound) streams, while working-class students go into other streams (Osborne 1999). This approach is problematic because the academic students tend to have access to more or better resources and often more challenging coursework that emphasizes education for the 'whole student.' By contrast, those dealt out of academic courses tend to be exposed to curriculum considered to be more practical – often at the expense of a 'liberal education,' which focuses on intellectual and social development. Some studies (see, for example, Rist 1970; Churchill and Kaprielian-Churchill 1991) suggest that streaming reflects social class – not ability or intelligence.

Despite all the evidence that points to disadvantages of and inequities resulting from streaming, it continues to appear prominently in education policy in many jurisdictions, and for several reasons. The education system is structured such that streamed courses are the only viable option, given class size and teacher preparation. More recently, and particularly in Ontario prior to school reform in the 1990s, de-streaming has not been successful. Groups of students of varying ability were thrown together in the same classroom, but teachers were not given supports to make de-streaming work (Osborne 1999). Robertson, Cowell, and Olson (1998) concluded that teachers viewed Ontario's grade nine de-streamed curriculum in the early and mid-1990s as difficult to adapt within their classrooms, though according to this research, students disagreed about the value of de-streaming as it was practised. Although more than half the students responding in this study preferred not to be streamed, the 'high-achieving' students tended to prefer a streamed model (Robertson, Cowell, and Olson 1998).

Nearly all policy actors raised the issue (independently and without prompting) that non-university-bound students were left out in the policy outcomes. In Ontario, as illustrated in table 7.1, fewer than half of all students went on to post-secondary education upon completing high school in 1999 (Statistics Canada 2002). Of that 49 per cent, nearly half attended a community college, one-third attended university, and the balance attended a range of other non-university post-secondary institutions such as technical, trade, or vocational schools, or private training schools. This reality of educational attainment suggests that a curriculum catering to university-bound students addresses the needs of only 15 per cent of students at best. Moreover, the needs of students who do not complete secondary school are not addressed. The Auditor General of Ontario (2003) also reports a similar finding, though the language used differs ('weaker' versus 'non-university-bound'): 'Educators also expressed concerns about the suitability of the new curriculum for weaker students. Recent studies and test results indicated that many students are still not succeeding under the new curriculum and that revisions to the curriculum or teaching strategies or both are required to help these "at-risk" students succeed' (123).

However, some policy actors disagreed with this concern. Bureaucrat Marcellas felt that the Harris government approached the curriculum reforms with the view that secondary education in Ontario served university-bound students well (following an approach they wanted to continue), but they also wanted to improve the quality of education for others. Previous reports, including the *Royal Commission on Learning*, Marcellas noted, were critical of guidance and career education, and graduation requirements were criticized for being too difficult. Similarly, political staffer Will discussed the issue of the non-university-bound student as a concern:

We were satisfied from our feedback from stakeholders that we were leaving a third of our high school students behind in these two streams. There was a need for a third. There was absolute, abject resistance from establishing a third stream. Complete, utter resistance that the applied stream was a big enough tent to capture those people. A number of stakeholders were convinced that

Table 7.1   Educational attainment of 18- to 20-year-olds no longer in high school, 1999

	No post-secondary (%)	Post-secondary continuing students (%)	Post-secondary graduates (%)	Post-secondary leavers (%)
Ontario	45	49	2	4
Canada	38	52	4	6

Source: Statistics Canada 2002

there was a bunch of kids and it's proven to be true. We couldn't get a third stream. We met a wall of resistance. Everything we did was counter-intuitive to what you were thinking a Conservative government would do ... I personally tried to get the premier to weigh in ... I am not the only one. The trustee associations were very, very worried. (Will, political staffer)

Despite Will's remarks, the Ministry of Education's 'official' position was that measures were in place to address the needs of all students. For instance, a ministry press release (June 2000) reads, 'The range and content of all the [workplace] courses will give students sound and comprehensive preparation for a variety of jobs, training programs and careers. With this new curriculum, students will graduate with a good understanding of the field they are pursuing, industry and government standards, health and safety issues, environmental concerns, career opportunities and specifics of a trade.'

The entire issue of the new 'streams' was considered problematic by all. In fact, research at the time revealed that fewer than one-quarter of Ontarians actually supported a return to streaming at the secondary school level, suggesting that policy actors echoed the general sentiments of Ontarians (Livingstone, Hart, and Davie 1996). To understand policy actors' concerns, an overview of the streaming that appears in policy texts is necessary. Under the previous system, grade nine courses were de-streamed, while grades ten through twelve contained three streams: basic, general, and advanced. Under the new curriculum policy, grade nine and ten courses had two streams: academic (coded as D) and applied (coded as P), with some elective courses coded as open (O). Academic courses purported to develop students' knowledge and skills through the study of theory and abstract problems, while applied courses focused on the essential concepts of a subject and developed students' knowledge and skills through practical applications and concrete examples. Familiar situations were used to illustrate ideas, and students were given more opportunities to experience hands-on applications of the concepts and theories they studied. Finally, open courses prepared students for further study in a subject and were considered appropriate for all students. For grades eleven and twelve, new courses were streamed on the basis of students' post-secondary destination:

- University ('U') preparation courses aimed to equip students with the knowledge and skills they needed to meet the entrance requirements for university programs.
- University/college ('M') preparation courses aimed to equip students with knowledge and skills needed to meet university and college entrance requirements.
- College ('C') preparation courses aimed to equip students with the knowledge and skills they needed to meet college, apprenticeship, or other training admission requirements.
- Workplace ('E') preparation courses aimed to equip students with the knowledge and skills they needed to meet the expectations of employers, or certain apprenticeship and training programs admission requirements.
- Open ('O') courses aimed to broaden students' knowledge and skills in subjects that reflected their interests and to prepare them for active and rewarding participation in society.

Students could move into a different stream by taking 'transfer courses' if their plans changed. Non-university-bound students, then, would be those intending to pursue college (and would therefore enrol in M, C, and O courses), or those preparing to enter the workforce upon graduation (and would therefore enrol in E and O courses).

This coding arose out of the course menus developed prior to the official start of the curriculum policy process. The ministry failed to state an explicit rationale for how or why they coded courses in a particular way. Though core subjects (mathematics, English, geography, and history) were coded for all 'destinations,' other subjects were more limited. For example,

- Business studies courses were coded O, M, C, and W (U was visibly absent)
- Arts courses (dance, music, visual arts, and media arts) lacked U codes
- International languages were coded U and O streams, while Latin was only coded U

- Pure sciences (physics, biology, and chemistry) were coded C
  and U, while a general workplace preparation science course was
  coded E
- Philosophy was coded O in grade 11, and U in grade 12

Alone, this arbitrary coding may appear inconsequential. But when coupled with student and teacher perceptions of coding, a troublesome picture emerged, contrary to the ministry's claim that the new curriculum provided more opportunities. Though there is no systematic evidence, anecdotal evidence suggests that course coding may dissuade non-university-bound students from pursuing certain options they may consider above their abilities – and even cause teachers to perceive students labelled 'workplace' as unable to perform in U courses. For example, a non-university-bound student who completed the 'open' grade 11 philosophy (HZB3O) might avoid the grade 12 philosophy course because it was coded U. General social science courses (Introduction to Anthropology, Psychology, and Sociology [HSP3M] and Challenge and Change in Society [HSB4M]) as well as Canadian and World Politics (CPW4U) were coded college and university, seemingly unavailable to workplace-destined students who might avoid courses not coded with an E. As a result, non-university-bound students risked getting a very different education from their counterparts – possibly missing out on interesting and engaging subject matter that could contribute to personal and intellectual development.

Based on the credits that a student did or did not earn, post-secondary opportunities might have been eliminated. For instance, a student who earned all or mostly E credits lacked the requirements for college admission. By contrast, many non-university-bound students did have opportunities to gain workplace experience through school-to-work programs (such as the Ontario Youth Apprenticeship Program or OYAP, co-op education), though these were not new features of curriculum policy. College admission criteria required M, C, and U courses for entry into programs. Universities tended to require a set number U-coded courses for admission (only some universities would accept M-coded courses), while M, C, E and O courses were not counted. Participation in school-to-work programs restricted elective course enrolment and might also result in similar loss of post-secondary options.

Though, as I illustrate here, coding bore relevance to students' post-secondary opportunities, there may in fact have been few differences in course content, despite the streams reflected in the code. Evidence suggests that confusion about the distinctions among these streams emerged upon the release of policy documents – a concern writers shared. Writers were quick to point out that the differences between academic and applied were never well clarified to them during the writing process – and thus the grade nine and ten curriculum policy documents produced did not reflect significant variances. Hardy's remarks about the confusion over stream distinctions were representative of many other writers:

> I know the one thing that struck me in my mind the most [was] that they were saying, 'We're moving away from general, advanced, and basic. We're going to be going to applied and academic.' And we weren't too sure what that meant. The only instruction they gave us was, 'We want to make sure that there is same content, but more abstract for academic and more concrete and hands-on for applied.' That was it, so OK, so it looks like we're looking at the same content, so we'll just distinguish between more higher-speaking skills for probably the academic and more basic kind of concepts for the applied . . .
>
> The only instructions we were getting is, 'Distinguish between applied and academic,' and we kept saying, 'OK, what happens to the kids when we make them applied?' But that was never approached . . . they are going to make applied so the basic level skills or the kids leave school? You know, they [students who struggle] can't make it in high school, they get to sixteen and they [drop out and] go work . . . The big complaint that I got from colleagues – and looking back on it, it was very justified – is that the applied course was still pretty much a watered-down academic. Still too much content, far too many expectations – we're killing these kids. And the kids who didn't make the applied, they were put in there, like our former basic-level students, didn't have a prayer. Didn't have a hope in this course. And we were expecting failure results there too.

Others describe the elimination of the 'basic' stream as detrimental to certain student populations:

> The one big concern that we had which leads me to that outcome is around the area of the workplace stream, and basic. There was a lot of concern within the writing teams that we voiced that students with basic needs were going to be left in the dark, and that the workplace stream would not be viewed by most as we thought it should be . . . And they [the ministry] did what they wanted to do . . . We thought there could be more opportunities for transition from school to work, rather than school to university, or even college. There was a lot of concern about that. And we felt that

would help a lot of the students who would have taken more of the basic courses in the previous world ... I think the outcome was that they lost opportunity for basic-level kids. (Mike, project manager)

You can talk to all of those kids who used to get a general diploma from high school, who used to go through the basic level, and who don't have anything wrong, who have not graduated, who have dropped out and have paid. (Danielle, consultation participant)

There was nothing for that because they didn't want that third stream – the basic, we used to call that the basic stream. There was nothing for that and there was nothing to say, workplace people are telling you they need skilled labour ... Nobody paid attention. To this day, they say, 'Oh, yeah that's a nice idea.' And that was it – but nobody ever wrote anything about it ... I can't understand why they wouldn't encourage kids to do this. And they are so worried about the dropout rate. If you're so worried about the dropout rate, well, you've got something where everybody says this is what you should be doing, but nobody's addressing it. (Alison consultation participant)

Data collected after the enactment of SSR reveal that policy actors' fears about the fate of students in the workplace stream were realistic. Both Alison Taylor (2005) and Suzanne Majhanovich (2005) report high failure rates in applied courses (as they were in the general and basic streams in previous curricula), and the graduation rate of the first cohort through the new system was low (over one-fourth of students in the first cohort were unlikely to graduate, as the result of high failure rates in applied courses). At the same time, failure rates in the university stream in grades eleven and twelve decreased, suggesting that the ministry continued to serve university-bound students well. A critical-democratic policy, by way of its concern with social justice, would indeed address the needs of these diverse students.

Equalization of Social Cleavage: Social Justice as an Educational Goal?

Policies must address social exclusion between the elites and excluded marginalized groups to achieve the critical-democratic ideal. Policy actors raise several outcome areas pertinent to the equalization of social cleavage. The term *social cleavage* originates from the 1967 work of Seymour Lipset and Stein Rokkan, who define its three aspects: social division separates people along at least one key social characteristic such as occupation, status, religion, or ethnicity; groups included or excluded are conscious of their collective identity and willing to act on that basis; and formal institutions respond to the interests of those on one side of the division.

Because of its central role in critical democracy, social justice must be privileged in critical-democratic education. Indeed, Kathy Hytten argues that a curriculum for (critical) democracy cannot exist without a strong social justice component: 'Social justice is an integral feature of democratic life, as democratic societies are, at least in the ideal, just societies. They strive for equity, self-determination, and freedom. They educate students to become just citizens' (2006, 221). To that end, several criteria may be used to evaluate educational policies with respect to their social justice orientation: how, to what extent, and why do education policies support, interrupt, or subvert:

- Exploitative relationships (capitalist, patriarchal, racist, heterosexist, disablist, etc.) within and beyond educational institutions?
- Marginalization and inclusion within and beyond the education system?
- Promotion of relationships based on recognition, respect, care, and mutuality, or produce powerlessness (for education workers or students)?
- Practices of cultural imperialism? And which cultural differences should be affirmed, which should be universalized, and which rejected?
- Violent practices within and beyond the education system? (Gerwirtz 1998, 482)

Social justice is central to achieving the ideal of critical democracy. Thus, institutions striving for critical-democratic policy outcomes ought to explicitly prioritize social justice as a goal. In the case of education policy, critical-democratic curriculum policy texts ought to openly include social justice in their learning outcomes. Beginning with the elimination of the Anti-Racism, Equity, and Access Branch prior to the beginning of the process, social justice was simply not a priority from the political leadership, confirmed by the memorandum revealed by MPP Howard Hampton in the Legislative Assembly (Legislative Assembly, *Debates and Proceedings* [23 April 1997]). This is consistent with the neoliberal and neoconservative ideologies that guided the Common Sense Revolution, and consistent with trends in many jurisdictions where other priorities guide educational efforts at the expense of social justice. As Hytten points out, 'While there have always been educators calling for a social justice approach toward education, this vision has never been a dominant one. This is especially true in our current climate, where teachers are increasingly asked to focus on a very narrow set of goals, in particular raising standardized test scores' (2006, 224).

Thus, the emphasis on standardization, measurement, and preparation for careers reflected in Ontario's curriculum policy texts, as well as many features of the process itself, undermine social justice. The absence of 'thick' social justice across all subject areas, and all policy documents is thus no surprise.

Absence of Equity and Social Justice Focus

The government's decision to eliminate the Anti-Racism, Equity, and Access Branch within the Ministry of Education was the first indication of the political decision to exclude social justice from new curriculum policy. Of all policy actors interviewed, only one bureaucrat brought up the elimination of this branch, stating, 'I know that once the Harris government came in, it was basically decimated – that whole floor, the equity floor.'

When asked about the presence of equity, diversity, and social justice in curriculum policy documents, two bureaucrats described how subsequent revisions to the curriculum (under the Liberal government that took office in 2003) are very different and address equity and diversity, though they didn't specifically comment on the policy documents central to this research. Several writers and consultation participants described their perceptions about an absence of equity, diversity, and social justice in greater detail than bureaucrats. Curtis, a consultation participant, was very aware of and concerned with these issues, and provided some context:[6]

> If you take a look at where issues around equity and diversity were within programs, initially, again, we had come through a period with the previous government, with the NDP, where these were considered key policy pieces and therefore were in all of the documentation. There were content pieces that were completely left out when the policy documents were generated, simply because, you know, they were considered to be ideological positions, and this government decided, 'No, we're not going to go there.'
>
>   I'm thinking so much about what they did with anti-racist education. Really, it was meant, initially, to be woven into the entire operation of

secondary schools. Well, what they did was simply to take that out and put it into the front of the document as a standardized paragraph that would accompany all of the policy documents. It was their way of saying, well, look, we've got it in our policy documents, but the reality is, you didn't teach to that any longer . . .

I felt, and I think others have shared this with you, there was a very concerted effort on the part of the government to not allow the issues around, as I say, equity, issues around peace education, issues that had to do with class and gender to be part of the programming. So what you ended up with in a lot of the policy documents is, again, knowledge and skills were very clearly defined, but all of those other peoples seem to have been left on the cutting room floor, so to speak.

A few writers echoed Curtis's perceptions about the shift from equity to equality, thus excluding equity from the curriculum policy:

Equality and equity is not on treating everybody the same, it's treating everybody the way that they need to be treated to get to the same place. And that was clearly not part of this curriculum. It's like they thought that every child in the schools was like their children . . .

I was thinking about inclusiveness and diversity, and the need for thinking about our identities that we bring to questions of public importance, and how we move through the challenges of increasing diversity within a social justice context. (Scott, writer)

A curriculum that was really focused primarily on skills . . . would help them become employable. I don't deny that that's a critical role for schools to play, but it seemed that . . . there was an imbalance. (Justin, writer)

Policy actors' perceptions revealed an absence of equity, diversity, and social justice in the content as well as from the over-arching aims of the process. Clearly, diversity, equity, and social justice were not priorities articulated in the framing of the issues, and they appeared to have been excluded in favour of a standardized, skills-focused curriculum. In the sections that follow, I first describe the issue of 'value-neutrality' raised within the context of content-rich policy texts. I then explore the concern that non-university-bound students were disadvantaged by the new streaming model. I then investigate the degree to which social justice was reflected in policy documents. Finally, I explore the perception that insufficient support and supplemental learning materials were available to support enactment.

Concluding Comments

As a whole, curriculum policy texts as outcomes produced during the Common Sense Revolution neither embodied nor promoted any form of democracy in education. The policy texts created were prescriptive and standardized in an effort to be 'value-neutral.' Moreover, these outcomes as perceived by policy actors in the process, when triangulated with other data, revealed considerable shortcomings in the policy texts when viewed through a critical-democratic lens. Policy actors criticized the resulting curriculum policy for failing to meet the needs of all students resulting from the streaming approach used. Not surprisingly, the policy texts failed to address equity, diversity, and social justice, as well as democracy in education, since these simply were not priorities for the government or for most policy actors involved. Like the process, then, the policy text outcomes fell short of the critical-democratic ideal. For the most part, policy actors were pleased with the policy texts produced as improvements over previous curriculum policy. However, problems with lack of continuity as well as concern that the curriculum policy failed to address the needs of non-university-bound students emerged. Interviews with policy actors revealed the absence of a social justice focus in policy texts. Policy actors raised issues surrounding enactment of the new curriculum policy, especially concern about rushed enactment and the lack of resources and supports for educators. These concerns were supported by other sources.

Thus we revisit the question of whether we need to have a democratic policymaking process to achieve *education for democracy* and *democracy in education*. The analysis presented here suggests that a policy process that lacks democratic features *and* privileges certain types of educational priorities (e.g., streaming, a career focus at the expense of worker and citizen empowerment) that are at odds with democratic ideals leads to curriculum policy texts in which education *for* democracy and democracy *in* education are absent. Is it possible to construct a viable critical-democratic process that would achieve education *for* democracy and democracy *in* education in policy texts? In the next chapter, I present and discuss possibilities and alternatives for critical-democratic policymaking.

8   An Exploration of Possibilities: Porto Alegre, Brazil, as an Analytic Foil Contrasting Ontario

One of the reasons that conservative policies dominate is because teachers and others are not given realistic alternatives that actually work.
— Michael Apple 2001b, iv

If we understand democracy in its critical and strong sense, we must broaden the scope of participation beyond that which exists in many contemporary institutions.
— Landon Beyer 1993

Popular participation 'teaches' the state to better serve the population.
— Luis Amando Gandin and Michael Apple 2004, 174

The Ontario experience described in the case study provides but one approach to curriculum policy formulation – one that, despite some positive outcomes, failed to embody a democratic and inclusive approach to policy production. This approach to policy development presents the question, is there a viable way to democratize policymaking? One particular jurisdiction, Porto Alegre, highlights some very real possibilities for different approaches to policy formulation that approach a critical-democratic ideal through meaningful citizen engagement, inclusion, and a concern for social justice in both process and outcomes. Many lessons can be learned from Porto Alegre's experience that offer insight into ways in which the critiques of Ontario I presented might be addressed. Most importantly, Porto Alegre illustrates how citizens can reclaim their voice in the policy process, leading to efficient and effective policy production that reflects critical-democratic ideals.

Porto Alegre's unique approach to policy production (and particularly its participatory budgeting) has attracted considerable international attention. The municipality received the International Best Practice award for local governments at the 1996 United Nations Habitat Conference. Hosting the World Social Forum for several years, beginning in January 2001, catapulted Porto Alegre onto the international stage (Baiocchi 2005), leading to increased popular and academic attention. Since that time, it has continued to be studied by researchers, reported in the media, and recognized by a variety of non-governmental organizations, including a positive evaluation by UNESCO (2000), and attention from World Bank – which has taken to distributing brochures promoting this model of participatory policy to other countries (Gret and Sintomer 2005).

This chapter describes Porto Alegre's policy production based on secondary research and accounts published by others, as well as government documents. Rather than presenting a case study, this chapter offers an analytic foil against which Ontario's policy production under the Common Sense Revolution is contrasted. While the critique offered in the previous chapter problematizes policy production in the case study, the purpose of contrasting Porto Alegre against Ontario to suggest that other approaches are indeed feasible. By no means, however, does Porto Alegre represent a miracle solution to democratization of policy production. Indeed, it runs up against its own problems and limitations, which I will address in this chapter, to balance the potential of several important lessons that might be applied to other jurisdictions. Moreover, its success depends upon unique local contextual factors, which I describe in this chapter, which underscore that its applicability to other jurisdictions must be approached cautiously. While Porto Alegre may offer an example of critical-democratic policymaking, the literature on policy borrowing (see, for example, Halpin and Troyna 1995; Levin 1998; James and Lodge 2003; Phillips and Ochs 2003) reminds us that such endeavours require a full exploration of context applicability.

As an analytic foil, Porto Alegre provides a striking contrast to Ontario, though at the same time some similarities allow for a robust comparison. Both Ontario and Porto Alegre undertook large-scale education reforms, which included a reformulation of curriculum policy (that is, new courses and new curriculum policy, not revisions to existing policy). Both processes occurred during the mid- to late 1990s. Despite these similarities, differences affect the analysis. First, while Ontario's education policy is provincial in scope, Porto Alegre's is municipal.

Second, Ontario's curriculum reform included secondary and elementary education (though only secondary was studied in this research), while Porto Alegre's reform was at the Fundamental level (roughly equivalent to Ontario's elementary education).

Porto Alegre, Brazil

Porto Alegre, the largest city in and capital of the state of Rio Grande Do Sul in southern Brazil, had a population of 1.3 million in 2000 (Miños 2002). Founded in the mid-1700s by colonists from the Portuguese Azores, its location at the junction of five rivers makes it an important port, as well a major industrial and commercial centre in Brazil (Brazilian Embassy 2005). Despite enjoying a high rate of literacy (96%), Porto Alegre is a community marked by social inequality (Wainwright 2003). In 1981, one-third of Porto Alegre's population lived in slums (Wainwright 2003), with fewer than half of all citizens having access to sanitation and sewers (Gandin and Apple 2004). Contrasting the large proportion of those in abject poverty, fifteen families owned almost all the urban land available for development in Porto Alegre (Wainwright 2003). In an interview, Roberto Savio, founder of the World Social Forum, describes Porto Alegre's diversity this way: 'Porto Alegre is made up of all people – old and young, women and men, indigenous groups, peasants, trade unions, of all colours, it represents a huge diversity of peoples' movements. I would say that there is no domination although there are many groups who wish to dominate' ('Porto Alegre' 2005, 119).

Despite a long tradition of authoritarian politics in Brazil that were dominated primarily by a small, wealthy sector of society, a successful labour movement during the 1980s resulted in the election of the Workers' Party (Partido dos Trabalhadores, or PT) in Porto Alegre in 1989. The Workers' Party established 'an elaborate and successful system of grass roots participation in municipal governance' (Koonings 2004, 80) and is best known for its participatory budgeting. The participatory budget process has operated successfully in Porto Alegre, receiving worldwide attention over the past decade. The Workers' Party was re-elected three times and in 1998 took control of Rio Grande do Sul, with a population of 10 million, launching a similar process there. However, in 2004, the Workers' Party was defeated by the Popular Socialist Party in a very close, run-off election (Tribunal Regional Eleitoral do Rio Grande do Sul 2004).[1]

Porto Alegre has a corporatist political system in which legislative power is given to civic assemblies that represent economic, industrial, agrarian, and professional groups. The approach to citizen participation in policy decisions used in Porto Alegre 'stands apart from many other similar attempts to institute some version of civic governance' (Baiocchi 2001, 43), because it devolved substantial power to participants. In the late 1990s after success in participatory budgeting, participatory policymaking was applied to a number of other thematic areas, including education.

Arenas for Discourse: Creating Citizen and Government Capacity through *Orçamento Participativo*

Porto Alegre received substantial international attention for its success in creating a participatory budgeting process to overcome problems of citizen participation while involving those usually 'in the margins' in policymaking. Soon after taking power in 1988, the Workers' Party initiated an innovative experiment in radical social democracy through the introduction of participatory budgeting, through the OP. The party envisioned an open and democratic process in which citizens meet, deliberate, and make decisions about budgetary matters. To that end, the OP process is founded on three principles:

* All citizens are entitled to participate, and community organizations have no special status.
* Participation is governed by a combination of direct and representative democracy rules and takes place through regularly functioning institutions whose internal rules are decided upon by participants.
* Resources are allocated according to an objective method based on 'general criteria' (substantive criteria established by the participatory institutions to rank priorities) and 'technical criteria' (technical or economic viability as defined by the executive and federal, state, or city legal 'norms') (Santos 1998).

This form of participatory budgeting relies on 'actual conversations between people that meet the standards of open-endedness and public mindedness' (Baiocchi 2001, 96). Observers point out that Porto Alegre's participatory budgeting model is an exercise in joint governance by municipal bodies as well as citizens who assume direct decision-making power within levels of a participatory pyramid. The three levels are: (1) neighbourhood, (2) regional (sixteen sectors into which the city is divided, and six thematic areas), and (3) municipal.

While the OP is now considered well-functioning, its start was less than ideal and it evolved by trial and error (Viero and Cordeiro 2003; Santos 2005; Baiocchi 2006). The first iteration was met with cynicism and suspicion, and resulting participation rates were moderate. As well, the process was initially resisted by the 'economic elite,' largely in the form of 'hostile media coverage' (Wood and Murray 2007, 29). 'Clientelism,' the exchange of favours for voters to influence their political action, permeated Brazilian politics for many years, and the OP overcame it in order to function smoothly (Santos 2000, 2005; Azevedo and Schugurensky 2005; Baiocchi 2005). The OP developed a series of strategies to prevent clientelism transparently. Once citizens recognized that the process was legitimate and that clientelism had been minimized, participation rose annually, from only 976 participants in 1990 to over 28,000 in 2000 (Menegat 2002). Baiocchi (2001)[2] argues that participation in the OP is inclusive of groups usually marginalized, citing that in 1998, 'low educated persons' accounted for 60 per cent of participants, 'persons of low income' accounted for 33 per cent of participants, and the amount of participation[3] was relatively equal, regardless of these demographics. While he found no evidence of racial disparity, Baiocchi (2001) does acknowledge that women were not as well represented as men. The perceived inclusiveness of the process is reflected in the words of one community activist in Porto Alegre: 'It is not the suits who come here and tell us what to do. It is us. I am a humble person. I have participated since the beginning. And like me, there are many more poor people like me who are there with me, debating or helping in whatever way possible. And so I think the OP is enriching in this way, because it makes people talk, even the poorest ones. It has not let the suits take over' (Baiocchi 2001, 51).

For the purpose of this discussion, it is useful to understand the structure of the OP process, which occurs annually. Each year, the OP cycle begins in March and April with an initial round (*primeira rodada*) of twenty-two plenary meetings – one in each of the sixteen regions, as well as one for each of six thematic areas. The thematic areas are (1) transportation and circulation, (2) education and leisure, (3) culture, (4) health and social welfare, (5) economic development and taxation, and (6) city organization and urban development. The *primeira rodada* meetings end with a vote to elect regional delegates (one for every twenty participants) who will represent the delegates at the next round of meetings (*rodadas intermediáras*). Delegates create lists outlining priorities and issues to take to the next level of budgeting based on participant deliberation.

Next, a second round of intermediary meetings between April and June allow debate and deliberation, prioritization, and further election of delegates. These are small-scale meetings in neighbourhoods or within thematic working groups. During this round, the municipal government supplements meetings with technical information to assist participants in making decisions. As well, the government presents their own priorities, which citizens deliberate and vote on. Minutes document the proceedings of all meetings. Participants apply criteria and formulae to identify priorities from the issues discussed. These priorities are then passed on to the municipal government for consideration during the next round.

The second round (*segunda rodada*) occurs in June and July, providing a forum for discussion of proposals generated in the first round. Municipal bureaucrats also introduce investment proposals during this round. Deliberation of proposals occurs at plenary debates, ending with the election of members to the Participatory Budget Council (Conselho do Orçamento Participativo, or COP). Each regional and thematic party sends up to two delegates and two substitute (*suplentes*) members. As well, participants vote on any unresolved issues. Finally, a point system[4] is used to rank priorities for the Investment Plan. Negotiation and collaboration can occur among members in order to prioritize. Two or more regions can jointly prioritize a project that affects them so that it receives a higher level of consideration in a given year (Viero and Cordeiro 2003).

From August onwards, the COP organizes a city-wide round of meetings among delegates. In August and September, proposals are discussed at weekly COP meetings, where the executive consolidates citizens' demands with 'institutional demands' proposed by the municipal government. Points are awarded to proposals based on three criteria: proportion of population of the region proposing the demand, degree of 'need' for the demand, and priority of the demand relating to the investment selected by the region (Santos 2005). During this period, the COP also trains newly elected councillors to ensure that they understand the process and the criteria for resource distribution. By 30 September each year, the COP must present a budget proposal to the mayor. In October and December, the COP discusses and votes on the proposed budget, then establishes a detailed Investment Plan that specifies which projects will be undertaken in which neighbourhoods and city-wide.

While the procedural aspects of the OP are relevant, it is also important to consider qualitative aspects of citizens' involvement. The literature documents how OP meetings operate. Perhaps most notably, Gianpaulo Baiocchi provides insight into the way that citizens conduct themselves and understand their own participation in the process; his work illustrates the level of sophistication that citizens – many of whom are from the margins of society – understand their participation and the process itself. As well, Baiocchi's work illustrates the diversity in the ways in which grassroots associations organize and conduct themselves. For example, many neighbourhood associations regularly hold social events (e.g., parties, barbeques, and activities for children) as part of their activities. Many hold political events, such as debates, meetings with the mayor or municipal departments, and petitions. Despite what might appear on the surface to be political association, participants in the OP consider 'politics' to be separate from the community work of the OP. In fact, in their view, 'politics' has place in the community association. As one community activist explained, 'In the [neighbourhood] association, no one has a [political] party. It is like a religion: you have ours, I have mine, and we do not discuss it. In the association, our party is our community' (Baiocchi 2005, 124).

Despite the lack of perceived politics, participants expect disagreement and deliberation. Conflict is an important feature of the OP. Santos (2000, 500) identifies persistent 'conflict and mediation between technical and political issues, as well as between knowledge and power' as main features. As such, OP participants at all levels must (and do) acquire the skills to work with conflict towards a common goal.

An important role of the OP has been facilitating learning among policy actors. Indeed, many Porto Alegrans view the OP as a school of democracy in itself (Wilkinson 2007). Those working in government learn from the process. Specifically, elected officials and municipal employees had to learn to work in a new fashion, negotiating with citizens rather than imposing decisions based on technical criteria (Abers 2000). For instance, bureaucrats with technical engineers (e.g., municipal engineers) had to change their communication styles and their 'dismissive attitudes' towards citizens to ensure that they were understood in the OP process (Santos 1998, 2005). To that end, the municipal government introduced the Program of Internalization of Participatory Budgeting in 1997 to ensure that municipal bureaucrats infused OP into their everyday work. The program relies on workshops to ensure bureaucrats understand all elements of the process (Santos 1998).

Through participation, citizens learn the requisite skills for collective action, which include running meetings and negotiating compromises. 'Avoiding personal quarrels and learning to work with rules guiding speech and voting' were significant things that citizens had to learn in order for the OP to function (Abers 2000, 185). As well, citizens learn to help one another learn and to support one another. An activist interviewed by Gianpaulo Baiocchi explained, 'Those who come for the first time are welcome, we have a lot of patience for them, there is no problem, we let them make demands during technical meetings, they can speak their mind and their anxieties. We have patience for them because we were like that once ... You have the responsibility of not abandoning him, of staying with him. That is the most important thing' (Baiocchi 2001, 65). This conception of the 'other' at a community meeting suggests that even opponents have a certain type of respect for one another, even when they disagree with the tone or content of the other's remarks. Reciprocal respect for the other is consistent with Mouffe's conception of agonism and thus suggests that at least some participants embody the critical-democratic ideal in the way that they view fellow OP participants.

Citizens who participate in the process also acquire 'privileged' knowledge, including the intricacies of government, and 'expert' or technical knowledge relating to specific projects (Abers 2000; Baiocchi 2005, 2006). This includes not only information that directly affects their neighbourhoods and neighbourhood associations, but also information about social policy issues central to the municipality's thematic assemblies.

Critiques of the OP

While the OP undeniably achieved success since its inception in Porto Alegre, it is not without challenges and areas for improvement. In their 2005 research, Marian Gret and Yves Sintomer outline some of the challenges and shortcomings of the OP. First, for example, while women tend to be well represented in participatory budgeting, feminist issues have not been addressed in resulting decisions. Second, immigrant groups tend to be under-represented. Third, the system is complex and citizen knowledge of it is shaky, despite their participation. Finally, participatory policymaking requires considerable time on the part of participants, which leads to some being unable or unwilling to attend meetings – particularly those in extreme poverty or those who have significant responsibility in the home (see, for example, Wilkinson's 2007 research on women's participation).

Because the OP is a political contract between the elected officials and the people, and not a right or process guaranteed by law, sustaining the OP in Porto Alegre is perceived as a challenge (Santos 1998). Thus, tensions have arisen about its legitimacy and sustainability, particularly among some elected officials in the late 1990s (Santos 1998). Despite the 2004 Workers' Party defeat, participatory budgeting remains in place – in fact, in their election campaign, the opposition promised to preserve and improve the OP (Baiocchi 2006).

Benjamin Goldfrank's 2005 comparative analysis of participatory policy experiments in Port Alegre, Caracas, and Montevideo illustrates a variety of outcomes, depending on the context. Whereas Porto Alegre's OP was a success, a similar attempt in Caracas failed, and yet another in Montevideo had mixed success. Two factors explain the mixed results, according to Goldfrank's analysis. First, the degree of national decentralization and resources for municipal governments and the level of institutionalization of local opposition parties affect the ability of participatory policymaking to be successful. Second, these conditions shape the design, such that the degree of legitimate participation varied from one jurisdiction to the next. The more legitimate the participation (e.g., absence of manufactured consent, elimination of clientelism) in a jurisdiction, the greater the lasting citizen involvement (Goldfrank 2005).

Education in Brazil

Public education in Brazil is simultaneously governed by federal, state, and municipal governments. At the national level, in 1995 Brazil saw its first minister of education since the 1930s with the appointment of an economist and former rector of a university, Paulo Renato de Souza, as minister (Schwartzman 2004). Education is organized into five levels: infant (early childhood education up until the age of six), fundamental (years one through eight), secondary (years nine through eleven), higher, and postgraduate. The first three levels (infant, fundamental, and secondary) are often referred to as 'basic' education, and the last two as 'higher' education (Soares 2004). Infant and fundamental education are the co-responsibility of municipalities and states, secondary edu-cation is the responsibility of states (though the federal government mandates a national curriculum), and higher education is a federal responsibility. However, in practice, some municipalities such as Porto Alegre take on greater (or all) responsibility for fundamental education (Gandin 2002).

Basic education is compulsory for children aged seven to fourteen and is free to all Brazilians at any age. Though there is universal access to basic schooling, grade repetition and truancy rates are high (Soares 2004), transition to higher education is low, with high rates of non-completion. In 2001, 43 per cent of eighteen-year-olds were out of school (Schwartzman 2004), and just over 50 per cent of students complete basic education (deCastro and Tiezzi 2004).

Education funding is outlined in the Brazilian Constitution of 1988, which allocates 18 per cent of federal resources and 25 per cent of state and municipal government resources for education (Schwartzman 2004). A National Fund for Basic Education (Fundo de Manutenção e Desenvolvimento do Ensino Fundamental e Valorização do Magistério, or FUNDEF) was established to ensure that resources are actually spent on education and to reduce regional differences by allocating per-pupil and per-teacher floors (Schwartzman 2004). FUNDEF was the first step towards decentralization and autonomy in regional areas, since states and/or municipalities have some degree of control over the use of funds, provided they conform to the 'floor' formulae (Schwartzman 2004). Private schools exist in Brazil, and have enrolments of nearly 10 per cent of students in fundamental education programs (Gandin 2002).

Minister of Education deSouza, during his appointment between 1995 and 2002, was responsible for several federal reforms. He re-established the National Institute of Educational Research (Instituto Nacional de Estudos e Pesquisas Educacionais) as a government agency to collect education statistics. To facilitate data collection, the National Institute of Educational Research introduced three large-scale assess-ment systems for the basic, secondary, and higher levels of education (Schwartzman 2004). Reforms to secondary school were undertaken to 'improve and expand secondary education in tune with the demands of the productive sector and with the developmental needs of the country, society and citizens' (deCastro and Tiezzi 2004, 93). These included a revised national curriculum, the National Curriculum

Directives (*Diretrizes Curriculares Nacionais,* or DCN) (Myers 2005).The ministry identified the key aims of the reforms as (deCastro and Tiezzi 2004, 94):

- Expanding the system to attain universality progressively
- Redefining the role of secondary education in the education process as a whole
- Improving supply
- Improving the quality of education

Brazil, along with other Latin American countries, has been criticized for a neoliberal approach to education (Myers 2005). The stated aims of the secondary school reforms reflect a neoliberal concern with labour supply to meet corporate demands, and a focus on quality education, evident in the 1999 National Curricular Guidelines for Secondary Education (*Parâmetros Curriculares Nacionais Ensino Médio,* or PCNEM). The introduction of standardized assessments (which, at the secondary level include a high-stakes test, *Exame Nacional do Ensino Médio* or ENEM) reflects a neoconservative stance, as defined in chapter 2. Moreover, the national educational policies contain the 'rhetoric of neo-liberalism' which 'insists on the importance of education to solve the problems of capitalism' (Gandin 2006, 219). This rhetoric results in the application of business models to schooling, replacing equity and social justice in education with a focus on individual ability and effort (Gandin 2006).

Reforms during the early 1990s also increased the level of decentralization for the infant and fundamental levels by placing responsibility for all aspects of infant and fundamental education on municipalities and states. This decentralization placed responsibility for local budgeting, school organization, and curriculum at the local level. In Porto Alegre, the Workers' Party was able to take control of fundamental education through this decentralized approach to schooling and used this opportunity to challenge the neoliberal policies at the local level. Luis Armando Gandin and Michael Apple report that Porto Alegre's principal goal for education at the time of reform was a radical democratization in the municipal schools along four thematic axes: management of the school, curriculum, principles for living together, and evaluation (Gandin and Apple 2004).

During the inception of the Citizen School project, local school councils deliberated and made recommendations in each of the four thematic axes. An astounding 60,000 citizens participated in these meetings (Hatcher 2002). School councils generated recommendations that were brought forward to the Municipal Congress of Education (discussed in the sections that follow) by an elected representative, and brought back to the schools for further discussion, and so forth, over the course of eighteen months (Azevedo 2000).

Policy Deliberation: Replication of the OP to Create the Citizen School

In Porto Alegre, the Workers' Party established the Citizen School (*Escola Cidadã*) using an approach to policy formulation that grew from the successful participatory budgeting process, which relied heavily on citizenship participation. In response to low student success rates, the government sought to create a radically different educational experience for the infant and fundamental levels over which the municipality had jurisdiction. The resulting public school structure was named the Citizen School. The official framing of the Citizen School project is described on the Municipal Education Secretariat's (*Secretaria Municipal de Educação*, or SMED) website: 'To the Popular Administration, to democratize is to construct, with participation, a project of education that has social quality, is liberating and transformative, where the school is a laboratory of practice, exercise and achievement of rights, of formation of autonomous, critical and creative historic subjects, full citizens, identified with ethical values, willing to construct a social project that has as a center of attention the practice of justice, of freedom, of respect and fraternal relationship among men and women and a harmonic relationship with nature' (Gandin and Apple 2004, 179).

Prior to the introduction of the participatory process, the SMED made all local decisions about education (Wilkinson 2007). Luis Armando Gandin (2002, 238) identifies citizens' 'preparedness to participate' in education reforms as a direct result of technical knowledge and 'augmentative capacity' that evolved through their participation in the OP.

The education policy reforms leading to the creation of the Citizen School began in March 1994, with four phases completed in eighteen months. Porto Alegre's curriculum policy formulation was part of a larger education reform effort that encompassed four broad 'thematic axes': (1) management of the school, (2) curriculum, (3) principles for living together, and (4) evaluation. Upon completion of the centralized policy, local enactment entailed specific curriculum development. That is, individual school communities 'fleshed out' the broad curricular areas (called thematic complexes) mandated centrally. In the document 'Principles and Directives,' the municipal government of Porto Alegre articulated five principles to guide the policy process, which provide insight into their conception of educational purpose (Hatcher 2002):

- Education is a right of all, with particular emphasis on the situation of those who throughout history have been denied this right.
- Popular participation is a method of management of public policy in the field of education, stimulating and guaranteeing the conditions for the collective construction of the education we want.
- Dialogue is an ethical-existential principle of a humanist and solidaristic project, which respects differences and the plurality of visions of the world, while also being critical and proactive in the face of social inequalities and injustice.
- Radicalization of democracy[5] is the strategic objective of a government of the left, committed to the interests of the majority, the popular classes, stimulating co-management of the public sphere as a step towards popular sovereignty and control over the state.
- Utopia is a motivating vision of the education and school we want and also of the project of socio-economic development which is both possible and necessary for the great majority of the excluded and the exploited in the capitalist system.

Phase 1: Establishing School Councils – Mobilizing Neighbourhood Participation

Based on lessons learned from the successful OP, the SMED launched the first phase of education policy formulation at the neighbourhood level by mobilizing school communities, public organizations, and higher education institutions by creating school councils (*conselhos escolares*). School councils, legislated by the municipality in 1992 and enacted in 1993, are central to the institutional structure, as well as to the process of curriculum policy formulation and enactment. They hold deliberative power over administrative, financial, and educational matters. Each school council must include elected representation of teachers, parents, students, staff, and administrators, with elections every two years. The number of representatives in each category varies, depending on school enrolment (Gandin 2002), ranging from five in a school of fewer than 100 pupils, to a maximum of nineteen in the largest school (Gandin 2002; Wilkinson 2007). Thus, a school with higher enrolment has a proportionately larger school council. School councils decide which global projects are to be taken on by the school, establish principles of administration, allocate funds, and monitor the implementation of decisions (Gandin 2002).

To discourage clientelism, proposals introduced by school councils require the collective support of the majority of school council members and must conform to a set of principles, procedures, and standards agreed upon by members of the school council. These strategies have been used successfully in the OP, as described earlier in this chapter (Santos 2000, 2005; Azevedo and Schugurensky 2005; Baiocchi 2005). To ensure compliance, SMED representatives are assigned locally to monitor local practices (as further discussed later in this chapter).

Phase 2: Municipal Congress of Education – Establishing Regional Participation

In the second phase, local school representatives gathered within the sixteen municipal regions established for the OP. Each formulated regional proposals, which were eventually submitted to the Constituent Congress of Education (*Congresso Constituinte*, or CCE) in Phase 3. Within the regional proposals, local educational practices were brought forward by school council representatives, discussed, and analysed. The practices discussed included teaching methods, evaluation, class councils, and community participation in school management (Azevedo 2000). As was the case with the OP process, some degree of learning was necessary for citizens involved, to engage in the type of 'ideal' deliberation envisioned by the SMED and government: 'At the beginning, many school council representatives used to express their own personal opinions, rather than the opinions of their constituencies. To reduce this problem and increase accountability, the Project stimulated teachers, administrators, students and parents to organize around their unions and associations ... To be adopted, a proposal must have the support of the majority of the school community, and must be consistent with a set of administrative and pedagogical principles, procedures and norms that arise from the dialogue among the four constituencies' (Azevedo and Schugurensky 2005, 48–9).

By the end of the first cycle in 1995, twenty-five issues were identified, including school non-attendance and retention, democratic management, violence, education in rural areas, professional development, and scientific knowledge versus popular knowledge (Azevedo 2000). The concept of 'scientific' knowledge, perhaps somewhat a misnomer, refers to conventional academic knowledge. This is contrasted with the conception of 'popular knowledge,' which is 'knowledge that is connected to the lives of the most disadvantaged members of our communities' and often not considered legitimate in formal education policy arenas (Gandin and Apple 2003, 193). The twenty-five issues were then taken to the CCE in the third phase of the process for further elaboration.

Phase 3: Building the Constituent Congress of Education

The SMED established the Constituent Congress of Education (Congresso Constituinte Escolar, or CCE) as a forum for regions to present their proposals for longer-term planning. Elected delegates attend the CCE, representing every segment of the city, including school council representatives, unions, and representatives from other levels of educational (Gandin 2002). According to Gandin (2002), the CCE was put into place in order to ensure that the SMED adheres to the collective will of the neighbourhood and regional communities.

To maintain of transparency, the proposals are compiled into documents that are available on the SMED website, detailing not only the proposals and their objectives, but also the names of *proponentes* (those who proposed each one), including names of schools and in some cases individuals. The representatives who are present vote on the proposals. The resulting outcomes of the CCE represent the policy that will govern schools for the next four years. The rationale for its establishment is that '[the Constituent] Congress of Education was developed by the Popular Administration to guarantee that even the centralized action that originates in the SMED is itself based on democratic decision-making. One of the central aims of the SMED is to guarantee that the decentralized local School Councils operate to achieve the larger goals for the education of the city, but with due recognition that these larger goals were themselves forged through a democratic process' (Gandin and Apple 2004, 181).

The first CCE took place in 1995, with CCEs conducted every four years thereafter to ensure that the Citizen School continues to address local priorities. Through participatory deliberation, 700 delegates constructed ninety-eight principles that were to be implemented in the reform during that first CCE. SMED members were not allowed to vote, in order to preserve citizen-focused decision-making. Three priorities for education guided them (Gandin 2002): democratization of access to school, democratization of knowledge, and democratization of management.

Several significant policy directions arose out of the first CCE. First, a fundamental change was made to school organization. Rather than the traditional system of grades (e.g., first grade, second grade, and so forth), school was reorganized into cycles of formation, whereby students progress through three cycles of three years each: childhood, pre-adolescence, and adolescence. This way, students are grouped with others in their age group and stay with that cohort for a three-year block. This configuration was established to address the high failure rate, which led to students being held back into classes with students much younger than they. Grouping students by age was intended to motivate all students while 'fight[ing] against the common sense idea that there are prerequisites to be learned without which it is impossible to apprehend the forms of knowledge in the next line' (Gandin 2002, 138). Azevedo (2000, 129) explains that this approach 'sees learning as a process in which preparatory periods do not exist; instead there is a permanent process of development.'

The resulting CCE policies changed the way that curriculum expectations are understood. Rather than traditional subject disciplines, curriculum is organized into thematic complexes. Interdisciplinary curriculum areas (social expression, biological, chemical and physical sciences, socio-historic, and logic-mathematical) bring thematic complexes to life: 'The starting point for the construction of curricular knowledge is the culture(s) of the communities themselves, not only in terms of content but in perspective as well. The whole educational process is aimed at inverting previous priorities and instead serving the historically oppressed and excluded groups' (Gandin and Apple 2002b, 267).

The thematic complexes provide very general guidelines for curriculum policy. Rather than having specific learning outcomes (as we see in the Ontario curriculum), thematic complexes create a starting point for instructional topics to be identified at the school level. This ensures that the curriculum addresses things that are meaningful to students and to the local (neighbourhood) community. The SMED requires that 'knowledge areas' address questions such as *why? for what?* and *how?* (Gandin 2002, 143). The use of 'the Decalogue' (a ten-step guide to curriculum construction described below) and the emphasis on problematizing assumptions ensures that inequities are not reproduced, but rather are addressed explicitly in the school environment through curriculum inquiry.

Phase 4: Elaborating the Internal Regulations for Schools Locally

This phase represents mobilization of the principles created in the CCE through participation via school councils. Specific curricula in Porto Alegre are formulated at the school level through school council deliberations, which involve input from parents, students, support staff, and teachers on an ongoing basis. Decisions are based on direction from the CCE. Thus, schools cover the same curricular themes, but how they bring those themes to life through examples, projects, and resources varies on the basis of unique needs and characteristics of the school community.

To equip participants with the technical knowledge necessary to carry out this aspect of curriculum policy formulation, the SMED offers two supports: municipal meetings of the school councils, and a permanent program of continuing education for participants inside schools. According to Azevedo (2000), the municipal meetings provide a forum to share the types of knowledge necessary to manage schools. At the same time, they allow the explanation of the differences of interests between the various groups, particularly students, teachers, and parents. School councils are encouraged to follow ten steps, nicknamed 'The Decalogue,' in the construction of the curriculum (Gandin 2002, 140–1):

1. Acknowledge and study the context of where the school is situated through participatory action research by the school collective, usually led by teachers
2. Read and analyse research findings; select the statements that are significant and representative of the community's aspirations, interests, conceptions, and cultures
3. Define a 'thematic complex' by determining the phenomenon that organizes the most significant information and research
4. Elaborate principles of the knowledge areas within the thematic complex selected
5. Collectively select and broaden a conceptual matrix for the curriculum

6. Create a graphic representation of the complex
7. Elaborate work plans in every knowledge area, cycle, and years in the cycle
8. Circulate plans among participants and compose interdisciplinary strategies within and among cycles
9. Evaluate and periodically replan through systematic meetings by cycles, years in the cycle, and area
10. At the end of the cycle, problematize the lived thematic complex in order to find the focus of the next thematic complex

Using the principles outlined in 'The Decalogue,' school councils bring the thematic complexes to life, making decisions on specifically how these complexes are approached in their communities. These important decisions are made through discussion and dialogue with members of the school community – teachers, parents, administrators, and students. Specific examples are discussed in the Outcomes section later in this chapter.

Institutional Culture: Inverting the Structure

In 1993, the new secretary of education looked at ways to restructure the SMED to establish a connection between progressive educational goals, the participatory policymaking structure to come, and the institutional structure of the SMED itself. To do this, the SMED had to 'invert the logic and create administrative structures that were subordinate to pedagogical and political needs' by dismantling the existing 'vertical structure' (Gandin 2002, 124). The resulting structure, enacted in 1994, had two administrative units within the SMED: Pedagogical and Administrative Supervisions (Gandin 2002). Two new entities were created to increase the level of decentralization and lead to a more participatory approach to education policy and administration. First, a centralized multidisciplinary team was created to offer guidance to schools on pedagogical issues. Second, institutional action groups (IAGs) were responsible for the relationships between schools and communities, mobilizing school communities in their efforts to create participation. This structure changed in 1997, after conflicts arose between multidisciplinary teams and IAGs. To address the problems, multidisciplinary teams were eliminated, and the IAG role was enhanced to include subject expertise (Gandin 2002).

IAG advisors spend time in schools each week, serving as liaisons between the SMED and the schools. As well, IAGs serve an accountability function, ensuring that schools enact the policy agreed upon by the school councils. Gandin (2002) explains that conflicts arise when IAG advisors do not permit changes to a school council's plans – even when changes are small and sometimes warranted. The rationale for this particular IAG function, in the words of the secretary of education, is, 'We are really serious about the rights of the students. The schools cannot claim their autonomy to disrespect the rights of the students. We are a public institution and therefore we have a social obligation to guarantee that we respect the rights that were achieved with a lot of struggle. If the students have the right to X number of hours of classes, they will have to have this amount of hours' (Gandin 2002, 232).

To address the need for technical expertise required to participate in school council, municipal meetings provide a forum for school council members to learn in order to 'enhance both the quantity and quality of the participation of parents' (Gandin 2002, 131). The municipal meetings, open to parents, teachers, students, and staff, allow individuals and groups to share ideas and information about education.

The SMED's guiding institutional values place priority on including participants' perspectives. This commitment to inclusion of perspectives and allowing citizens to make ultimate education policy decisions guides how the SMED approaches enactment of new policies. For instance, while Gandin (2002) reports some resistance among teachers (such as organizing their classes, curriculum, and evaluation in the same way they had prior to the new policy enactment, thus rejecting school council decisions) during the enactment of new policies, the secretary of education describes how the SMED tailored the enactment process to address needs of teachers who struggled with reforms: 'We respected [teachers'] pace; they demanded more time, we gave them more time; they asked for more meetings specific to discuss this, we offered the meetings; they wanted more support from our advisors, we offered them that too' (Gandin 2002, 224–5). Certainly the SMED could benefit from supporting teachers to encourage acceptance of the new policies. Rather than pushing acceptance with punitive measures, the SMED focused on accommodation through longer timelines and additional learning opportunities via meetings to explain processes.

Citizen Engagement: It's Our Policy to Make

In Porto Alegre, policy formulation processes flow directly out of the ingrained principles and practices of the OP. However, the lens through which education is viewed in Porto Alegre is not necessarily consistent with the Brazilian federal conception of educational purpose. As described earlier, Brazilian national education goals and policy papers tend to reflect a neoliberal stance (Gandin 2002; Myers 2005). Gandin attributes some of the Workers' Party success in establishing the Citizen School within a broader neoliberal policy context: 'Because neoliberal policies cannot merely be imposed, but must also win the consent of agents involved in education, spaces are created where it is possible to construct alternative practices. The Citizen School rearticulates these spaces and turns them into opportunities for its project . . . it uses spaces and gaps created by neoliberal policies and creeds to launch an alternative project' (Gandin 2006, 220–1).

Certain terms often associated with neoliberal education discourses (and that appear in the Brazilian national policy statements) are reframed locally through education reform in Porto Alegre (Gandin 2002, 2007; Gandin and Apple 2002a). Specifically, autonomy and decentralization are reconceptualized by the popular movement, though these terms continue to face struggles over meaning. While decentralization and the accompanying autonomy given to states and municipalities may have been intended as a neoliberal strategy, as Gandin asserts, the Workers' Party seized the opportunity to 'construct a system that does not have to follow any federal curricular directives' (Gandin 2006, 221) by applying the OP process to all aspects of elementary schooling. By contrast, other Brazilian jurisdictions 'complained about the neo-liberal effects of decentralization which gave them more responsibility without more resources' (Gandin 2006, 221). In doing so, Porto Alegre transformed a system that might have retained the status quo to a new and unique formation of education, one that emphasizes the municipal values of democratic citizenship.

While accountability is another concept often associated with neoliberalism, as discussed in greater detail in chapter 2, Porto Alegre's reframes it in the education policy formulation context. Though there is accountability in the national education policy (for example, standardized testing and reporting mechanisms), the SMED identified a different kind of accountability for the Citizen School project. At all levels of education policy formulation in Porto Alegre, all policy actors (including the SMED) are accountable for addressing democratic decision-making criteria. The SMED utilizes the IAGs to ensure this occurs. As well, the formation and use of the CCE provides an additional mechanism for democratic accountability – that is, ensuring that the SMED indeed addresses the needs and decisions of the participants in policy formulation.

Reframing the Lexicon, Summits, and Dialogue

The literature suggests that the citizens of Porto Alegre were generally in favour of educational change (see Gandin 2002, 2007, and the various works of Gandin and Apple). The high level of dropouts, coupled with poor levels of literacy, suggest that Porto Alegre's schools were not serving its citizens and certainly not contributing to the achievement of participatory parity. For instance, a teacher interviewed by Luis Armando Gandin (2002, 224) stated, 'We all know that the traditional school was not offering quality education for our students. The change was necessary.'

With a perceived public need for change, Porto Alegre used symbolic language to frame the solution, disrupting the neoliberal rhetoric operating at the federal level, which I just described. First and foremost, the move to name the project the Citizen School was symbolic. As Gandin (2006, 222) explains, 'Speaking of citizen as opposed to client or consumer is a conscious move to insert political words in the discussion.' As well, some of the research identifies a conceptual concern about common sense – particularly significant to a comparative analysis with Ontario where a Common Sense Revolution drove reform efforts. Gandin (2002) explains the dual meaning of *common sense* in Porto Alegre. On one hand, there is a positive conception of common sense, as described by Santos (1998), which refers to the cultural knowledge of the community and of students. The terms *popular knowledge* and *community wisdom* better represent the positive conception of common sense (Gandin 2002). On the other hand, a negative connotation of common sense appears throughout Gandin's interviews and document analysis. This second conception of common sense is associated with a 'distorted vision' or 'false consciousness' (Gandin 2002, 221) of how things are, one at odds with critical thought. He reports a perceived 'need of replacing common sense with more politicized and critical thought' (218). Gandin cites several examples of rejection of the term *common sense* among participants and in SMED texts.[6] Contradiction and confusion about the two conceptions of common sense, Gandin (221) warns, 'can indirectly help to reproduce the undesirable model of the teacher who has the "right" knowledge and the student who is there only to absorb.' In response, Porto Alegre's education policy reflects a rejection of common sense in the latter conception of the term.

Input at Many Levels

The absence of specific Porto Alegre's education policy actors' narratives makes it difficult to provide a full picture of the design dynamics at play, particularly with respect to local curriculum formulation. While individual experiences in participation most certainly vary, evidence presented in the literature suggests that there are many opportunities for citizens to be involved at the neighbourhood, regional CCE level in Porto Alegre. A Porto Alegre teacher who participated in case study research describes participation in curricular formation at the school level this way: 'The community participated a lot, it was really integrated, since the school was an achievement of the Participatory Budget, so it has mobilized them and brought them to the discussions, so they also wanted the school they achieved to be a different school, that fulfilled their expectations and that they desired that their children experienced life inside the school' (Diehl et al. 2006, 3).

The evidence further suggests that citizens' involvement in formulating education policy builds on their knowledge, skills, and experiences acquired through the historical OP process in the community. The participants' experiences as described in this chapter suggest that the culture of participatory policymaking in Porto Alegre is consistent with Chantal Mouffe's conception of agonism, whereby participants respect one another's right to participate, even though they may not agree with each other's positions. As well, disputes over issues and prioritization are ultimately settled by voting, particularly at the CCE. This suggests that Porto Alegre's policy process acknowledges that consensus cannot always be reached – though compromise is achieved through social learning when rival positions are given due consideration and deliberation is able to take place. For instance, another teacher interviewed describes how, at the school level, deliberations took place over how to address the problem of dropouts in that school: 'In March ... we took a month to study the [proposals] and building our school proposal ... there were some teachers and the SMED that defended the non-retention, and that was really discussed, there was consensus, and that was achieved in the time of the regiment by the rest of the community' (Diehl et al. 2006, 3–4). This example illustrates how, at least within this school, time allotted for the discussion of issues is important to members of the school community (in this case, a month for the discussion of dropouts). The cyclical nature of the policy process – which includes school council elections every two years and CCEs every four years – ensures repeated renegotiation of priorities and directions.

Outcomes: Creating Flexibility, Building Citizen Capacity, Increasing School Participation

While the education policy process in Porto Alegre described here addresses aspects of elementary education including budgeting, school management, evaluation, and curriculum, the scope of my research limits the discussion to matters of the curriculum. By creating a two-tiered curriculum process – where thematic complexes are mandated by the results of the CCE (the top tier), but elaborated upon and conceptualized at the school level (the second tier) – Porto Alegre's curriculum policy contains built-in flexibility, which allows school councils to shape what is taught in schools to address the needs of students and the local community. Moreover, the broader community identifies local needs (not education 'experts' alone). Educators work with students and parents to ensure that the curriculum is relevant. To do this, school councils collect and analyse stories from the community, then identify the most significant words to determine priorities (Azevedo and Schugurensky 2005). This ensures that popular knowledge and local priorities play a central role in a school's curriculum. From these, key concepts are chosen to relate the focus of curriculum to the priorities emerging, which are connected to the thematic complexes (Azevedo and Schugurensky 2005). The thematic complexes are social expression, biological and physical sciences, socio-historic, and logic-mathematical (Gandin 2002). The use of an example of the Socio-Historic Curricular Thematic Complex demonstrates how thematic complexes are brought to life within the school.

As the example illustrates, thematic complexes have the capacity to address social justice, as envisioned by Nancy Fraser (2007, 2010) and Landon Beyer (1993). The use of thematic complexes in Porto Alegre's curriculum policy emerges out of the theoretical work of Moisei Pistrak (complexes that were featured in soviet schools) and Paulo Freire (subject generators) (Pistóia 2001). Thematic complexes allow flexibility. When coupled with principles outlined in 'The Decalogue' to apply thematic complexes in schools, justice aims are directly prioritized. As a result, those members of society who usually are marginalized when it comes to 'official knowledge' reflected in curriculum policy gain the

Socio-Historic Curricular Thematic Complex

One of Porto Alegre's schools organized its thematic complex in the socio-historic area in order to examine questions directly linked to the interests and problems of the community.

At the centre of the thematic complex was the issue of the community's standard of living.

Three sub-themes were listed: rural exodus, social organization, and property. In the rural exodus sub-theme, the issues reflected the origin of the community – living now in a favela, but originally from the rural areas. This is a common story in the favelas, where people who had nothing in the rural areas came to the cities only to find more exclusion.

In these sub-themes, the issues discussed were migration movements, overpopulation of the cities, an 'unqualified' working force, and marginalization. In the sub-theme social organization, the issues are distributed in terms of temporal, political, spatial, and socio-cultural relations. The issues, again, represent important questions in the organization of the community: the excessive and uncritical pragmatism of some in the associations, the connections with the neighbourhood associations and the OP, and cultural issues such as religiosity, body expression, African origins, dance groups, and 'samba schools.' In the third sub-theme – property – the issues were literally linked to the situation of the families in the favela, living in illegal lots with no title, having to cope with the lack of infrastructure, while fighting for their rights as citizens.

This example shows the real transformation that is occurring in the curriculum of the schools in Porto Alegre. The students are not studying history or social and cultural studies through books that never address the real problems and interests they have. Through the thematic complexes, the students learn history by beginning with the historical experience of their families. They study important social and cultural content by focusing on and valorizing their own cultural manifestations. A real shift is occurring, because the focus is not on the 'core/official' knowledge organized around dominant class and race visions of the world, but on the real problems and interests of the students and the community. It is important to note that these students will ultimately still learn the history of Brazil and the world, 'high' culture, etc., but this will be seen through different lenses. Their culture will not be forgotten in order for them to learn high-status culture. Rather, by understanding their situation and their culture and valuing it, these students will be able to simultaneously learn and have the chance to transform their situation of exclusion.

Source: Adapted from Gandin and Apple (2004). Used by permission.

opportunity to have their perspectives and voices heard. In this way, the two-tiered curriculum policy process fosters social justice in education. Equally important is the type of learning that takes place in schools, described by Jose Clovis de Azevedo, in which there is 'consideration of the student as a real, concrete, historic subject, bearer of culture and of wisdoms that can't be artificially abstracted in the process of knowledge construction. This implies overcoming the conception of knowledge as a thing, ready, finished, disdained to the culture context, in the life of the student subject, that can be transferred to those who know and those who don't know' (Azevedo 2007, 31). As Azevedo illustrates in this passage, Citizen School curriculum construction is very different from the traditional, 'official' knowledge contained in curriculum policy documents in most jurisdictions, including Ontario. This is a conscious move away from outcomes-based learning that requires students to be 'right' or 'wrong.' In this way, students are active participants in learning, since they engage with and construct knowledge to be relevant to them and their communities.

However, students are not the only citizens who learn within the broader Citizen School process. Participation in the education process provides an education in itself – another venue (beyond the OP) for the citizens of Porto Alegre to learn about one another and about this particular policy area. Moira Wilkinson (2007) found that school council members are aware of various learnings that arise from their participation. For example, a parent member describes her experience of learning from school council meetings: 'I get to learn, because everything for me is a lesson, about learning ... I keep learning and sometimes, I just listen, to learn. We are learning, you know? Because I was never on the Council [before], so I'm learning a lot. It's more about learning, we sort of stay listening more so we can learn' (Wilkinson 2007, 189).

Finally, Porto Alegre provides additional supports for citizen to learn about educational issues. The SMED produces booklets called *Cadernos*

Pedagógicos. Each issue contains essays written by individuals on topics pertinent to education policy, offering a variety of perspectives.
Similarly, Porto Alegre hosts a conference, the World Education Forum,
regularly. While the World Education Forum is open to presenters
and participants from outside of Porto Alegre, it is another important,
SMED-organized opportunity for citizens to learn about education,
including an international perspective.

In addition to the benefits to those who participate in policy formulation and these learning opportunities, recent data suggest that
one outcome of the Citizen School is greater student success. As
described earlier in this chapter, rates of non-completion and failure in Porto Alegre and Brazil were high. Gandin (2006) reports
that between 1988 and 2002, Porto Alegre's enrolment in fundamental education increased by 232 per cent, while the national average
increased by only 22 per cent. As well, the number of public schools
increased by 126 per cent – with the majority of new schools built in
the favelas of Porto Alegre. The dropout rate in fundamental education fell from over 9 per cent in 1989 to 1 per cent of students in 2003
(Gandin 2006).

Challenges and Critiques of Citizen
School Policy Formulation

As I described in this chapter, Porto Alegre has achieved considerable success in instituting participatory approaches to policy production, and received international attention for those accomplishments.
However, as with any process, the policy production in Porto Alegre
experienced its share problems and challenges. In this section, I will
discuss some of those challenges, as well as critiques.

First, and despite the potentially progressive structure and curriculum policy content, various members of the school community resisted
enactment of the new model of schooling (Gandin 2002). Some parents
resisted the new structure of schooling, with questions: 'Where are my
son/daughter's grades? Why does s/he not have his/her notebook full of
content that I recognize?' (Gandin 2002, 241).

Teachers also resisted. Some were reluctant to 'create a classroom
environment based on involvement with knowledge connection rather
than fear of low grades,' because this required them to give up the lever
of power offered by controlling students through grading (Gandin
2002, 223). Nevertheless, Gandin observes that the thematic complex

approach 'has been producing excellent results in terms of the dialogue that it establishes between the culture of the community and the knowledge offered by the school. According to the SMED, this is happening even in the schools who did not easily accept the change. In fact I talked to some teachers who initially resisted the thematic complex and now embrace it as a method of connecting with the communities and forcing themselves to study their own areas again' (2002, 223–4). To ensure that schools enact the changes required by the policy and appearing in their own school plans, the IAGs serve a 'policing' function in which they report back to the SMED. As well, the IAGs monitor school council activity to ensure that decisions made adhere to the principles of democratic decision-making.

Second, some research critiques the level of citizen inclusion within school councils. Moira Wilkinson's 2007 research on women's participation in Porto Alegre school councils reveals some problematic aspects. The process of election of a maximum number of school council members, and delegates for regional and municipal meetings, limits opportunities for participation. She also reports that in at least some school councils, administrators encourage certain parents to nominate themselves for election to the council – and some parents do not have the courage to nominate themselves without external encouragement. Finally, she observes that, particularly among women, responsibilities in the home can deter participation in school council work.

Discussion and Contrast

As an analytic foil, the preceding description of Porto Alegre's policy production process reveals a different approach to curriculum policy development during the 1990s in stark contrast to Ontario's. The differences begin with how each jurisdiction conceptualizes educational purpose. While the two statements of educational purpose in Porto Alegre and Ontario contain a few commonalities (e.g., Ontario emphasized the need for access to education, while in Porto Alegre education is stated as a right), these statements reflect distinct differences in tone and educational intent. Ontario focused on preparation for the workforce and 'responsibilities of citizenship.' By contrast, Porto Alegre's statements refer to the central role that education can play in overcoming exploitation and building a radical democracy, and dealing with social justice explicitly. These statements openly acknowledge the political role of education. By contrast, some Ontario policy actors emphasized their goals of value-neutrality, suggesting that education is or can be apolitical. The emphasis on value-neutral and standardized curriculum ignored the very real issues of inequality in Ontario, thus minimizing the importance of social justice education.

When we look at the approach to curriculum policy development as it relates to broader education policy reforms, a difference emerges. In Ontario, the development of curriculum policy occurred in isolation from other education policy initiatives – though all were guided by the Common Sense Revolution, which provided the broad vision of the reforms as a whole. That is to say, while in Ontario all aspects of educa-tion were reformed, the actual policy formulation of each (curriculum, educational finance, etc.) occurred in isolation. By contrast, in Porto Alegre, education policy was developed as a whole, and curriculum was not separated from school management, evaluation, and cooperation.

A difference emerges in policy actor inclusiveness. Whereas Ontario relied on inclusion of policy elites and a highly centralized, top-down, and politicized decision-making process, Porto Alegre took a more democratic alternative to involve citizens in all phases of development on a voluntary basis. Writing teams who made successful bids created Ontario's curriculum policy centrally, thus eliminating the potential for many to participate in curriculum policy deliberation. The Ministry of Education limited Ontarians' opportunities to participate in stake-holder consultations. There were some opportunities for individuals and groups to respond to draft documents posted in writing, but the degree to which Ontarians were aware of such opportunities is unclear. Even those policy actors who participated at the centre of the process did not necessarily nor universally feel that their points of view were considered by the decision-makers, and clearly some concerns voiced (e.g., the issue of streaming discussed in chapters 8 and 9) were not reflected in policy. The centrally produced curriculum documents were enacted in a top-down fashion. By contrast, Porto Alegre devel-oped criteria and organizers centrally (through using a participatory decision-making structure and voting at the CCE) and allowed elabora-tion of specifics at the school level, using the established criteria. The well-established OP framework paved the way for citizen capacity to participate in Porto Alegre. As such, Porto Alegre's political practice actually involves citizens – not elites selected by governments – and as such results in a 'thicker' conception of democracy.

Transparency was evident in Porto Alegre – ranging from the detailed proposals at the CCE, which included the names of groups or individuals who proposed them, to their universal availability through the SMED's website. By contrast, Ontario did not disclose the names of those who wrote curriculum policy, or the groups who participated in stakeholder consultations.

Most importantly, Porto Alegre demonstrated that a participatory public policy process in education that empowers active citizen participation is actually possible. The involvement of the most vulnerable citizens is consistent with Paulo Freire's philosophy: 'Truly, only the oppressed are able to conceive of a future totally distinct from their present, insofar as they arrive at a consciousness of a dominated class. The oppressors, as the dominating class, cannot conceive of the future unless it is the preservation of their present as oppressors. In this way, whereas the future of the oppressed consists in the revolutionary transformation of society, without which their liberation will not be verified, the oppressor's future consists in the simple modernization of society, which permits the continuation of class supremacy' (1972, 32).

This conception appears to be consistent with the critical-democratic ideal, though greater detail would be necessary to judge if that is so. This Brazilian experience of participatory democracy provides us with a vision of an alternative way of formulating education policy. Beyond creating more active citizens, Porto Alegre's curriculum policy process actually mobilized the population and put curricular decisions into the hands of the people, with as many as 60,000 participants. As Richard Hatcher points out, the process connects 'pedagogy and politics, the classroom and the wider society, social change and individual change' (Hatcher 2002).

Outcomes provide another area for discussion. I draw attention to two aspects of outcomes: policy text content and student outcomes. In Ontario, the result was highly prescriptive, standardized, and outcomes-based curriculum policy that was unilaterally enacted across the province, without accommodation of local needs and priorities. Through their standardization, these curriculum policy texts called for all students to meet the same expectations – regardless of individual or community diversity. As the evidence suggests, social justice was neither an official nor informal concern within Ontario's policy process. Porto Alegre's process involved a more bottom-up approach that required school-level decision-making about curriculum organization, content, and priorities within centrally established guidelines articulated through the thematic complexes. Social justice outcomes were explicitly stated and thus became part of the accountability framework that guided the policy formulation. The Porto Alegre approach's built-in flexibility allows schools to adapt curriculum to meet the needs of individual students and school communities: 'One of the most effective tools for resolving the frequent disconnect between the cultural and social frameworks of communities and schools is the use of educational thematic units, built around a central concern for the community ... These thematic units become a locally based and locally owned instrument designed to construct and distribute knowledge that is socially relevant for the educational community' (Fischman and McLaren 2000, 172).

As I explained, Ontario policy actors expressed concern about the lack of opportunity for non-university-bound students' success, which was confirmed by secondary data and statistics indicating higher failure and dropout rates among students. In Porto Alegre, particular attention was paid to inclusion in order to reduce the level of dropouts and increase student engagement. Data presented earlier in this chapter suggest that Porto Alegre's school enrolments increased, and students were succeeding at higher rates.

Finally, participants' civic learning provides another basis for comparison. In order to equip participants with the knowledge and skills to participate, Porto Alegre built citizen capacity to participate in educational decision-making through the CCE, regional meetings, and school council participation, as well as continuing education programs for those involved. Of course, there was an initial level of citizen capacity through the already established OP. While the data currently available are not sufficient to provide details about the content and structure of Porto Alegre's education policy deliberations, that the OP process appears to foster opportunities for agonistic exchange among participants.

By contrast, Ontario failed to provide concerted guidelines, education, or training for policy actors. As some of the Ontario policy actors interviewed for this research noted, they learned a great deal from their role in the process but would have benefited from additional, structured learning about the process of policymaking, as well as about content specifically.

The possibility of transferring Porto Alegre's successful policy-formulation processes to Ontario is alluring. Porto Alegre's experience awakens the hope that inclusive and democratic policymaking could be a viable alternative for other jurisdictions. Indeed, Porto Alegre achieved a relatively efficient and (relative to multi-million dollar contracts) inexpensive process comparable to Ontario's during the same timeframe. However, we see from the critiques of the OP presented earlier in this chapter that the participatory model had mixed success when applied in other jurisdictions. Contextual factors play an enormous role in the ability of a jurisdiction to successfully engage the public in policy formulation. There are some similarities between Ontario and Porto Alegre – centralized government and an over-arching neoliberal environment at various levels of government. However, Ontario has several unique characteristics that problematize a shift to participatory policymaking. These include an absence of existing citizen capacity, a bureaucracy shaped by NPM, and questionable levels of citizen engagement.

Concluding Comments

This chapter offered insight into a different approach to curriculum policy production, which serves as an analytic foil to the Ontario case study. Porto Alegre's process offers an alternative to conventional, government-driven policymaking, which characterized Ontario's education policy process during the 1990s, as well as that of other North American jurisdictions. This description of Porto Alegre's policy production illustrated features that conform to the critical-democratic ideal – though it represents but one of many possible ways in which policy production can be designed to address democracy through meaningful citizen engagement. Most notably, Porto Alegre highlights ways in which citizens can effectively reclaim their right to participation in the process in a way that is both efficient and leads to more socially just outcomes. The 'inverted' policymaking structure that led to the creation of Porto Alegre's Citizen School is rooted in the municipality's history of and collective capacity in participatory budgeting, which suggests that moving towards a more critically democratic model of policy production must start small and grow. Citizens learned over time, and, despite mistakes and challenges, they continued to refine the process. Citizens were not the only groups who had to engage in learning and reconceptualization of their democratic roles. Likewise, the government and bureaucracy had to shift their roles, moving from a more conventional decision-making role to that of civic educators and facilitators. While other research points to challenges in transferring this policy process to other jurisdictions, it is clear that movement towards critical-democratic policymaking is both possible and viable if the people have the will to push forward.

9   Conclusion

The debates about the curriculum that occur in a democracy at any given time will reveal both how that democracy interprets itself, and how that interpretation is being challenged and revised in order to bring into being a more genuinely democratic form of life than that which currently exists.

– Wilfred Carr 1998, 324

To make room for dissent and foster the institutions in which it can be manifested is vital for democracy.

– Chantal Mouffe 2000c, 150

Seeking to foster citizen engagement without political reform is a mug's game. The forces distancing citizens from conventional politics are far too powerful for that. In any case, it is not the duty of citizens to bend themselves to the needs of political institutions, but the responsibility of institutions and political leaders to adapt themselves to what their people require. What is more, that is good democratic practice; in a democracy, popular will is the foundation stone upon which good government is constructed.

– David Cameron 2002, 47

Ontario's Common Sense Revolution was a critical event in Canadian public policy and politics. It represented changes not only to policy content, but also to the way in which policy formulation occurred. While some have applauded the NPM style of policy production for its alleged efficiencies, this privatized approach represents a step away from democracy. Rather, the social evolution of policy production can be radicalized by rejecting traditional, representative democracy and demanding a participatory, critical-democratic approach. Such change, as Porto Alegre illustrates, is very real and very possible.

In this chapter, I explore the lessons learned from Ontario's education policy production during the Common Sense Revolution and look to those possibilities. The challenge facing the realization of critical-democratic policy production hinges on encouraging citizens to devise and demand structures and criteria that encourage policy actors to participate in ways consistent with critical-democratic ideals, even if they may not share those ideals. Such structures are akin to the rules of parliamentary activity and must include basic principles or values (such as inclusion) and accountability measures to ensure they are addressed. These structures serve as arenas for discourse and deliberation and must allow for civic learning. Finally, citizens must recognize the relationship between education and democracy. Education *for* democracy and democracy *in* education may provide the only hope for realizing the possibility of citizen demands for a different way of conceptualizing policy formulation, as we see in Porto Alegre. Democracy in schools must foster substantive social justice (as I outlined in chapter 1) and the exploration of alternative approaches to citizen involvement. To achieve real change in education policy process consistent with critical democracy, a number of considerations and features would be necessary, some of which I address in this chapter.

Documentation and Critique

This book provided both documentation and critique of an important moment in the evolution of Ontario's education policy production – but more importantly, it shed light on possibilities for a more democratic approach to public policy. Despite the shortcomings of the production process and policy texts from a critical-democratic perspective, Ontario's formulation of curriculum policy yielded some positive impacts on the policy actors who were involved, albeit many unintended. This point is important, because it illustrates the civic benefits of involvement and social learning. Policy actors tended to view the overall experience as a positive one that resulted in a great deal of learning – ranging from better understanding of government, to better understanding of and respect for rival positions. Policy actors' experiences and areas of personal learning varied, depending upon the type of involvement they had and the degree to which they had access to dialogue and exchange with others. Some aspects of policy actors' experience (learning from their opponents, engaging in dialogue) approached the type of agonistic deliberation consistent with the critical-democratic ideal, pointing to the very real possibility of agonistic exchanges, even within existing structures.

Changes to Ontario's broad public policy production process were evident in curriculum reform, as I have shown. Like so many other jurisdictions, Ontario experienced waves of educational change in decades preceding SSR. However, the scope, tone, and speed of reforms introduced by the Harris government under the Common Sense Revolution were unprecedented. Divisive actions and policy changes shook up the province and deliberately eliminated equity-focused policy and programs, thus reducing the degree to which Ontario engaged in socially just social policy. The environment surrounding educational reforms – including curriculum policy formulation – was nothing less than tumultuous, characterized by conflict with teachers. A fundamental shift in framing educational issues also occurred, with the introduction of business metaphors in which education was a 'business' whose 'customers' were parents and students. These reflected the prevailing neoliberal and neoconservative ideologies operating in the province. This framing defined the educational problems, and the solutions to them set the tone for curriculum policy production, which was characterized by neoliberal processes ranging from the NPM institutional culture within government, to the reliance on privatization to carry out policy functions.

While the process yielded positive gains of capacity and speed in policy production, these quantitative measures are far too narrow to address the many and less clear-cut criteria of democracy in process. While the privatization of policy functions is problematic, from a democratic perspective, certainly analysis by neoliberal criteria might yield a different conclusion. To be sure, the Ministry of Education was able to meet unthinkable time constraints in the production of policy texts; as well, the privatization undertaken allowed the ministry to compensate for a lack of internal capacity at least in part resulting from the NPM smaller government. However, when curriculum policy development is viewed as a political process characterized by dispute and negotiation, as envisioned by Walter Werner and Michael Apple, outsourcing fails to provide procedural opportunities to address the sorts of public conversation necessary to address tensions and conflict over what counts as knowledge. This is essential for a robust democratic policy process, and particularly for the contested terrain of curriculum.

My analysis suggests that, despite efforts to include stakeholders in the curriculum policy decisions, Ontario fell short of the critical-democratic ideal in its formulation. Chantal Mouffe's agonistic democracy, a central component in my elaboration of a critical-democratic policy process, relies upon the domestication of hostility into agonism, where participants view their opponents as adversaries (not enemies). It calls for the 'expression of dissent and institutions through which conflicts can be manifested' (Mouffe 2000c, 149). Ontario's curriculum policy formulation was grounded in neoliberal and neoconservative ideologies, with goals and processes that gave little or no explicit consideration of either critical democracy or agonism as features of the process.

Possibilities: Balancing Idealism and Realism

As Benjamin Levin and J. Anthony Riffel (1994) remind us, idealism must be balanced by realism if any progress is to be made. While my work here presents a prima face case for critical democracy as an ideal, and I argue that education and democracy ought to co-exist, I recognize that this view is not shared by all. From a realist perspective, the absence of these shared ideals poses some challenges to fundamental changes to education policy formulation and policy outcomes. However, some of the positive gains experienced by policy actors and my discussion of policymaking elsewhere suggest that idealism in indeed warranted – that citizens indeed have the interest, passion, and potential to engage in critical-democratic policy production.

The process undertaken by Porto Alegre offers possibilities for a different approach to policy formulation, as well as outcomes. This is not to say that Porto Alegre's approach is necessarily or easily transferable elsewhere. As I illustrated, attempts at similar processes in other jurisdictions have met with mixed results. This reflects need for a judicious approach to policy borrowing (see, for example, Levin 1998b; Halpin and Troyna 1995; James and Lodge 2003; Phillips 2003, 2006), since each jurisdiction poses unique characteristics and diverse citizen needs and priorities. However, this example underscores the fact that, if a government or a populace is serious about democratic inclusion and education reform, different ways of approaching policy formulation are not only possible, but potentially effective.

The literature documents cases of successful participatory policy processes mainly in municipalities (see, for example, Schneider and Ingram 1997; Button and Mattson 1999; Weeks 2000; Baiocchi 2001; Fields and

Feinberg 2001; Fung and Wright 2001), but to date neither critical-democratic nor agonistic approaches to policy formulation[1] has been investigated or described in significant detail. These cases of successful participatory policy processes illustrate that it is both feasible and possible to involve citizens in policymaking. Applying a critical-democratic model of policy formulation to a jurisdiction like Ontario requires reconsideration of the issues that can arise within societal, institutional, and policy formulation contexts, as I described in the case study analysis. Because the process design possibilities at all stages are numerous, and because, as James Bohman (1998) points out, participatory policymaking is not unified, a great deal of investigation remains to be done if we are to construct a viable, open-ended process.

The Case for Participation in Policy Production

There are several rationales for a more inclusive policy process. First, as I have argued throughout this book, meaningful citizen participation in policy formulation is essential to achieving a critical-democratic ideal. However, increased participation also makes political sense. Creating policy in a way that is perceived as fair has been empirically shown to lead to acceptance of outcomes as legitimate by citizens (see, for example, the meta-analysis by Tyler 2000[2] and the evidence presented in chapter 1) – thus a more democratic process can have self-serving ends for governments.

Second, increased participation has direct benefits to the participants involved. This research revealed how participation leads to civic learning and a sense of community as policy actors interact and learn about one another's perspectives, resulting in social learning. At the most basic level, however, policy actors in this study agreed that some form of preparation for participation in policy formulation would have been beneficial. This is consistent with Porto Alegre's experience in which citizens must learn to participate in deliberation, as well as in research reported by John Dryzek (2009). Consideration of the development of materials to assist those who participate in consultations should be undertaken by ministries. As well, infusing civic skills (ideally those associated with agonistic forms of exchange) into K–12 curriculum policy documents would ensure that citizens received some degree of preparation for participation in policy processes (consistent with the positions of Dryzek 2009 and Ruitenberg 2009). I discuss this in greater detail later in this chapter.

Third, participation can help overcome potentially dangerous stereotypes and rhetoric – very real among policy actors – which undermine agonistic deliberation and thus the critical-democratic ideal. These led to actors' dismissal of rival positions in Ontario. For example, the quote from one consultation participant who expected that his rivals would be 'tub thumpers' illustrates the sort of attitudes that some policy actors held during their involvement. However, once engaged in face-to-face discussion, some policy actors claimed that they were pleasantly surprised to overcome their stereotypes after having had a chance to interact with rivals. This anecdotal evidence suggests that venues for public deliberation can overcome these problems and this sort of dehumanization of opponents or rivals in the process, and points to the possibility of truly agonistic exchanges where the other is viewed as an adversary, not enemy.

Fourth, given the predominant neoliberal environment in many Western jurisdictions including Ontario (as I described in chapter 3), a more radical approach to democracy is necessary to overcome legitimacy problems associated with public policy. Communicative and collaborative approaches are simply not sufficient to confront neoliberalization. Instead, counter-hegemonic approaches concerned with addressing (rather than neutralizing) power imbalances are required. Critical-democratic policy production, because of its reliance on agonistic deliberation, provides a fruitful approach to achieve this (Purcell 2009).

Finally, on the basis of experiences of other jurisdictions who have adopted such approaches, participatory policy production can be both efficient and cost effective. Governments and bureaucrats might be interested in looking to Porto Alegre as an example of how a jurisdiction could move toward a model of greater and more meaningful citizen involvement for procedural frameworks that rely on an efficient cycle.

Role of Citizens in Reclaiming Their Right to Participate

Despite the secondary data I presented in chapter 6 suggesting some degree of political cynicism and apathy among Ontarians, there is potential to reinvigorate and re-engage them into political life. Scattered efforts in Ontario and in Canada aimed to engage in more participatory policymaking and decision-making. Examples include Toronto Community Housing (2005), which actually loosely based its model on Porto Alegre's OP, and efforts by the Liberal Party of Canada to utilize new media to engage party members across Canada in setting political priorities. At the time of writing, the terms of this pilot project are being negotiated. These attest to government interest in revisiting citizen engagement and involvement, and hints at public interest in reclaiming the right to participate. Like Ontario, Porto Alegre's societal context described in chapter 8 was also characterized by apathy and non-participation prior to the introduction of the OP. However, once Porto Alegrans were provided with opportunities for meaningful engagement after they made such demands, and developed the requisite democratic skills and capacities to participate, participation rapidly increased. The example of Porto Alegre also illustrates the power that citizens have to advocate for substantive change to governance and policymaking. The enthusiasm reported by those interviewed for this research offers some indication that there may be interest in greater participation in Ontario, though a lack of opportunity to participate in policy results in this interest remaining concealed.

Ontarians must first wholeheartedly buy into the idea of participatory policy formulation, and, like Porto Alegrans, demand it. To achieve the critical-democratic ideal, citizens and government alike must share a commitment to social justice – in process and policy outcomes. As Porto Alegre illustrates, a commitment to participation builds over time, especially in an environment of political apathy or government distrust: one cannot expect a successful first attempt at critical-democratic policy formulation. For instance, building the civic skills necessary to participate takes time and effort, as it did in Porto Alegre. As well, until citizens see the results of their peers' participation, they may not be motivated to participate. Thus, if Ontario were to engage in critical-democratic policymaking, it would be necessary to start small, with a single policy issue, and with the expectation that participation might be poor at the outset. As the process progressed, Ontarians would need to carefully consider strategies to include a wider representation of citizens in order to be inclusive. Such strategies would entail identifying which groups are under-represented and marginalized, and engaging in specific outreach to include them.

Inverting the Role of Government and Bureaucrats

To achieve critical-democratic policy formulation, the government and ministries would have to accept a revised role in policymaking, not unlike Porto Alegre's inverted structure. First, bureaucrats' roles would have to change; instead of exercising their existing role in providing advice to government on substantive matters, they would become facilitators of citizen learning and of deliberation. Their role would have to include the creation of educational opportunities for citizens to acquire civic skills and to learn about technical issues related to policy area(s) under consideration. Such educational opportunities would have to take place before a critical-democratic policy process commences, so that citizens were prepared for deliberation. Bureaucrats would need to accept a change in their role from decision-makers to facilitators, similar to the transformation that occurred in Porto Alegre, Brazil. This would require a surrender of power traditionally held within governments and their institutions. However, unless power is redistributed, true citizen participation in public policy cannot be realized. Without substantive action resulting from citizens' input, deliberation and agonistic exchanges become meaningless.

Appropriate procedures must also be developed for policy formulation, while privatization of policy formulation as a profit-making enterprise must be avoided. As I emphasized earlier, a critical-democratic policy process must be phased in, beginning with one policy area, in order to build citizens' capacity for effective participation, and gradually be expanded to different policy areas. Initially, reasonable timeframes for deliberation would need to be established by the government to ensure that the critical-democratic policy process contributes to the solution of policy problems as required. Then guidelines or rules for civil conduct would need to be established and agreed upon, as I laid out at the beginning of this book and also as envisioned by Simona Goi in her 2005 research.

An important implication surrounds the concept of agonism. While many have called attention to agonism as an ideal form of deliberation for public discourse and policy formulation (Mouffe 1997, 2000a, 2000b, 2005; Goi 2005; Crowder 2006; among others), the structures, institutions, and conditions necessary to achieve agonism remain unclarified, as I discussed in chapter 1. Along the lines of the work presented here, some empirical work examines and critiques existing arenas for public discourse against an ideal of agonism (for example, Pløger 2004, Goi 2005). Others such as Lincoln Dahlberg (2001, 2007) and Peter Dahlgren (2005) postulate ways in which information and communication technologies engage new modes of agonism. Despite this emerging body of work, a conceptual framework has not evolved to describe conditions and criteria that might facilitate agonism. Further development of such a conceptual framework would contribute to the growing interest in this approach to critical-democratic participation.

Without fundamental shifts to bureaucracy at the institutional level, critical-democratic policy processes that include agonism cannot be realized. Indeed, 'to respect and work with agonism is processually possible, but requires a political and planning ethos we yet have to develop' (Pløger 2004, 88). The structure of policy production must ensure that Ontarians from all regions of the province have opportunities to participate. A multi-tiered approach (similar to Porto Alegre's deliberations at the neighbourhood, regional, and municipal levels, with votes at the end of each, and with elected representatives moving forward to the next round) might be adapted to suit the province. Careful government oversight and/or intervention would likely be necessary in the first iterations to ensure that participants were engaging in authentic and agonistic deliberation, and to discourage undesirable strategies such as clientelism and co-optation. A point system (similar to Porto Alegre's) might be used to assign weight to proposals that move forward and to reward appropriate conduct in deliberations. While voting and a point system may appear to be a form of representative (as opposed to critical) democracy, the process of agonistic exchange leading up to a vote changes its nature. As well, Chantal Mouffe's agonistic ideal calls for adopting temporary solutions until the next time the policy problem is considered. A voting system might also contribute to a degree of efficiency necessary for the critical-democratic policy process to result in timely recommendations. With these possibilities for change in mind, the subsections that follow suggest theoretical implications arising from Ontario's experience and Porto Alegre's success, areas for further research, and implications for praxis.

Finally, a government serious about involving citizens in policy formulation must consider ways in which they can help citizens acquire the requisite skills and dispositions to be meaningfully engaged in agenda-setting and policy production (recognizing that citizens must have developmental opportunities to acquire requisite civic and substantive issue expertise). Citizens must acquire a basic understanding of the arenas available for public discourse, the importance of respect for rivals and their respective positions, an understanding of power, a recognition that consensus is not possible, the ability to express oneself in a public venue, and technical understanding of policy areas. As in Porto Alegre, such learning might be accomplished best through practice – and likely would require multiple opportunities over time for the citizenry to learn. Schools would also play a critical role in addressing this type of learning, which I discuss later in this chapter.

Tensions between Bureaucracy and Democracy: A Shared Commitment to Democracy as a New Accountability

In addition to embracing values associated with critical-democratic policy formulation, both citizens and the government must share a commitment to democracy as a form of accountability if we are to achieve the ideals set out in chapter 1. There are varied conceptions of accountability in the literature. Indeed, accountability poses two questions: accountable to whom and for what? The scope and meaning of accountability extends in numerous directions – ranging from being called to account for one's actions, to institutional control of individuals, to outcomes stemming from those behaviours. Accountability can be understood within two broad categories to organize the multitude of its meanings: a technical-managerial form of accountability that depends on measurement, and a more general meaning that depends on responsibility, carrying connotations of answerability (Biesta 2004, 234).

Helen Ingram argues that institutional structures – especially governments – must be accountable for representing democratic values in processes, including inclusiveness and diversity (Ingram 2000). Such accountability is crucial to ensure democracy in governance and in policy formulation. Similarly, the critical-democratic ideal calls for accountability for an inclusive policy formulation process and for curriculum policy outcomes that reflect the ideals of a critical democracy (inclusive, focused on social justice, and reflecting democracy *in* education and education *for* democracy).

While accountability was certainly a priority during Ontario's curriculum policy formulation, it was a narrow, managerial form, rather than accountability to socially just and democratic practice. While policy actors described multiple conceptions of accountability about their own role in the process,[3] they failed to articulate a conception of critical-democratic accountability, either in process or product. That is, policy actors did not identify any perceived accountability to ensure that the process was inclusive, or reflected aims concerned with (critical) democracy in education (e.g., civic learning and a commitment to social justice).

To truly conform to the critical-democratic ideal, explicit accountability for democratic inclusiveness and social justice would need to replace – or complement, at the very least – the managerial form, and as demonstrated by the curriculum policy process in Porto Alegre. Accountability played a central role in Ontario's curriculum policy production. James, a participant in stakeholder consultations, said that the task of curriculum reform was 'based on an entirely straightforward concept of accountability' in that producing a new set of more prescriptive curriculum policy documents would fulfil the government's commitment defined in the 'Common Sense Revolution.' Policy actors, when asked about their accountabilities in the process, not surprisingly, expressed accountability *to* others, rather than *for* a democratic process or outcome.

On the one hand, the critical-democratic ideal calls for strong accountability for an inclusive policy formulation process, and on the other, for a policy text that reflects ideals of a critical democracy (inclusive and focused on social justice). Where accountabilities are perceived to be for democratic process and/or democratic outcomes that emphasize social justice, the process conforms to the critical ideal. Thus, criteria include explicit accountability, which might include involving members of the community in meaningful ways through agonistic exchanges and mandating social justice as a criterion for policy outcomes, which would vary, depending on the policy area.

Imagining Possibilities: Forums and Structures for Participation and Arenas for Meaningful Discourse

A surmountable challenge to achieving critical-democratic policy is to devise structures and criteria that encourage *all* citizens-as-policy-actors to act in ways consistent with critical-democratic ideals, even if they do not share those ideals. Such structures are akin to the rules of parliamentary activity and must include basic principles or values (such as inclusion), and accountability measures to ensure they addressed. Venues or arenas for public participation are necessary for a critical-democratic policy process. As in Porto Alegre, a variety of venues can operate at a variety of different levels to achieve more inclusive and meaningful participation.

Arenas for public discourse allow citizens to confront and discuss policy issues that affect them (see, for example, Wildavsky 1979; Ingram 2000). The critical-democratic ideal rests on authentic and inclusive arenas for discourse. As Tatsuo Inoue explains, 'Promoting people's participation in the political process is necessary but not sufficient for the establishment of democratic practices. The quality of the process matters' (2003, 1).

Venues or arenas for public participation are necessary for a critical-democratic policy process. This ideal calls for a fundamental rethinking of public spaces necessary for agonistic discourse and debate. Currently, governments underutilize public political spaces, opting instead for the use of 'official' arenas for input controlled by the state and with limited public access, usually reserved for elites (Glynos 2002). By contrast, Peter Dahlgren envisions 'a constellation of communicative spaces in society that permit the circulation of information, ideas, debates – ideally in an unfettered manner – and also the formation of political will (i.e., public opinion)' (Dahlgren 2005, 148).

In the spirit of Dahlgren's vision, a variety of venues can operate at many different levels to achieve more inclusive and meaningful participation. Public political spaces can be informal and citizen driven (for example Porto Alegre's neighbourhood associations), led by non-profit community organizations (for example, the Public Conversation Project described by Simona Goi 2005),[4] or formal, government-driven spaces (similar to Porto Alegre's congresses). Alternately, new media can be used to provide additional forums for members of the public to gather online to deliberate and experience agonistic exchanges. Internet-democracy research and commentary addresses the concept 'counter-publics,' which take into account the democratic role of radical exclusion and associated counter-discursive struggles over the limits of legitimate deliberation occurring online (see, for example, Dahlberg 2007; Boler 2008). Arenas for critical-democratic discourse that include agonistic exchange must satisfy four criteria (Goi 2005):

• Accessibility – structured so that issues such as economic status, educational level, or occupation are not obstacles to participation
• Inclusiveness – so that no perspective is excluded a priori
• Openness to reconsideration of rules of engagement – in which the structure is subject to contestation as much as the topics that are agonally contested
• Connection to the policymaking institutions – so that outcomes of agonistic exchange are considered in policy decisions through channels of communication to ensure decision-makers are aware of outcomes

There must also be arenas for discourse and deliberation that are both means to policy debate and places of civic learning. These might be existing formats (e.g., consultation sessions, town halls), or new formats that might rely on information and communication technologies as envisioned by Lincoln Dahlberg. Non-profit and public institutions, including universities, might play a role in creating forums, as in Simona Goi's Public Conversation Project. The use of technology and of non-government organizations has the potential to overcome problems of geography.

Finally, and especially given research on the role of the press, the media might be called upon to play a more robust role in citizen learning and deliberation (see, for example, Pettigrew and MacLure 1997; Kim, Wyatt, and Katz 1999; Kozolanka 2007). While the public political sphere may be limited, the media and especially newspapers play a role as arenas for discourse on education and other public policy. In chapters 2 and 3, I described how the media constructed educational issues at the time of SSR. Moreover, given John Dewey's (1927) vision of the democratic role of the press in a vibrant democracy,[5] how educational issues are framed in the media has particular significance. Empirical research suggests that exposure to news coverage on a given topic is positively correlated to quality of individual opinion, and the potential for consideration of alternate perspectives (Kim, Wyatt, and Katz 1999). In Ontario, 'the press plays an active part in the construction of educational issues for its various readerships. Newspapers do not just write about education, they also represent to their readers what education is about. As such, the press acts in an important educational role for the public' (Pettigrew and MacLure 1997, 392). In this way, a vibrant media[6] that allow space for the elaboration and critique of citizens' views is an essential component of a critical-democratic public sphere. With the emergence of new media forms and forums, possibilities for broader representation in the media are endless and can provide a space for citizens with diverse views and from various geographic areas to share perspectives and, at best, participate in agonistic communication.

The Role of Schools: Exploring the Critical-Democratic Ideal through Education *for* Democracy, Democracy *in* Education

Education is an inherently political activity. Through education, we learn to do and to be. Thus, a discussion of policy texts requires further investigation of how (critical) democracy and education relate to one another. There is no shortage of discussion in the literature about the relationship between education and democracy. Indeed, philosophers, theorists, and educators recognize the impact of education on democracy and civic life. Educational theory since Dewey conveys a widespread view that education ought to foster democracy and equip those being educated to participate successfully in a democratic society. An active citizenry requires a deep understanding of democratic principles and the ability and eagerness to be involved in purposeful and effective participation. Education, it is argued, is essential to fostering such understandings and enabling involvement through a curriculum for democracy, nurturing the development of a democratic mind (see, for example, Dewey 1916; Darling-Hammond 1996; Parker 1996; Gutmann 1999; Boler 2004; Olssen, Codd, and O'Neill 2004). However, this is not currently the practice in many jurisdictions, including Ontario, where a managerial conception of education has taken hold. The shift from a democratic to a managerial approach in education arises out of a fundamental reconfiguration of the relationship between government and citizens, away from mutual concern for common good and toward an economic relationship in which the citizen becomes the consumer (Biesta 2004). This is precisely how Education Minister John Snobelen described Ontario's educational context during the 1990s. This type of audit culture leads to a preoccupation with punitive measures, 'crowd[ing] out other conceptions of effectiveness and democracy' (Apple 2005, 15).

Recognizing the distinction between education *for* democracy and democracy *in* education provides further clarification. Education *for* democracy centres on using the educational system to develop cognitive and affective traits to prepare students for citizenship in a democracy. Democracy *in* education requires an educational structure that is democratic to all involved, including students, teachers, administrators, and the community. As such, education *for* democracy is a necessary, but not sufficient, component of democracy *in* education. John Dewey argues that both society and education ought to be democratic in content and style: 'A society which makes provision for participation in its good of all its members on equal terms and which secures flexible readjustment of its institutions through interaction of the different forms of associated life is in so far democratic. Such a society must have a type of education which gives individuals a personal interest in social relationships and control, and the habits of mind which secure social changes without introducing disorder' (1916, 99).

Along these lines, Benjamin Levin reminds us that 'the ideals underlying education are similar to those underlying democracy, suggesting that schools should embody the principles of democracy for students as part of a sound education' (Levin 1998b, 57). Despite the similarity of ideals between education and democracy that Levin identifies, a tensions arise when attempts are made to enact and/or operationalize democracy *in* education and education *for* democracy. The tensions of democratic education can be attributed to antiquated criteria used to conceptualize educational structures and their effectiveness (Carr and Hartnett 1996). Our collective 'educational traditions' are pre-democratic in that they were established when schools were intended for the privileged classes and served as an elite sorting system to exclude certain social groups. These pre-democratic criteria 'distort and constrain any rational debate about the democratic role of education' (12). The problem can be aptly summarized as 'a contradiction between the obvious need for members of a democracy publicly to debate the social and political principles underlying its educational policies and the obvious failure of those policies to address questions about the kind of education which genuine participation in such a public debate requires. It is only in a democracy which does not take seriously the need to equip its future members with the intellectual understandings, civic virtues or social attitudes necessary for participating in public debate, that democratic discussion of recent educational reforms can be treated as irrelevant or largely ignored' (3).

From the critical-democratic stance, both John Dewey and Paulo Freire envision the school as a fundamental venue for democracy to grow – a place for education *for* critical democracy. Kenneth Saltman offers specific criteria that characterize education for critical democracy:

- Encourage students to be intellectually curious and understand the historical and global dimensions of knowledge
- Raise questions about broader structures of power in relation to particular interpretations of truth
- Encourage students to develop the intellectual tools to transform the world around them in ways that make a more just and democratic society for everyone
- Enhance students' capacities to imagine a future in which present inequalities and injustices are overcome and in which history is not inevitable and predetermined, but rather, open to transformation through collective action
- Make hope a social and political project
- Make individual freedom an ideal fulfilled through helping others to be free (2005, 202–4)

Among other suggestions, Saltman also calls on educators to recognize the role of a critical pedagogy[7] to achieve these ends. At the heart of critical pedagogy is Paulo Freire's belief that education ought to empower students to recognize connections between their individual problems and experiences and social contexts in which they are embedded, within the goal of social transformation. Critical pedagogy contributes not only to learners' analysis of curriculum content, but also to the ideal forms of curriculum enactment in the classroom to achieve a critical-democratic learning environment. Because of its concern with active student involvement towards transformation, a significant component of critical democracy in the classroom is critical inquiry whereby 'students and educators develop knowledge, skills, values, dispositions and actions that are called for by a reconstructive conception of democracy' (McMahon and Portelli 1994, 70).

Approaching the issue of critical pedagogy pragmatically, Eric Freedman raises concern that approaches to critical pedagogy in the tradition of Paulo Freire and Henry Giroux are difficult to enact in today's schools. He proposes a 'democratic development of curriculum, not its implementation' (Freedman 2007, 467), citing the practical limitations of critical pedagogy in a highly institutionalized environment (that is, a truly democratic classroom is not possible in most schools, as institutional limitations discourage radical transformations of teachers' roles). His revision of Paulo Freire's critical pedagogy prescribes presenting 'multiple positions on salient public issues, and train[ing] students in a method of analysing these positions' by 'probing into the root causes of social inequalities' (467).[8] Similarly, Wendy Kohli envisions social justice education as a form of empowerment, in which equity is addressed overtly: 'Social justice education is a "praxis" that includes a theoretical account of oppression and privilege, as well as practical strategies for changing social institutions. Schools are primary sites for this critical transformation since they reproduce inequality. Educating students to overcome internalized forms of oppression – such as racism, sexism, classism and homophobia – offering them a framework for understanding the external structures that are the source of these different oppressions, and empowering students to become agents of change, are all important goals of social justice education' (2005, 100).

The perspectives suggest strong rationales for social justice education as a central component of a democratic education. Jeannie Oakes and Martin Lipton (2003) provide an account of three things that a socially just education should do. First, a socially just curriculum uncovers, examines, and critiques values and politics in curriculum and instruction. Second, it challenges educational common sense, specifically questioning why we do certain things and how they produce and reproduce inequalities, especially along the lines of race, class, gender, language, and sexual orientation. Third, it constructs empowering alternatives to address the reproduction of those inequalities. Landon Beyer adds an additional proposal: curriculum for social justice ought to be organized as themes, rather than as discrete subjects. This would allow for 'inquiries unhampered by artificial divisions of experience and subject matters' (Beyer 1993). In this vision, he also proposes that students and teachers collaborate on projects, and members of the community participate in the education process, including curriculum decisions. There must be a formalized accountability framework to ensure that components of an educational system reflect the aims of social justice. In Paul Carr's (2007) vision, a social justice accountability framework examines functional criteria for curriculum as well as other areas of education: inclusion, representation, decision-making processes, communication, funding, data collection, accountability and monitoring/review.

Clearly, a shift towards education that would value and foster critical democracy is no easy task. Beyond changes to education policy that I have argued throughout this book, several levels within the education system also play a role in transformation. First, at the most basic level, teachers and teacher educators ought look to this research to understand how Ontario's curriculum policy came to be and what other possibilities there are for democracy *in* education and education *for* democracy. If teachers and teacher educators share a vision of critical-democracy as an ideal, it follows that they ought to engage their students in explorations of alternative ways of constructing education policy as well as enacting education (and curriculum) policy in their classrooms, schools, and communities. By doing so, public schooling would provide an education *for* democracy, by engaging students in learning practices that increase their capacities as critical-democratic citizens. Indeed, Claudia Ruitenberg argues that, if we wish to achieve agonistic democracy, citizenship education in public schools must take this task seriously. She proposes three areas in which political education (under the rubric of citizenship education) must change: educating political emotions in a way that moves against masculinist rationalism, fostering an understanding of the political, and finally, developing political literacy to read the political landscape in a way that uncovers the social order (Ruitenberg 2009).

Second, school administrators play a significant role, since administrative practice ought to be intertwined with research and theory 'to support the type of schooling (and society) that values rather than marginalizes' (Brown 2004, 77). Indeed, educational administration has traditionally reflected a culture which marginalizes issues of social justice, and these accountabilities reinforce the managerial aspect of their roles (Marshall 2004). But, as the literature suggests, shifting greater emphasis on social justice among school administers is critical to change at the school level (Marshall 2004; Shields 2004; Cambron-McCabe and McCarthy 2005). Unless school administrators create school environments that encourage and allow democratic practice in education, as well as education *for* democracy, teachers and students will continue to face barriers to the lived experience of critical democracy and eliminate the possibility of schooling to prepare an active citizenry.

Postscript to the Common Sense Revolution: Temporary Glimmer of Democracy

The defeat of the Progressive Conservatives by the Liberal Party led by Premier Dalton McGuinty in 2003 ended the Common Sense Revolution. Despite the change in leadership, neither the Anti-Racism Secretariat nor its counterpart at the Ministry of Education, eliminated in 1995, has been restored. At the time of writing, the Ministry of Education continues to undergo a cyclical curriculum revision called Sustaining Quality Curriculum (SQC). This involves comprehensive review of curriculum policy documents, at the rate of several subjects per year. The curriculum policy documents are being rewritten, though the revision process differs somewhat from the curriculum development process described here. However, it continues to rely on 'policy elites' and excludes feedback from interested stakeholders not identified by the ministry.

I contacted the Ministry of Education in 2005 to inquire if I could provide feedback on draft curriculum policy documents during SQC in my role as an interested citizen. I was told that only those in official capacities were in a position to comment. Several weeks later, I was contacted through my position at OISE to provide feedback on the draft SQC policy documents, and within days of that, contacted yet again to provide feedback on the same draft policy in my capacity as a representative of my subject association. The ministry officials had no concerns that I (as an individual) was able to provide two separate feedback responses, since each represented a different professional capacity and a different professional organization. This underscored a perpetuation of elitist policy actor involvement.

However, the Ontario government has since embarked upon two initiatives to strengthen democracy in the province. First, the McGuinty Liberal government created an independent Citizens' Assembly through Regulation 82/06 of the Election Act in 2006. Consisting of 103 individuals randomly selected by Elections Ontario (one per provincial riding), the Citizens' Assembly met for seven consecutive weekends in 2006–7 and held public meetings to study Ontario's electoral system (Democratic Renewal Secretariat 2007). While the establishment of the assembly has been lauded by some (see, for example, Snider 2008), its scope is limited to procedural aspects of democracy, and the selection of participants limits Ontarians' opportunities to be involved.

Second, a Democratic Renewal Secretariat was established by the McGuinty Liberals in 2005 with the following mandate: 'The Democratic Renewal Secretariat (DRS) was created to reform and revitalize the democratic institutions of the province, and create new opportunities for citizen participation. The Democratic Renewal Secretariat supports the Minister Responsible for Democratic Renewal. It is responsible for policy development, coordination and implementation of initiatives in support of democratic renewal' (Democratic Renewal Secretariat 2007, 1). The secretariat had an annual budget of approximately $9 million, and a staff of twenty-five. Like the efforts of the Citizens' Assembly, those of the Democratic Renewal Secretariat's through 2007 were focused largely on election reform, though their mandate suggests a broader concern with citizen participation.

While the present focus of the Citizens' Assembly and the Democratic Renewal Secretariat may not conform to the ideals of inclusive and critical democracy, their establishment and continued existence suggested that the government of Ontario had some degree of concern for increased participation and democracy in the province. This step towards increased democratization held great promise. Regrettably, the Democratic Renewal Secretariat was in operation for only one term, ceasing to exist shortly after the 2007 election, when the Liberal party was successful in its second bid for provincial leadership.

Concluding Comments

While working on this project, I was consistently reminded of an anecdote told by Jane Roland Martin in her 1985 book, *Reclaiming a*

Conversation: The Ideal of the Educated Woman. An academic carefully and critically considered racial injustices but his concern was purely theoretical and he was not moved to act on these conclusions or concerns. She argues that a democratic society is simply not well served by such 'spectator-citizens.' My hope is that readers will not only be academically and theoretically interested in the research and findings, but be moved to act on the problems identified and the possibilities offered through the inclusion of Porto Alegre as an alternative example. Only by overcoming the passive role of the spectator-citizen, demanding change, and proposing alternatives will Ontarians or citizens in other jurisdictions move towards critical-democratic practices in governance, policy formulation, and education.

Appendix: Policy Formulation Timeline

Ontario's 'official' secondary school curriculum policy formulation process can be summarized in ten stages established and carried out by the Ministry of Education.

1. Background research*: November 1996–January 1997
2. Expert panels / stakeholder feedback*: February 1997–May 1997
3. Student symposium: April 1997
4. Synthesis paper: July 1997
5. Requests for proposal: November 1997–January 1998
6. Course menus: February 1998
7. Writing*: March 1998–January 1999
8. Feedback: June 1998–January 1999
9. Validation: February–May 1999
10. Release and enactment: Grades nine and ten in 1999, Grades eleven and twelve in 2000

* Outsourced

Notes

Preface

1 A number of researchers have studied aspects of Ontario's school reform, though this is the first to fully reconstruct the process of policy production in the province.

1. The Ideal of Critical-Democratic Policy Production

1 Gewirtz (1998, 469) provides a useful categorization of 'five faces of oppression': exploitation, marginalization, powerlessness, cultural imperialism, and violence.
2 Religious and moral arguments centre on doctrines that call for people to live their lives with concern for the needs of others. Legal justifications include preservations of rights and freedoms, such as those in the United States Bill of Rights, and in Canada's Charter of Rights and Freedoms. Political arguments centre on the idea that social justice builds an inclusive citizenry, and democratic institutions thrive when economic and political inequities are minimized (Merrett 2004).
3 Mouffe defines the political as 'the dimension of antagonism that is inherent in human relations' (Mouffe 2000b, 101).
4 Politics 'consists in domesticating hostility and in trying to defuse the potential antagonism that exists in human relations' (Mouffe 2000b, 101).
5 As Ruitenberg (2009) points out, psychoanalysts have illustrated that the suppression of fundamental desires and emotions does not eliminate them, but rather delays their manifestation.
6 Mouffe uses this term throughout in her body of work, referring to its appearance in Richard Rorty's work.

7 The sets of criteria include:

- Criteria central to a critical-democratic institutional culture
- Criteria to evaluate the degree to which rules and tools address the critical-democratic ideal of agonistic exchanges
- Criteria for power dynamics and the open acknowledgment of power and politicization
- Criteria for critical-democratic policy actor inclusion
- Criteria to evaluate the degree of citizen engagement
- Criteria for critical-democratic impacts on policy actors
- Criteria for critical-democratic curriculum decisions
- Criteria to evaluate educational policies on their social justice orientation

2. The Politics of 'Common Sense' Policy Production

1 This term is usually associated with the advocacy coalition approach widely used in political science research. Schneider and Ingram (1997, 73), however, use it to describe the societal context that shapes other aspects of policy formulation.
2 *Red Tory* is a political tradition in Canada, referring to conservatives who are committed to liberal social policy.
3 Under the legislation, every public sector employer with more then ten employees and every private sector with more then fifty employees had to design and implement a plan that would eliminate barriers to the hiring and promotion of individuals from the designated groups.
4 The Legislative Assembly of Ontario has 103 seats representing ridings across the province. Elected members of the Legislative Assembly are commonly called members of the provincial Parliament (MPPs). Following the Westminster system, the leader of the party that holds the largest number of seats in the Legislative Assembly is the 'Premier and President of the Council' (Executive Council Act R.S.O. 1990), though is referred to as simply the premier. The premier appoints members to the Cabinet (or Executive Council), who are deemed 'ministers of the Crown,' serving as ministers for their respective ministries.
5 Levin and Young (2000) reported that the 'confrontational' rhetoric during reforms in England also invoked the language of 'crisis' to justify large-scale reforms.
6 As I reported earlier, Livingstone, Hart, and Davie's (1996) research suggests the satisfaction level with Ontario schooling was just over 50 per cent.

Two years later, Livingstone, Hart, and Davie (1998) found that perceptions about the Harris government's education reforms varied, depending upon political affiliation – more than half of those who support the Progressive Conservative Party thought that the changes improved education quality in Ontario, while one-third of Liberal supporters hold this view, and even fewer NDP supporters.

Political staffer Will recalls that most of the voters with whom he spoke said, 'I hate the fact that [Mike Harris] amalgamated Toronto, I hate the fact that he did this or that. But this guy did what he said he would do and I love him for that and that is why I am going to vote for him again.'

7 This is based on evidence from the interviews conducted with policy actors, my examination of media coverage and secondary research, and Kozolanka's (2007) exhaustive analysis of the role of the media at this time.

3. Restructuring Education

1 Section 93 of the British North America Act of 1867 began with the words, 'In and for each province the Legislature may exclusively make laws in relation to education.'

2 Grade 13 courses were 'replaced' by OAC in the 1980s, and OAC courses were phased out between 1999 and 2003 as a result of the Harris reforms to education.

3 In 2000, Secretary of the Cabinet Rita Burak stated, 'The OPS has a well-defined, long-standing culture and value set. Because of our size and history, we have enjoyed, for the most part, over the last forty years a truly non-partisan, representative public service.' Armstrong (1997) characterizes this commitment to public good via nonpartisan values as stewardship, contrasting this to very different values found among private sector or market-driven organizations.

4 Gidney (1999) suggests that democratization of schools includes initiatives such as more relevant curriculum – including vocational, domestic, and manual education – extension of school-leaving age, concern with contemporary problems and issues, and the objective of educating the whole child.

5 The Anti-Racism, Equity, and Access Branch was created within the Ministry of Education in 1992. As well, the ministry released a resource guide for anti-racism and equity education. In 1993, Memorandum 119 was issued, requiring all school boards to develop anti-racism and equity policies by March 1995 and to plan for implementation within five years. Carr (2006) explains: 'One of the shortcomings of the Ministry of Education's Anti-racism and Ethno-cultural Equity Education Branch was that almost

all of the staff, the majority of whom were racial minorities, came from the school board sector, and they did not have experience in government, which represented a radically different institutional culture. The Branch was not seen to be an integral part of the Ministry but, rather, an outside entity, almost a "special interest group," and this fact disadvantaged it greatly.'

6 The election of the Liberal government in 2003 resulted in the elimination of the teacher testing program.

7 A closer examination of the resulting curriculum policy documents would be necessary to further define the citizenship aim, though such analysis is beyond the scope of this research.

8 Directions include, but are not limited to, standardized literacy testing and increased standardization of curriculum.

4. Hidden Privatization in the Institutional Culture: Policy Actors or 'Hired Guns'?

1 The ministry revised Ontario's elementary school curriculum prior to SSR.

2 The ministry provided a number of requirements for each team. First, ways to differentiate between student learning expectations between streams (academic and applied for grades nine and ten; workplace, college, and university for grades eleven and twelve) was an important area of communication. Nearly all writers comment that the instructions, particularly for academic and applied streams, changed several times during the process, leading writers to conclude that in the beginning, the ministry may not have been certain what the distinctions between streams were. However, interviews reveal that some policy-writing team members felt those distinctions were never made perfectly clear.

Second, the ministry defined a very specific format for courses (referred to by some as a 'template'), which required that each course contain three to five strands, each representing a unit or theme of study. Each strand contains five overall expectations. Each overall expectation represents a sub-organizer within the strand, appearing as a heading. Each sub-organizer contains three to five specific expectations. At some point during the writing process, teams received lists of verbs to be used for overall and specific expectations.

3 Named after American automobile manufacturer Henry Ford, Fordism is a manufacturing philosophy that aims to achieve higher productivity by standardizing output, using conveyor assembly lines and breaking work into small de-skilled tasks. The concept has been applied to white-collar work, implying standardization and efficiency-oriented processes that de-skill bureaucratic or information industry work.

5. Policy Writers, Power, and Politicization: Were the Books Already Cooked?

1 This written narrative used the acronym OMET to refer to the Ontario Ministry of Education.

6. Citizen (Dis)Engagement in Selection and Consultations

1 This is based on an internal ministry memorandum I obtained from the Ontario archives from the manager of secondary school programs to the deputy minister, 20 December 1996.
2 The total number of participants in these sessions is not revealed. Only some organizations who participated are named: Ontario Literacy Coalition, Ontario Taxpayer's Federation, Ontario Federation of Labour, Ontario Parent Council, Ontario Secondary School Students Association.

7. Perceived Policy Outcomes and Their Absence of Democracy

1 Within this assessment paradigm, teachers report learning skills (works independently, teamwork, organization, work habits, and initiative) in a separate section of the report card, apart from academic skills, which are used exclusively for the course grade. Thus, the course grade reflects only the degree to which students meet learning expectations in the policy document. As well, the ministry prescribes a strategy for course-grade determination: 70 per cent of the grade is based on formative work, calculated using the mode; 30 per cent of the grade is based on summative evaluation (Ministry of Education 2000b).
2 I withhold this participant's identity here to protect anonymity, since the subject is revealed in this example.
3 Portelli and Vibert (2001) describe this as curriculum that centres on who we are and how we live well together, addressing questions about larger social and political contexts that are relevant to students' immediate, daily worlds, issues, and experiences.
4 Not unique to high school, this phenomenon is also common in college and university business courses.
5 Participants often used the term *non-university bound students*. This term is problematic, since it suggests that students' post-secondary destination is established early in high school, and that not be accurate. However, it does reflect the destination-focused streaming within the policy texts produced.
6 Note that the first portion of this quote also appears on p. 142 but warrants inclusion at length to better understand the context discussed in this section.

8. An Exploration of Possibilities: Porto Alegre, Brazil, as an Analytic Foil Contrasting Ontario

1 According to Baiocchi (2006), a number of reasons contributed to the PT's defeat: a well-planned campaign that capitalized on anti-incumbent sentiments by the opposition, a call for 'democratic alternation' (a tradition of alternating parties in power), dissatisfaction with the PT (under President Lula) at the national level, and a promise to maintain the OP and the World Social Forum. The incoming party was true to their word and preserved the OP.

2 Baiocchi's (2001) research utilized statistical data from the government, surveys of participants, and interviews with participants.

3 This was determined in response to a survey question, 'Do you speak at meetings?' with a frequency scale to capture the rate of participation (Baiocchi 2001, 51–2).

4 First priority receives five points, second priority four points, and so on, ending with the fifth priority receiving one point.

5 Mouffe also uses this term, describing radicalization of democracy as a process: 'The aim is to construct a "we" as radical democratic citizens, a collective political identity articulated through the principle of equivalence ... a radical democratic approach views the common good as a "vanishing point," something to which we must constantly refer when acting as citizens, but that can never be reached ... [common good functions] as a "social imaginary": that is, as that for which the very impossibility of achieving full representation gives to it the role of an horizon which is the condition of possibility of any representation within the space that it delimits' (Mouffe 1996, 325–6).

6 Gandin (2002, 218) cites the following phrases in documents:

- 'rupture with common sense'
- 'putting common sense into question'
- 'overcoming common sense'

9. Conclusion

1 It is true that Simona Goi (2005) describes how a forum can be devised for agonistic exchange, but her account is not tied directly to policy formulation.

2 Tyler (2000) concludes, on the basis of a review of research, that individuals are more willing to accept decisions when they feel that those decisions are

made through procedures they view as fair, where fairness is based on the following criteria: whether there are opportunities to participate; whether the authorities are neutral; whether people trust the motives of the authorities; and whether people are treated with dignity and respect during the process.

3 Policy actors interviewed tend to express accountability to others, rather than for a democratic process or outcome. The elected government officials, on the basis of remarks of political staffer Will, saw themselves as accountable to the voting public and accountable for implementing their election promises. This is also the view of bureaucrat Marcellas, who describes a shift from accountability to a 'public input' model of accountability, rather than to educators in past governments. Bureaucrats interviewed, for the most part, view accountability as primarily (if not solely) to their superiors – especially the elected officials. Consultation participants feel accountable to organizations they represent. Writing team members' responses reflected more complex notions of accountability. On the one hand, some use the term *hired guns* to describe their responsibility. However, writers also feel accountable to their peers as *guardians* of their subject, attempting to salvage what they feel was valuable. These writing-team-member conceptions tend to focus on the outcome in the form of policy text, rather than the process itself.

4 Goi (2005) describes Public Conversation Project (PCP), a non-profit organization founded in Massachusetts in 1989, as an example of a community-based forum for agonistic exchange. PCP was created as an experiment to investigate whether approaches used in family therapy could be transferred to or used with members of the public who hold opposing views on 'hot' public issues. Between 1990 and 1992, PCP held eighteen one-session dialogues on abortion, each involving four to eight participants who did not know each other ahead of time and held opposing views. According to Goi, the approach has since been repeated with other public issues in other jurisdictions, though not reported in research.

   Goi calls attention to the features of this model that reflect agonism. First, focusing conversations on one's position rather than persuading others reflects the agonistic concern of minimizing the repressive influence of consensus goals. Second, because the dialogue is intended to foster understanding rather than inflame hostility, antagonism is tamed. She suggests that to foster this kind of agonistic exchange, foundations and non-profit organizations that make up civil society ought be educated about the value of agonism, and encourage the development of financial support for projects.

5 Dewey's view, when he elaborates a Jeffersonian vision of democracy, emphasizes the creation of an informed and questioning citizenry through

education, and he grants a clear role for the press within this ideal of democracy. In this view, the media ideally entice the public to learn more about a subject.

Dewey admitted that 'a newspaper which was only a daily edition of a quarterly journal of sociology or political science would undoubtedly possess a limited circulation and narrow influence.' But, he predicted, the material in the newspapers he imagines would have such an 'enormous and widespread human bearing that its bare existence would be an irresistible invitation to a presentation of it which would have a direct popular appeal' (Dewey, qtd in Westbrook 1993, 311).

6 Of course, a full examination of the problems of today's centralized media structure is called for but is far beyond the scope of this work.

7 The term *critical pedagogy* – which first appears in 1983 in Henry Giroux's *Theory and Resistance in Education* (Darde, Baltodano, and Torres 2003) – is associated with Freire and Giroux, as well as Ira Shor and Peter McClaren.

8 Romas (2008) discusses the challenge of addressing social justice in the Ontario science curriculum. He recounts, 'There wasn't enough time to progress through the levels of learning, to more complex thought and analysis . . . How was I going to find time to incorporate teaching for social justice if I had to race just to get through the science material?' (43).

To address this, Romas uses current social issues (e.g., HIV/AIDS, water privatization, and alternative energy) as the 'examples' through which he taught conventional science topics. Similarly, Stocker and Wagner (2008) propose a number of equity issues and provide teachers with data sets to shift the focus of the curriculum towards critical pedagogy issues. Finally, Pinto (2005, 2006) illustrates a critical-pedagogical approach to the study of entrepreneurship in business education, in which learners actively unpack the 'cultural myths' common in business studies, with particular attention to ideologies, racial and gender equity, and power.

References

Abers, R. 2000. *Inventing Local Democracy: Grassroots Politics in Brazil.* Boulder, CO: Lynne Reiner Publishers.

Alemán, A.M.M. 2001. 'The Ethics of Democracy: Individuality and Educational Policy.' *Educational Policy* 15 (3): 379–403.

Anderson, S.E., and S. Ben Jaafar. 2003. 'Policy Trends in Ontario Education 1990–2003.' Working Paper, Sub-Project 2 of the Evolution of Teaching Personnel in Canada, SSHRC Major Collaborative Research Initiatives Project, 2002–6.

Apple, M.W. 1993. 'The Politics of Official Knowledge: Does a National Curriculum Make Sense?' *Teachers College Record* 95 (2): 222–41.

– 1996. *Cultural Politics and Education.* New York: Teachers College Press.

– 1999. 'The Absent Presence of Race in Educational Reform.' *Race, Ethnicity and Education* 2 (1): 9–16.

– 2001a. *Educating the 'Right' Way: Markets, Standards, God and Inequality.* New York: RoutledgeFalmer.

– 2001b. 'Educational and Curricular Restructuring and the Neo-Liberal and Neo-Conservative Agendas: Interview with Michael Apple.' *Currículo sem Fronteiras* 1 (1): i–xxvi.

– 2004. 'Creating Difference: Neo-Liberalism and Neo-Conservatives and the Politics of Educational Reform.' *Educational Policy* 18 (1): 12–44.

– 2005. 'Education, Markets, and an Audit Culture.' *Critical Quarterly* 47 (1–2): 11–29.

Armstrong, J.L. 1997. 'Stewardship and Public Service.' Paper prepared for the Public Service Commission of Canada. http://epe.lac-bac.gc.ca/100/200/301/psc-cfp/stewardship_public_service-e/pdf/stewardship_e.pdf.

Auditor General of Ontario. 2003. *2003 Annual Report of the Office of the Provincial Auditor of Ontario.* http://www.auditor.on.ca/en/reports_2003_en.htm.

Azevedo, J.C. 2000. 'Escola cidadã: políticas e práticas.' In *Porto Alegre, uma cidade queconquista: Artes e Ofícios,* coord. R. Pont, organiz. A. Barcelos, 111–22. Porto Alegre: Secretaria Municipal de Educação (SMED).

– 2007. 'Public Education: The Challenge of Quality.' *Estudos Avançados* 21 (60): 7–26.

Azevedo, J.C., and D. Schugurensky. 2005. 'Three Dimensions of Educational Democratization: The *Citizen School* Project of Porto Alegre.' *Our Schools / Our Selves* 15 (1): 41–58.

Babbie, E. 1992. *The Practice of Social Research.* 6th ed. Belmont, CA: Wadsworth Publishing.

Bäcklund, P., and R. Mäntysalo. 2010. 'Agonism and Institutional Ambiguity: Ideas on Democracy and the Role of Participation in the Development of Planning Theory and Practice – The Case of Finland.' *Planning Theory* 9 (4). DOI: 10.1177/1473095210373684.

Bächtiger, A., S. Niemeyer, M. Neblo, M.R. Steenbergen, and J. Steiner. 2010. 'Disentangling Diversity in Deliberative Democracy: Competing Theories, Their Blind Spots and Complementarities.' *Journal of Political Philosophy* 18 (1): 32–63.

Baiocchi, G. 2001. 'Participation, Activism, and Politics: The Porto Alegre Experiment and Deliberative Democratic Theory.' *Politics & Society* 29 (1): 43–72.

– 2005. *Militants and Citizens: The Politics of Participatory Democracy in Porto Alegre.* Stanford, CA: Stanford University Press.

– 2006. 'The Citizens of Porto Alegre.' *Boston Review* (March/April 2006). http://bostonreview.net/BR31.2/baiocchi.php.

Ball, S.J. 1994. *Education Reform.* Buckingham, UK: Open University Press.

– 1998. 'Big Policies / Small World: An Introduction to International Perspectives in Education Policy.' *Comparative Education* 34 (2): 119–30.

– 1999. 'Labour, Learning and the Economy: A Political Sociology Perspective.' *Cambridge Journal of Education* 29 (2): 195–206.

– 2009. 'Privatising Education, Privatising Education Policy, Privatising Educational Research: Network Governance and the "Competition State."' *Journal of Education Policy* 24 (1): 83–99.

Ball, S.J., and D. Youdell. 2007. *Hidden Privatization in Public Education: Preliminary Report.* Berlin: Education International 5th World Congress.

Barber, B. 2003. *Strong Democracy: Participatory Politics for a New Age.* 20th anniv. ed. Berkeley: University of California Press.

– 2004. 'Taking the Public out of Education.' *School Administrator* 61 (5): 10–13.

Bartlett, L., M. Frederick, T. Gulbrandsen, and E. Murillo. 2002. 'The Marketization of Education: Public Schools for Private Needs.' *Anthropology and Education Quarterly* 33 (1): 5–24.

Basu, R. 2004. 'The Rationalization of Neoliberalism in Ontario's Public Education System, 1995–2000.' *Geoforum* 35 (4): 621–34.

Bedard, G.J., and S.B. Lawton. 2000. 'The Struggle for Power and Control: Shifting Policy-Making Models and the Harris Agenda for Education in Ontario.' *Canadian Public Administration* 43 (3): 241–69.

Beetham, D. 1997. 'Market Economy and Democratic Polity.' *Democratization* 4 (1): 76–93.

Beilharz, P. 1989. 'Social Democracy and Social Justice.' *Journal of Sociology* 25 (1): 85–99.

Benford, R.D., and D.A. Snow. 2000. 'Framing Processes and Social Movements: An Overview and Assessment.' *Annual Review of Sociology* 26: 611–39.

Berg, A., and E. Berg. 1997. 'Methods of Privatization.' *Journal of International Affairs* 50 (2): 357–91.

Beyer, L.E. 1993. 'Pursuing Social Justice through Education: Schooling for a Critical Democracy.' *Synthesis/Regeneration* 5. http://www.greens.org/s-r/05/05-14.html.

– 1998. 'Can Schools Further Democratic Practices?' *Theory into Practice* 27 (4): 262–9.

Biesta, G.J.J. 2004. 'Education, Accountability, and the Ethical Demand: Can the Democratic Potential of Accountability Be Regained?' *Educational Theory* 54 (3): 233–50.

Birchfield, V. 1999. 'Contesting the Hegemony of Market Ideology: Gramsci's "Good Sense" and Polanyi's "Double Movement."' *Review of International Political Economy* 6 (1): 27–54.

Birdsall, N., and J. Nellis. 2002. 'Winners and Losers: Assessing Distributional Impacts of Privatization.' *World Development* 31 (10): 1617–33.

Blaug, R. 2002. 'Engineering Democracy.' *Political Studies* 50 (1): 102–16.

Blizzard, C. 1995. *How the Tories Took Ontario*. Toronto: Dundurn.

Bohman, J. 1998. 'Survey Article: The Coming of Age of Deliberative Democracy.' *Journal of Political Philosophy* 6 (4): 400–25.

Boler, M. 2004. *Democratic Dialogue in Education: Troubling Speech, Disturbing Silence*. New York: Peter Lang Publishing.

– 2008. *Digital Media and Democracy*. Cambridge, MA: MIT Press.

Box, R.C. 1999. 'Running Government Like a Business: Implications for Public Administration Theory and Practice.' *American Review of Public Administration* 29 (1): 19–43.

Brazilian Embassy in Washington. 2005. Home page. Retrieved 5 November 2005. http://www.brasilemb.org/.

Brennan, R. 1995. 'Minister Plotted "to Invent a Crisis": Snobelen Video Spurs Angry Calls for Him to Resign.' *Toronto Star,* 13 September.

Brown, K.M. 2004. 'Leadership for Social Justice and Equity: Weaving a Transformative Framework and Pedagogy.' *Educational Administration Quarterly* 40 (1): 77–108.

Burak, R. 2000, February 8. 'The Challenges Facing the Ontario Public Service.' Paper given at Public Policy Forum, Ottawa. Retrieved 23 June 2003. http://www.ppforum.com/english/publications/publications.

Burch, P.E. *Hidden Markets: The New Education Privatization.* New York: Routledge.

Button, M., and K. Mattson. 1999. 'Deliberative Democracy in Practice: Challenges and Prospects for Civic Deliberation.' *Polity* 31 (4): 609–37.

Caldwell, B.J. 1999. 'Market, Choice and Public Good in School Education.' *Australian Journal of Education* 43 (3): 257–73.

Cambron-McCabe, N., and M.M. McCarthy. 2005. 'Educating School Leaders for Social Justice.' *Educational Policy* 19 (1): 201–22.

Cameron, D. 2002. 'The Landscape of Civic Engagement in Ontario.' Paper prepared for the Panel of the Role of Government. http://www.law-lib. utoronto.ca/investing/reports/rp1.pdf.

Cameron, D., C. Mulhern, and G. White. 2003. 'Democracy in Ontario.' Paper prepared for the Panel of the Role of Government. http://www.law-lib. utoronto.ca/investing/reports/rp35.pdf.

Canadian Press Newswire. 1995. 'Snobelen Confident of Excelling at Post.' 4 July.

Caputo, R.K. 2002. 'Social Justice, the Ethics of Care, and Market Economies.' *Families in Society* 83 (4): 355–65.

Carozza, L. 2007. 'Dissent in the Midst of Emotional Territory.' *Informal Logic* 27 (2): 197–210.

Carr, P.R. 2006. 'Social Justice and Whiteness in Education: Color-Blind Policy-making and Racism.' *Journal for Critical Education Policy Studies* 4 (2). http:// www.jceps.com/?pageID=article&articleID=77.

– 2007. 'Standards, Accountability and Democracy: Addressing Inequities through a Social Justice Accountability Famework.' *Democracy and Education* 17 (1): 7–16.

Carr, P.R., and T.R. Klassen. 1997. 'Different Perceptions of Race in Education: Racial Minority and White Teachers.' *Canadian Journal of Education* 22 (1): 67–81.

Carr, W. 1998. 'The Curriculum in a Democratic Society.' *Curriculum Studies* 6 (3): 323–39.

Carr, W., and A. Hartnett. 1996. *Education and the Struggle for Democracy.*
    Buckingham, UK: Open University Press.
Chambers, S. 2003. 'Deliberative Democratic Theory.' *Annual Review of
    Political Science* 6: 307–26.
Chua, A.L. 2000. 'The Paradox of Free Market Democracy: Rethinking
    Development Policy.' *Harvard International Law Journal* 41 (2): 287–379.
Churchill, S., and I. Kaprielian-Churchill. 1991. 'Ethnicity, Language and
    School Retention in Ontario: The Unfinished Agenda.' In *Reform and
    Relevance in Schooling: Dropouts, De-streaming and the Common Curriculum,*
    ed. D.L. Allison and J. Paquette, 531–45. Toronto: Ontario Institute for
    Studies in Education.
Clarkson, S. 2002. *Uncle Sam and Us: Globalization, Neoconservatism, and the
    Canadian State.* Toronto: University of Toronto Press.
Cohen, J. 1989. 'Deliberation and Democratic Legitimacy.' In *Debates in Contem-
    porary Political Philosophy: An Anthology,* ed. D. Matravers and J. Pike, 342–60.
    London: Routledge.
– 2001. *Alien Invasion: How the Harris Tories Mismanaged Ontario.* Toronto:
    Insomniac.
'The Common Sense Revolution.' 1994. http://web.archive.org/web/20051124195225/
    http://www.ontariopc.com/feature/csr/csr_text.htm.
Corson, D. 2002. 'Teaching and Learning for Market-Place Utility.' *International
    Journal of Leadership Education* 5 (1): 1–13.
Crawford, K. 2000. 'The Political Construction of the "Whole Curriculum."'
    British Educational Research Journal 26 (5): 615–30.
Crittenden, G. 2001. 'The Harris Kremlin: Inside Ontario's Revolutionary
    Politburo.' In Cohen 2001, 57–66.
Crowder, G. 2006. 'Chantal Mouffe's Agonistic Democracy.' Paper presented
    at the Australian Political Studies Association Conference, 25–7 September
    2006, University of Newcastle. http://www.newcastle.edu.au/Resources/
    Schools/Economics%20Politics%20and%20Tourism/APSA%202006/
    POLSOCTHEORY/Crowder,%20George.pdf.
Curtis, B., D.W. Livingstone, and H. Smaller. 1992. *Stacking the Deck: The
    Streaming of Working-Class Kids in Ontario Schools.* Ottawa: Our Schools /
    Our Selves.
Dahl, R.A. 1998. *On Democracy.* New Haven, CT: Yale University Press.
Dahlberg, L. 2001. 'The Internet and Democratic Discourse: Exploring the
    Prospects of Online Deliberative Forums Extending the Public Sphere.'
    Information, Communication & Society 4 (4): 615–33.
– 2007. 'The Internet, Deliberative Democracy, and Power: Radicalizing the
    Public Sphere.' *International Journal of Media and Cultural Politics* 3 (1): 47–64.

Dahlgren, P. 2005. 'The Internet, Public Spheres, and Political Communication: Dispersion and Deliberation.' *Political Communication* 22 (2): 147–62.

– 2007. 'Civic Identity and Net Activism: The Frame of Radical Femocracy.' In *Radical Democracy and the Internet*, ed. L. Dahlberg and E. Siapera, 318–28. London: Palgrave Macmillan.

Darder, A., M. Baltodano, and R.D. Torres. 2003. *The Critical Pedagogy Reader.* New York: Routledge.

Dare, Bill. 1997. 'Harris's First Year: Attacks and Resistance.' In *Open for Business, Closed to People,* ed. D. Ralph, A. Regimbald, and N. St.-Amand, 20–7. Halifax: Fernwood Publishing.

Darling-Hammond, L. 1996. 'The Right to Learn and the Advancement of Teaching: Research, Policy, and Practice for Democratic Education.' *Educational Researcher* 6 (6): 5–17.

Davies, S. 2002. 'The Paradox of Progressive Education: A Frame Analysis.' *Sociology of Education* 75 (4): 269–85.

deCastro, M.H.G., and S. Tiezzi. 2004. 'The Reform of Secondary Education and the Implementation of ENEM in Brazil.' In *The Challenges of Education in Brazil*, ed. C. Brock and S. Schwartzman, 89–115. Oxford: Symposium Books.

DeFaveri, I., and N. Kach. 1987. 'An Outline of Some Current Educational Issues.' In *Essays on Canadian Education,* ed. N. Kach, K. Mazurek, R.S. Patterson, and I. DeFaveri, 141–60. Calgary: Detselig.

deLeon, L., and P. deLeon. 2002. 'The Democratic Ethos and Public Management.' *Administration & Society* 34 (2): 229–50.

deLeon, P. 1997. *Democracy and the Policy Sciences.* Albany: State University of New York (SUNY) Press.

Delgado, R. 2011. 'Rodrigo's Reconsideration: Intersectionality and the Future of Critical Race Theory.' *Iowa Law Review* 96: 1247–88.

Democratic Renewal Secretariat. 2007. *Results-Based Plan Briefing Book: 2007–08.* Toronto: Queen's Printer. http://www.ontla.on.ca/library/repository/ser/266519/2007-2008.pdf.

Dewey, J. (1916) 1966. *Democracy and Education: An Introduction to the Philosophy of Education.* New York: Free Press.

– 1927. *The Public and Its Problems.* New York: Holt.

Diehl, V.R.O., L.O. Silva, M.C.C. Guinther, and M.V. dos Santos. 2006. 'Curricular Context in Education Cycles: The Impact of Education Changes on the Pedagogical Actions of Physical Education Teaching.' *Fiep Bulletin / Foz do Iguaçu* 76:246–49. Retrieved 1 June 2008. http://www.esef.ufrgs.br/f3p-efice/fiep%20vera.pdf.

Dryzek, J.S. 2005. 'Deliberative Democracy in Divided Societies.' *Political Theory* 33 (2): 218–42.

– 2009. 'Democratization as Deliberative Capacity.' *Comparative Political Studies* 42 (11): 1379–1402.

Dua, E., and A. Robertson. 1999. *Scratching the Surface*. London: Women's Press.

Dyer, R. 1997. *White*. London: Routledge.

Earl, L.M., S. Freeman, S. Laskey, S. Sutherland, and N. Torrance. 2002. *Policy, Politics, Pedagogy and People: Early Perceptions and Challenges of Large-Scale Reform in Ontario Secondary Schools*. Report for the Ontario Secondary School Teachers' Federation for the International Centre for Educational Change.

Elections Ontario. n.d. 'Statistics from the Records (1975–2003).' http://results.elections.on.ca/results/history/statistics/stats_5.jsp?flag=E.

Erman, E. 2009. 'What Is Wrong with Agonistic Pluralism?' *Philosophy & Social Criticism* 35 (9): 1039–62.

Fielding, J. 2002. 'Tales from the Crypt or Writing the Ontario Canadian World Studies Curriculum.' *Our Schools / Our Selves* 11 (3): 77–84.

Fields, A.B., and W. Feinberg. 2001. *Education and Democratic Theory: Finding a Place for Community Participation in Public School Reform*. New York: SUNY Press.

Fischer, F. 1993. 'Reconstructing Policy Analysis: A Postpositivist Perspective.' *Policy Sciences* 25 (3): 333–40.

– 1998. 'Beyond Empiricism: Policy Inquiry in Postpositivist Perspective.' *Policy Studies Journal* 26 (1): 129–46.

Fischer, F., and J. Forester, eds. 1993. *The Argumentative Turn in Policy Analysis and Planning*. Durham, NC: Duke University Press.

Fischman, G.E., and P. McLaren. 2000. 'Schooling for Democracy: Toward a Critical Utopianism.' *Contemporary Sociology* 29 (1): 168–79.

Fleury, S.C. 2005. 'Social Studies for an Empire: Thoughts on Where Did Social Studies Go Wrong?' *Social Studies* 96 (4): 163–70.

Forester, J. 1993. *Critical Theory, Public Policy and Planning Practice: Toward a Critical Pragmatism*. New York: SUNY Press.

Fraser, N. 2007. 'Feminist Politics in the Age of Recognition: A Two-Dimensional Approach to Gender Justice.' *Studies in Social Justice* 1 (1): 23–35.

– 2008. 'Abnormal Justice.' *Critical Inquiry* 34: 393–422.

– 2010. 'Injustice at Intersecting Scales: On "Social Exclusion" and the "Global Poor."' *European Journal of Social Theory* 13 (1): 363–71.

Freedman, E.B. 2007. 'Is Teaching for Social Justice Undemocratic?' *Harvard Educational Review* 77 (4): 442–73.

Freeman, S.R. 2003. *The Cambridge Companion to Rawls*. Cambridge: Cambridge University Press.

Freire, P. 1972. *Pedagogy of the Oppressed*. London: Penguin Books.

– 1978. *Pedagogy in Process*. New York: Seabury.

Fung, A., and E.O. Wright. 2001. 'Deepening Democracy: Innovations in Empowered Participatory Governance.' *Politics & Society* 29 (1): 5–41.

Gandin, L.A. 2002. 'Democratizing Access, Governance, and Knowledge: The Struggle for Educational Alternatives in Porto Alegre, Brazil.' PhD diss., University of Wisconsin – Madison.

– 2006. 'Creating Real Alternatives to Neoliberal Policies in Education: The Citizen School Project.' In *The Subaltern Speak: Curriculum, Power and Educational Struggles*, ed. M.W. Apple and K.L. Buras, 217–42. New York: Routledge.

– 2007. 'The Construction of the Citizen School Project as an Alternative to Neoliberal Educational Policies.' *Policy Futures in Education* 5 (2): 179–93.

Gandin, L.A., and M.W. Apple. 2002a. 'Can Education Challenge Neo-Liberalism? The Citizen School and the Struggle for Democracy in Porto Alegre, Brazil.' *Social Justice* 29 (4): 26–41.

– 2002b. 'Thin versus Thick Democracy in Education: Porto Alegre and the Creation of Alternatives to Neo-Liberalism.' *International Studies in Sociology of Education* 12 (2): 99–115.

– 2003. 'Educating the State, Democratizing Knowledge: The Citizen School Project in Porto Alegre, Brazil.' In *The State and the Politics of Knowledge*, ed. M.W. Apple, 193–219. New York: RoutledgeFalmer.

– 2004. 'New Schools, New Knowledge, New Teachers: Creating the Citizen School in Porto Alegre, Brazil.' *Teacher Education Quarterly* 31 (1): 173–98.

Gewirtz, S. 1998. 'Conceptualizing Social Justice in Education: Mapping the Territory.' *Journal of Education Policy* 13 (4): 469–84.

Gewirtz, S., and A. Cribb. 2002. 'Plural Conceptions of Social Justice: Implications for Policy Sociology.' *Journal of Education Policy* 17 (5): 499–509.

Gidney, R.D. 1999. *From Hope to Harris*. Toronto: University of Toronto Press.

Gilbert, M.A. 1997. 'Prolegomenon to a Pragmatics of Emotion.' Presented at First International Conference of the Ontario Society for the Study of Argumentation, St Catharines, ON, 16–20 May.

– 1999. 'Language, Words and Expressive Speech Acts.' *Proceedings of the Fourth International Conference of the International Society for the Study of Argumentation*, ed. F. van Eemeren, R. Grootendorst, J.A. Blair, and C.A. Willard, 231–34. Windsor, ON: Ontario Society for the Study of Argumentation.

– 2001. 'Emotional Messages.' *Argumentation* 15 (3): 239–50.

Gillborn, D. 2005. 'Education Policy as an Act of White Supremacy: Whiteness, Critical Race Theory and Education Reform.' *Journal of Education Policy*
20 (4): 485–505.

Girard, D., and J. Ruimy. 1997. '"Mr Fixit" Set to Deal with Teachers: Johnson
Willing to Compromise as He Takes Over Education Hot Seat.' *Toronto Star*,
11 October.

Giroux, H. 1983. *Theory and Resistance in Education*. London: Heinemann.

Glass, R.G. 2000. 'Education and the Ethics of Democratic Citizenship.' *Studies
in Philosophy and Education* 19: 275–96.

Glynos, J. 2003. 'Radical Democratic Ethos, or What Is an Authentic Political
Act?' *Contemporary Political Theory* 2: 187–208.

Goi, S. 2005. 'Agonism, Deliberation, and the Politics of Abortion.' *Polity* 37 (1):
54–82.

Goldfield, M., and B.D. Palmer. 2007. 'Canada's Workers Movement: Uneven
Developments.' *Labour / Le Travail 59*. http://www.historycooperative.org/
journals/llt/59/goldfield.html.

Goldfrank, B. 2005. 'The Politics of Deepening Local Democracy: Decentralization, Party Institutionalization, and Participation.' Paper presented at the
annual meeting of the American Political Science Association, Washington, DC, 1 September 2005. http://citation.allacademic.com/meta/p_mla_
apa_research_citation/0/4/2/6/0/pages42602/p42602-1.php.

Gret, M., and Y. Sintomer. 2005. *The Porto Alegre Experiment: Learning Lessons
for Better Democracy*. Toronto: Fernwood.

Gualmini, E. 2008. 'Restructuring Weberian Bureaucracy: Comparing Managerial Reforms in Europe and the United States.' *Public Administration* 86 (1):
75–94.

Gutmann, A. 1999. *Democratic Education*. 2nd ed. Princeton, NJ: Princeton University Press.

Gutmann, A., and D. Thompson. 2004. *Why Deliberative Democracy?* Princeton:
Princeton University Press.

Habermas, J. 1984. *Reason and the Rationalization of Society*. Vol. 2 of *The Theory
of Communicative Action*. Boston: Beacon.

Halpin, D., and B. Troyna. 1995. 'The Politics of Policy Borrowing.' *Comparative Education* 31: 303–10.

Hargreaves, A., P. Shaw, D. Fink, C. Giles, and S. Moore. 2002. *Final Report:
Secondary School Reform: The Experiences and Interpretations of Teachers and
Administrators in Six Ontario Secondary Schools*. http://fcis.oise.utoronto.ca/
~icec/cfreport1.pdf.

Harney, S. 2002. *State Work: Public Administration and Mass Intellectuality*. Durham,
NC: Duke University Press.

Hatcher, R. 2002. 'Democracy and Education: The Experience of Porto Alegre and Rio Grande do Sul, Brazil.' *Education and Social Justice* 4 (2): 47–64.

Heck, R.H. 2004. *Studying Educational and Social Policy: Theoretical Concepts and Research Methods.* Mahwah, NJ: Lawrence Erlbaum.

Hefetz, A., and M. Warner. 2004. 'Privatization and Its Reverse: Explaining the Dynamics of the Government Contracting Process.' *Journal of Public Administration Research and Theory* 14 (2): 171–90.

Henig, J.R. 1994. *Rethinking School Choice: Limits of the Market Metaphor.* Princeton, NJ: Princeton University Press.

Hogan, P. 2000. 'Virtue, Vice and Vacancy in Educational Policy and Practice.' *British Journal of Educational Studies* 48 (4): 371–90.

Hucker, J. 1997. 'Antidiscrimination Laws in Canada: Human Rights Commissions and the Search for Equality.' *Human Rights Quarterly* 19 (3): 547–71.

Hyslop-Margison, E.J. 2000. 'Alternative Curriculum Evaluation: A Critical Approach to Assess Social Engineering Programs.' *Online Issues: Centre for the Study of Curriculum and Instruction* 6 (1). http://www.ccfi.educ.ubc.ca/publication/insights/archives/v06n01/hyslop-margison.html.

Hyslop-Margison, E.J., and A. Sears. 2006. *Neo-Liberalism, Globalization and Human Capital Learning: Reclaiming Education for Democratic Citizenship.* Dordrecht, Netherlands: Springer.

Hytten, K. 2006. 'Education for Social Justice: Provocations and Challenges.' *Educational Theory* 56 (2): 221–36.

Ibbitson, J. 1996. 'The New Blue Machine: Mike Harris's *Right Young Things* Are Setting the Political Agenda in Ontario.' *Ottawa Citizen,* 3 February.

– 1997. *Promised Land: Inside the Mike Harris Revolution.* Toronto: Prentice-Hall.

– 1998. 'Ontario Rushes to New High-School Curriculum: Tories Are About to Launch the Country's Biggest Curriculum Rewrite Ever, and They've Given Themselves 17 Months to Do It.' *Hamilton Spectator,* 31 January.

Ingram, H. 2000. 'Research Agenda for Public Policy and Democracy.' Irvine: University of California Centre for the Study of Democracy. http://escholarship.org/uc/item/8g67t2jw.

Inoue, T. 2003. 'Two Models of Democracy: How to Make Demos and Hercules Collaborate in Public Deliberation.' Paper presented at IVR-2033 World Congress, University of Lund, Sweden, 12–18 August. http://www.ivr2003.net/Abstracts/inoue.pdf.

Ireson, J., and S. Hallam. 1999. 'Raising Standards: Is Ability Grouping the Answer?' *Oxford Review of Education* 25 (3): 343–58.

Jackman, M. 2006. 'Canadian Charter Equality at Twenty: Reflections of a Card-Carrying Member of the Court Party.' *Policy Options* 27 (1): 72–7.

James, O., and M. Lodge. 2003. 'The Limitations of "Policy Transfer" and "Lesson Drawing" for Public Policy Research.' *Political Studies Review* 1: 179–93.

Keil, R. 2002. '"Common-Sense" Neoliberalism: Progressive Conservative Urbanism in Toronto, Canada.' *Antipode* 34: 578–601.

Kim, J., R.O. Wyatt, and E. Katz. 1999. 'News, Talk, Opinion, Participation: The Part Played by Conversation in Deliberative Democracy.' *Political Communication* 16: 361–95.

Kincheloe, J.L. 1999. 'Critical Democracy in Education.' In *Understanding Democratic Curriculum Leadership*, ed. J.G. Henderson and K.R. Kesson, 70–83. New York: Teachers College Press.

Kogan, M. 1985. 'Education Policy and Values.' In *Policy-Making in Education*, ed. I. McNay and J. Ozga, 11–38. Oxford: Pergamon.

Kohli, W. 2005. 'What Is Social Justice Education?' In *Key Questions for Educators*, ed. W. Hare and J.P. Portelli, 98–100. Halifax: Edphil Books.

Kohn, M. 2000. 'Language, Power and Persuasion: Toward a Critique of Deliberative Democracy.' *Constellations* 7 (3): 408–29.

Koonings, K. 2004. 'Strengthening Citizenship in Brazil's Democracy: Local Participatory Governance in Porto Alegre.' *Bulletin of Latin American Research* 23 (1): 79–99.

Kozolanka, K. 2007. *The Power of Persuasion: The Politics of the New Right in Ontario*. Montreal: Black Rose Books.

Ladson-Billings, G. 1998. 'Just What Is Critical Race Theory, and What's It Doing in a "Nice" Field Like Education?' *Qualitative Studies in Education* 11 (1): 7–24.

– 2009. 'Race Still Matters: Critical Race Theory in Education.' In *The Routledge International Handbook of Critical Education*, ed. M.W. Apple, W. Au, and L.A. Gandin, 110–22. New York: Routledge.

Leighton, D. 2002. 'Searching for Politics in an Uncertain World: Interview with Zygmunt Bauman.' *Renewal* 10 (1): 14–18.

Lemisko, L.S., and K.W. Clausen. 2006. 'Connections, Contrarieties, and Convolutions: Curriculum and Pedagogic Reform in Alberta and Ontario, 1930–1955.' *Canadian Journal of Education* 29 (4): 1097–126.

Levin, B. 1997. 'The Lessons of International Education Reform.' *Journal of Education Policy* 12 (4): 253–66.

– 1998a. 'The Educational Requirement for Democracy.' *Curriculum Inquiry* 28 (1): 57–79.

– 1998b. 'An Epidemic of Education Policy: (What) Can We Learn from Each Other?' *Comparative Education* 34 (2): 131–41.

– 1998c. 'The Rhetoric of Education Reform.' Paper presented to the Canadian Society for the Study of Education, Ottawa, May 1998.

- 1999. 'Class and Equity in a New Era of Education Policy.' *British Journal of Educational Studies* 47 (3): 313–16.
- 2005. *Governing Education.* Toronto: University of Toronto Press.
Levin, B., and J.A. Riffel. 1994. 'Dealing with Diversity: Some Propositions from Canadian Education.' *Education Policy Analysis Archives* 2 (2). http://epaa.asu.edu/ojs/article/view/665.
Levin, B., and J. Young. 2000. 'The Rhetoric of Educational Reform.' *Journal of Comparative Policy Analysis* 2 (2): 189–209.
Lipset, S.M, and S. Rokkan. 1967. *Party Systems and Voter Alignments.* New York: Free Press.
Livingstone, D.W., D. Hart, and L.E. Davie. 1996. *Public Attitudes towards Education in Ontario 1996.* Toronto: OISE in association with University of Toronto Press.
- 1998. *Public Attitudes towards Education in Ontario 1998.* Toronto: OISE in association with University of Toronto Press.
Locke, J. 2006. 'Obstruction in the Legislature: The Struggle for Power between the Government and the Opposition.' Paper presented at the Canadian Political Science Association Annual Conference, Toronto, 2 June.
Looney, A. 2001. 'Curriculum as Policy: Some Implications of Contemporary Policy Studies for the Analysis of Curriculum Policy, with Particular Reference to Post-Primary Curriculum Policy in the Republic of Ireland.' *Curriculum Journal* 12 (2): 149–62.
López, G.R. 2003. 'The (Racially Neutral) Politics of Education: A Critical Race Theory Perspective.' *Educational Administration Quarterly* 39 (1): 68–94.
Loxley, A., and G. Thomas. 2001. 'Neo-Conservatives, Neo-Liberals, the New Left and Inclusion: Stirring the Pot.' *Cambridge Journal of Education* 31 (3): 291–301.
Lugg, C.A. 1998. 'Political Kitsch and Education Policy.' Paper presented at American Educational Research Annual Meeting, San Diego, 13 April.
Lupton, G. 1997. 'Angry Teachers Take Their Stand.' *Kingston Whig–Standard,* 28 October.
Majhanovich, S. 2002. 'Conflicting Visions, Competing Expectations: Control and De-Skilling of Education – A Perspective from Ontario.' *McGill Journal of Education* 37 (2): 159–77.
- 2005. 'Educational Decentralisation: Rhetoric or Reality? The Case of Ontario, Canada.' In *International Handbook on Globalisation, Education and Policy Research,* ed. J. Zajda, 599–612. Dordrecht, Netherlands: Springer.
Mallan, C. 2002. 'Rehired, at Twice the Rate of Pay: Ministers Question Findings – 40 Ministry Staff Leave, Then Return in Private Roles; Auditor Uncovers Wild Spending at Queen's Park.' *Toronto Star,* 4 December.

Manzer, R.A. 1994. *Public Schools and Political Ideas: Canadian Educational Policy in Historical Perspective.* Toronto: University of Toronto Press.

– 2003. *Educational Regimes and Anglo-American Democracy.* Toronto: University of Toronto Press.

Marginson, S. 2006. 'Engaging Democratic Education in the Neoliberal Age.' *Educational Theory* 56 (2): 205–19.

Marshall, C. 2004. 'Social Justice Challenges to Educational Administration: Introduction to a Special Issue.' *Educational Administration Quarterly* 40 (1): 3–13.

Martin, J.R. 1985. *Reclaiming a Conversation: The Ideal of the Educated Woman.* New Haven, CT: Yale University Press.

– 1992. 'Critical Thinking for a Humane World.' In *The Generalizability of Critical Thinking: Multiple Perspectives on an Educational Ideal,* ed. S. Norris, 163–80. New York: Teachers College Press.

McGann, Anthony. 2005. 'The Problem of Consensus in Habermas and Rawls: Rethinking the Basis of Deliberative Democracy.' Paper presented at the annual meeting of the American Political Science Association, Washington, DC, 1 September. http://citation.allacademic.com/meta/p_mla_apa_rese arch_citation/0/3/9/8/9/pages39891/p39891-1.php.

McMahon, B., and J.P. Portelli. 2004. 'Engagement for What? Beyond Popular Discourses of Student Engagement.' *Leadership and Policy in Schools* 3 (1): 59–76.

Menegat, R. 2002. 'Participatory Democracy in Porto Alegre, Brazil.' *Participatory Learning and Action Notes* 44: 8–11.

Merrett, C.D. 2004. 'Social Justice: What Is It? Why Teach It?' *Journal of Geography* 103 (3): 93–101.

Ministry of Education. 1996. 'Understanding and Participating in Curriculum Change.' http://www.edu.gov.on.ca/eng/document/discussi/curricul.html.

– 2000a. 'Backgrounder: Highlights of the New High School Program.' News release, June.

– 2000b. *The Ontario Curriculum Grades 9 to 12: Program Planning and Assessment.* Toronto: Queen's Printer.

Miños, D.C. 2002. *Porto Alegre, Brazil: A New, Sustainable and Replicable Model of Participatory and Democratic Governance.* The Hague. http://www.tni.org/sites/www.tni.org/archives/archives/chavez/portoalegre.pdf.

Mouffe, C. 1996. 'Feminism, Citizenship and Radical Democratic Politics.' In *Social Postmodernism: Beyond Identity Politics,* ed. L. Nicholson and S. Seidman, 332–56. Cambridge: Cambridge University Press.

– 1997. 'Decision, Deliberation and Democratic Ethos.' *Philosophy Today* 41 (1): 24–30.

– 2000a. 'Deliberative Democracy or Agonistic Pluralism.' Reihe Politikwis-
    senschaft Political Science Series, Institute for Advanced Studies, Vienna.
    http://users.unimi.it/dikeius/pw_72.pdf.
– 2000b. *The Democratic Paradox.* London: Verso.
– 2000c. 'Politics and Passions: The Stakes of Democracy.' *Ethical Perspectives*
    7: 146–50.
– 2005. *On the Political.* London: Routledge.
Morton, D. 1997. *'Sic Permanet:* Ontario People and Their Politics.' In White
    1997a, 3–18.
Myers, J.P. 2005. 'Politics, Ideology and Democratic Citizenship Education:
    The Pedagogy of Politically Active Teachers in Porto Alegre, Brazil and
    Toronto, Canada.' PhD diss., University of Toronto.
Natale, C. 1998. 'Social Darwinism Comes to the Classroom.' *Our Schools / Our
    Selves* 55 (9): 26–42.
National Anti-Racism Council of Canada. 2002. 'Racial Discrimination in
    Canada: The Status of Compliance by the Canadian Government with
    the International Convention on the Elimination of All Forms of Racial
    Discrimination.' http://www.ocasi.org/index.php?qid=786&catid=117.
Newman, J. 2002. 'Putting the "Policy" Back into Social Policy.' *Social Policy
    and Society* 1 (4): 347–54.
Nussbaum, M. 1999. 'Women and Equality: The Capabilities Approach.' *Inter-
    national Labor Review* 138 (3): 227–51.
Oakes, J. 2005. *Keeping Track: How Schools Structure Inequality.* 2nd ed. New
    Haven, CT: Yale University Press.
Oakes, J., and M. Lipton. 2003. *Teaching to Change the World.* 2nd ed. Boston:
    McGraw-Hill.
O'Farrell, L. 2001. 'Writing Arts Curriculum in a Public Sector–Private Sector
    Partnership.' Paper presented at the UNESCO Meeting of Experts, Arts
    Education in Latin America and the Caribbean, Uberaba, Brazil, October.
Olson, J. 2009. 'Friends and Enemies, Slaves and Masters: Fanaticism, Wendell
    Phillips, and the Limits of Democratic Theory.' *Journal of Politics* 71 (1):
    82–95.
Olssen, M. 1996. 'In Defense of the Welfare State and of Publicly Provided Edu-
    cation.' *Journal of Education Policy* 11 (3): 337–62.
Olssen, M., J. Codd, and A. O'Neill. 2004. *Education Policy: Globalization, Citi-
    zenship and Democracy.* London: Sage.
Omi, M., and H. Winant. 1994. *Racial Formation in the United States: From the
    1960s to the 1990s.* New York: Routledge.
O'Neill, S. 2000. 'The Politics of Inclusive Agreements: Towards a Critical Dis-
    course Theory of Democracy.' *Political Studies* 48: 503–21.

Ontario English Catholic Teachers Association (OECTA). 1998. 'Secondary School Reform Process: OECTA Interim Analysis.' http://www.oecta.on.ca/wps/portal/publications/items?WCM_GLOBAL_CONTEXT=/web+content/OECTA/Resource+Library/Position+Papers+and+Briefs.

– 2003. 'Three Strikes and You're Out: The Experts Give Secondary School Reform a Failing Grade.' http://www.oecta.on.ca/wps/portal/publications/items?WCM_GLOBAL_CONTEXT=/web+content/OECTA/Resource+Library/Position+Papers+and+Briefs.

Ontario, Legislative Assembly. 1997a. *Debates and Proceedings.* 21 January. (John Snobelen, MPP). http://hansardindex.ontla.on.ca/hansardeissue/36-1/l148.htm.

– 1997b. *Debates and Proceedings.* 23 April. (Howard Hampton, MPP). http://hansardindex.ontla.on.ca/hansardeissue/36-1/l179.htm.

– 1998a. *Debates and Proceedings.* 29 April. (Lyn McLeod, MPP). http://hansardindex.ontla.on.ca/hansardeissue/36-2/l004b.htm.

– 1998b. *Debates and Proceedings.* 7 October. (Howard Hampton, MPP). http://hansardindex.ontla.on.ca/hansardeissue/36-2/l040a.htm.

Orum, A.M., J.R. Feagin, and G. Sjoberg. 1991. 'Introduction: The Nature of the Case Study.' In *A Case for the Case Study,* ed. J.R. Feagin, A.M. Orum, and G. Sjoberg, 1–16. Chapel Hill: University of North Carolina Press.

Osborne, K. 1999. *Education: A Guide to the Canadian School Debate – Or Who Wants What and Why?* Montreal: Penguin/McGill Institute.

Parker, L., and G. Gould. 1999. 'Changing Public Sector Accountability: Critiquing New Directions.' *Accounting Forum* 23 (2): 109–35.

Parker, W.C. 1996. *Educating the Democratic Mind.* New York: SUNY Press.

Patterson, R.S. 1987. 'The Canadian Response to Progressive Education.' In *Essays on Canadian Education,* ed. N. Kach, K. Mazurek, R.S. Patterson, and I. DeFaveri, 61–75. Calgary: Detselig.

Patton, M. 1990. *Qualitative Evaluation and Research Methods.* 2nd ed. Thousand Oaks, CA: Sage.

Perl, A. 2000. 'Can the State Think for Itself? Implications of Consultants' Rise in Policy Analysis.' Paper presented at the 2000 Annual Meeting of the American Political Science Association, Chicago, 3 September.

Perl, A., and D.J. White. 2002. 'The Changing Role of Consultants in Canadian Policy Analysis.' *Policy Organisation & Society* 21 (1): 49–73.

Pettigrew, M., and M. MacLure. 1997. 'The Press, Public Knowledge and the Grant Maintained Schools Policy.' *British Journal of Educational Studies* 45 (4): 392–405.

Pettit, P. 2008. 'Three Conceptions of Democratic Control.' *Constellations* 15 (1): 46–55.

Phillips, D. 2003. 'Processes of Policy Borrowing in Education: Some Explanatory and Analytical Devices.' *Comparative Education* 39 (4): 451–61.
– 2006. 'Investigating Policy Attraction in Education.' *Oxford Review of Education* 32 (5): 551–59.
Pinto, L.E. 2005. '*The Apprentice:* A Critical Approach to Media Portrayal of Business in the Classroom.' *Orbit* 35 (2): 31–3.
– 2006. 'Critical Thinking and the Cultural Myth of the Entrepreneur.' *Our Schools / Our Selves* 16 (1): 69–84.
– 2007. 'Textbook Publishing, Textbooks, and Democracy: A Case Study.' *Journal of Thought* 40 (3): 99–121.
Pistóia, L.H.C. 2001. 'Um estudo de caso em uma proposta curricular e interdisciplinar na Rede Municipal de Ensino de Porto Alegre.' PhD diss., Universidade Federal do Rio Grande Do Sul.
Pløger, J. 2004. 'Strife: Urban Planning and Agonism.' *Planning Theory* 3 (1): 71–92.
Portelli, J.P. 2001. 'Democracy in Education: Beyond the Conservative or Progressivist Stances.' In *Philosophy of Education: Introductory Readings,* ed. W. Hare and J.P. Portelli, 3rd ed., 279–94. Calgary: Detselig.
Portelli, J.P., and R.P. Solomon. 2001. *The Erosion of Democracy in Education.* Calgary: Detselig.
Portelli, J.P., and A.B. Vibert. 2001. 'Beyond Common Educational Standards: Toward a Curriculum of Life.' In Portelli and Solomon 2001, 63–82.
'Porto Alegre 2005: An Interview with Roberto Savio.' 2005. *Development* 48 (2): 119–21.
Prentice, A. 2004. *The School Promoters: Education and Social Class in Mid-Nineteenth Century.* Toronto: University of Toronto Press.
Purcell, M. 2009. 'Resisting Neoliberalization: Communicative Planning or Counter-Hegemonic Movements?' *Planning Theory* 8 (2): 140–65.
Radin, B.A. 2000. *Beyond Machiavelli: Policy Analysis Comes of Age.* Washington: Georgetown University Press.
Ramírez, M.D. 2003. 'Privatization in Mexico and Chile: A Critical Perspective.' In *International Handbook on Privatization,* ed. D. Parker and D.S. Saul, 262–90. Cheltenham, UK: Edward Elgar Publishing.
Rawls, J. 1971. *Theory of Justice.* Cambridge: Harvard University Press.
Reddick, R.N. 2004. 'History, Myth, and the Politics of Educational Reform.' *Educational Theory* 54 (1): 73–87.
Reshef, Y. 2007. 'Government Behaviors and Union Protest: Systemizing the Relationship.' *Journal of Labor Research* 28 (2): 375–95.
Rezai-Rashti, G.M. 2003. 'Equity Education and Educational Restructuring in Ontario: Global and Local Policy and Practice.' *World Studies in Education* 4 (1): 29–44.

Rist, R. 1970. 'Student Social Class and Teacher Expectations: The Self-Fulfilling Prophecy in Ghetto Education.' *Harvard Educational Review* 40 (3): 411–50.

Rizvi, F. 1998. 'Some Thoughts on Contemporary Theories of Social Justice.' In *Action Research in Practice: Partnerships for Social Justice in Education,* ed. B. Atweh, S. Kemmis, and P. Weeks, 47–56. London: RoutledgeFalmer.

Roberts, P. 1998. 'The Politics of Curriculum Reform in New Zealand.' *Curriculum Studies* 6 (1): 29–46.

Robertson, C.L., B. Cowell, and J. Olson. 1998. 'A Case Study of Integration and Destreaming: Teachers and Students in an Ontario Secondary School Respond.' *Journal of Curriculum Studies* 30 (6): 691–717.

Robertson, H.J. 1998. *No More Teachers, No More Books.* Toronto: McClelland & Stewart.

Romas, J. 2008. 'Science and Social Justice Are Not Mutually Exclusive.' *Our Schools / Our Selves* 17 (2): 43–52.

Rorison, B. 2002. 'National Revolution, Local Resistance: A Policy Analysis of the Revision of the Math Curriculum in Bayside County.' Presented at the convention of the University Council for Educational Administration in Pittsburgh, November. http://www.education.umd.edu/EDPL/papers/RorisonB.pdf.

Rosenberg, S.W. 2005. 'The Empirical Study of Democracy: Setting a Research Agenda.' Irvine: University of California Center for the Study of Democracy. Paper 05-03. http://escholarship.org/uc/item/78x7984g.

Ruitenberg, C.W. 2009. 'Educating Political Adversaries: Chantal Mouffe and Radical Democratic Citizenship Education.' *Studies in Philosophy and Education* 28 (3): 269–81.

Ryan, T.G., and P. Joong. 2005. 'Teachers' and Students' Perceptions of the Nature and Impact of Large-Scale Reform.' *Canadian Journal of Educational Administration and Policy* 38. http://www.umanitoba.ca/publications/cjeap/articles/ryan_joong.html.

Ryfe, D.M. 2005. 'Does Deliberative Democracy Work?' *Annual Review of Political Science* 8: 49–71.

Sabatier, P.A. 1991. 'Toward Better Theories of the Policy Process.' *PS: Political Science and Politics* 24 (2): 147–56.

Saint-Martin, D. 1998. 'The New Managerialism and the Policy Influence of Consultants in Government: An Historical-Institutionalist Analysis of Britain, Canada, and France.' *Governance: An International Journal of Policy and Administration* 11 (3): 319–56.

Saltman, K. 2005. *The Edison Schools: Corporate Schooling and the Assault on Public Education.* New York: Routledge.

Santos, B. 1998. 'Participatory Budgeting in Porto Alegre: Toward a Redistributive Democracy.' *Politics & Society* 26 (4): 461–510.

– 2005. 'Two Democracies, Two Legalities: Participatory Budgeting in Porto Alegre, Brazil.' In *Law and Globalization from Below: Towards a Cosmopolitan Legality,* ed. B. Santos and C.A. Rodriguez-Garavito, 310–38. London: Cambridge University Press.

Scanlon, E. 1997. 'Suggestions for Case Study Research Methods.' Retrieved 14 October 2004. http://www.gwbssw.wustl.edu/~csd/evaluation/casestudy/caseguide.html.

Schmidt, T. 2001. 'The Man behind Mike.' In *Alien Invasion: How the Harris Tories Mismanaged Ontario,* ed. R. Cohen, 67–71. Toronto: Insomniac.

Schneider, A.L. 1998. 'Institutions and Policies for Democracy: Improving Policy Design.' *Policy Currents* 8 (1): 9–12.

Schneider, A.L., and H. Ingram. 1997. *Policy Design for Democracy.* Lawrence, KS: University Press of Kansas.

Schwartzman, S. 2004. 'The Challenges of Education in Brazil.' In *The Challenges of Education in Brazil,* ed. C. Brock and S. Schwartzman, 9–39. Oxford: Symposium Books.

Sclar, E. 2000. *You Don't Always Get What You Pay For: The Economics of Privatization.* Ithaca, NY: Cornell University Press.

Shields, C.M. 2004. 'Dialogic Leadership for Social Justice: Overcoming Pathologies of Silence.' *Educational Administration Quarterly* 40 (1): 109–32.

Shudak, N.J., and R.J. Helfenbein. 2005. 'Contradicting the Contrarians: The Rhetoric of the Neoconservative Right in Social Studies Education.' *Social Studies* 96 (4): 149–56.

Sjoberg, G., N. Williams, T.R. Vaughan, and A. Sjoberg. 1991. 'The Case Study Approach in Social Research: Basic Methodological Issues.' In *A Case for the Case Study,* ed. J.R. Feagin, A.M. Orum, and G. Sjoberg, 27–79. Chapel Hill: University of North Carolina Press.

Skrla, L., J.J. Scheurich, J.F. Johnson, and J.W. Koschoreck. 2001a. 'Accountability for Equity: Can State Policy Leverage Social Justice?' *International Journal of Leadership in Education* 4 (3): 237–60.

– 2001b. 'Complex and Contested Constructions of Accountability and Educational Equity.' *International Journal of Leadership in Education* 4 (3): 277–83.

Smyth, J. 2001. 'Prepare Them for Work and Create Good Citizens, Too.' *National Post,* 8 September.

Smyth, J., and A. Dow. 1998. 'What's Wrong with Outcomes? Spotter Planes, Action Plans, and Steerage of the Educational Workplace.' *British Journal of Sociology of Education* 19 (3): 291–303.

Snider, J.H. 2008. 'Crackpot or Genius? Canada Steps onto the World Stage as a Democratic Innovator.' *Journal of Public Deliberation* 4 (1): 1–5.

Snobelen, J. 1995. 'Blueprint for Redesigned Education System.' *Toronto Star*, 17 August.

Snow, D.A., and L. Anderson. 1991. 'Researching the Homeless: The Characteristic Features and Virtues of the Case Study.' In *A Case for the Case Study*, ed. J.R. Feagin, A.M. Orum, and G. Sjoberg, 148–73. Chapel Hill: University of North Carolina Press.

Soares, F. 2004. 'Quality and Equity in Brazilian Basic Education: Facts and Possibilities.' In *The Challenges of Education in Brazil*, ed. C. Brock and S. Schwartzman, 69–88. Oxford: Symposium Books.

Statistics Canada. 2002. 'Youth in Transition Survey.' *Daily*, 23 January. http://www.statcan.ca/Daily/English/060705/d060705a.htm.

Stein, S.J. 2004. *The Culture of Education Policy*. New York: Teachers College Press.

Stocker, D., and D. Wagner. 2008. 'Talking about Teaching Mathematics for Social Justice.' *Our Schools / Our Selves* 17 (2): 69–82.

Sunstein, R. 1997. *Free Markets and Social Justice*. New York: Oxford University Press.

Tally, R.T. 2007. 'The Agony of the Political: A Review of Chantal Mouffe, *On the Political*.' Faculty Publications – English. Paper 10. http://ecommons.txstate.edu/englfacp/10.

Taylor, A. 2005. '"Re-Culturing" Students and Selling Futures: School-to-Work Policy in Ontario.' *Journal of Education and Work* 18 (3): 321–40.

Taylor, S. 1997. *Educational Policy and the Politics of Change*. New York: Routledge.

Taylor, S., and M. Henry. 2002. 'Globalization and Educational Policymaking: A Case Study.' *Educational Theory* 50 (4): 487–503.

Thien, D. 2007. 'Disenchanting Democracy, Review of *On the Political*.' *Area* 39 (1): 134–5.

Thornton, M.D. 2008. 'Please Get Emotional: Conservative Campaign Strategy and the Power of Emotion in the 1995 Ontario Election.' Paper delivered at the Annual Meeting of the Canadian Political Science Association, 6 June, Vancouver. http://www.cpsa-acsp.ca/papers-2008/Thornton.pdf.

Toronto Community Housing. 2005. *Community Management Plan, 2005–2007*. Toronto: Toronto Community Housing.

Travers, A. 2008. 'The Sport Nexus and Gender Injustice.' *Studies in Social Justice* 2 (1): 79–101.

Tribunal Regional Eleitoral do Rio Grande do Sul. 2004. 'Eleições Municipais 2004 2º Turno.' http://www.tre-rs.gov.br/eleicoes/2004/2t/RS88013.htm.

Trickey, J. 1997. 'The Racist Face of "Common Sense."' In *Open for Business, Closed to People*, ed. D. Ralph, A. Regimbald, and N. St-Amand, 113–21. Halifax: Fernwood Publishing.

Tyack, D. 1999. 'Democracy in Education: Who Needs It?' *Education Week* 19 (12): 42–7.

Tyler, T.R. 2000. 'Social Justice: Outcome and Procedure.' *International Journal of Psychology* 35 (2): 117–25.

UNESCO. 2000. 'The Experience of the Participative Budget in Porto Alegre, Brazil.' MOST Clearing House Best Practices. http://www.unesco.org/most/southa13.htm.

– 2003. 'Processes of Curriculum Policy Change: Building the Capacities of Curriculum Specialists in Educational Reform.' http://www.ibe.unesco.org/fileadmin/user_upload/archive/curriculum/Asia%20Networkpdf/vienrepor.pdf.

Viero, O.M., and A.P. Cordeiro. 2003. 'The Case for Public Provisioning in Porto Alegre. WaterAid and Tearfund. http://www.wateraid.org/documents/plugin_documents/pspbrazilweb.pdf.

Vincent, C. 2003. *Social Justice, Education and Identity.* London: Routledge-Falmer.

Wagle, U. 2000. 'The Policy Science of Democracy: The Issues of Methodology and Citizen Participation.' *Policy Sciences* 33: 207–23.

Wainwright, W. 2003. 'Making a People's Budget in Porto Alegre.' *NACLA Report on the Americas* 36 (5). http://proquest.umi.com.myaccess.library.utoronto.ca/ pqdlink?did=330597451&sid=2&Fmt=3&clientId=12520&RQT=309&VName=PQD.

Walton, D.N. 1992. *The Place of Emotion in Argument.* University Park, PA: Penn State University Press.

Weeks, E.C. 2000. 'The Practice of Deliberative Democracy: Results from Four Large-Scale Trials.' *Public Administration Review* 60 (4): 360–72.

Weis, L., L.P. Pruitt, and A. Burns, eds. *Off White: Readings on Power, Privilege, and Resistance,* 2nd ed., 313–30. New York: Routledge.

Welch, A.R. 1998. 'The Cult of Efficiency in Education: Comparative Reflections on the Reality and the Rhetoric.' *Comparative Education* 34 (2): 157–75.

Werner, W. 1991. 'Curriculum and Incertainty.' In *Social Change and Education in Canada,* ed. R. Ghosh and D. Ray, 2nd ed., 105–113. Toronto: Harcourt Brace Jovanovich.

Westbrook, R. 1993. *John Dewey and American Democracy.* Ithaca, NY: Cornell University Press.

White, G., ed. 1997a. *The Government and Politics of Ontario.* 5th ed. Toronto: University of Toronto Press.

– 1997b. 'The Legislature: Central Symbol of Ontario Democracy.' In White 1997a, 71–92.

– 1997c. 'Transition: The Tories Take Power.' In *Revolution at Queen's Park: Essays on Governing Ontario*, ed. S. Noel, 139–50. Toronto: James Lorimer.

– 2000. 'Revolutionary Change in the Ontario Public Service.' In *Government Restructuring and Career Public Service*, ed. E. Lindquist, 310–45. Toronto: IPAC.

– 2002. 'Change in the Ontario State 1952–2002.' Paper prepared for the Role of Government Panel. http://www.law-lib.utoronto.ca/investing/reports/rp8.pdf.

White, R. 1998. *Ontario since 1985*. Toronto: East End Books.

Wildavsky, A. 1979. *Speaking Truth to Power: The Art and Craft of Policy Analysis*. Boston: Little, Brown.

Wilkinson, M.N. 2007. 'Learning to Participate: Poor Women's Experiences in Building Democracy in Brazil.' PhD diss., Teachers College, Columbia University.

Winant, H. 2004. 'Behind Blue Eyes: Whiteness and Contemporary US Racial Politics.' In *Off White: Readings on Power, Privilege, and Resistance*, 2nd ed., ed. L. Weis, L.P. Pruitt, and A. Burns, 3–16. New York: Routledge.

Wolf, A. 1999. *Building Advice: The Craft of the Policy Professional*. Wellington, NZ: State Services Commission of the New Zealand Government.

Wolfe, D.A. 1997. 'Queen's Park Policy-Making Systems.' In *Revolution at Queen's Park: Essays on Governing Ontario*, ed. S. Noel, 151–64. Toronto: James Lorimer.

Wood, T., and W.E. Murray. 2007. 'Participatory Democracy in Brazil and Local Geographies: Porto Alegre and Belo Horizonte Compared.' *European Review of Latin American and Caribbean Studies* 83: 19–41.

Woolstencroft, P. 1997. 'More Than a Guard Change: Politics in the New Ontario.' In *Revolution at Queen's Park: Essays on Governing Ontario*, ed. S. Noel, 38–54. Toronto: James Lorimer.

Wrigley, T. 2003. 'Is "School Effectiveness" Anti-Democratic?' *British Journal of Educational Studies* 51 (2): 89–112.

Yin, R. 1994. *Case Study Research: Design and Methods*. 2nd ed. Beverly Hills, CA: Sage.

Zussman, D. 2000. 'Increasing Accountability in the Federal Public Service.' Paper presented at the CGA Canada Conference 2000, 27 January, Ottawa. http://old.ppforum.ca/common/assets/speeches/en/increasing_accountability.pdf.

Index